POLICING DRUGS

Policing Drugs

KARIM MURJI
Roehampton Institute London

Routledge
Taylor & Francis Group
LONDON AND NEW YORK

First published 1998 by Ashgate Publishing

Reissued 2018 by Routledge
2 Park Square, Milton Park, Abingdon, Oxon, OX14 4RN
711 Third Avenue, New York, NY 10017, USA

Routledge is an imprint of the Taylor & Francis Group, an informa business

Copyright © Karim Murji 1998

All rights reserved. No part of this book may be reprinted or reproduced or utilised in any form or by any electronic, mechanical, or other means, now known or hereafter invented, including photocopying and recording, or in any information storage or retrieval system, without permission in writing from the publishers.

Notice:
Product or corporate names may be trademarks or registered trademarks, and are used only for identification and explanation without intent to infringe.

Publisher's Note
The publisher has gone to great lengths to ensure the quality of this reprint but points out that some imperfections in the original copies may be apparent.

Disclaimer
The publisher has made every effort to trace copyright holders and welcomes correspondence from those they have been unable to contact.

A Library of Congress record exists under LC control number: 98073752

ISBN 13: 978-1-138-32568-5 (hbk)
ISBN 13: 978-1-138-32575-3 (pbk)
ISBN 13: 978-0-429-45026-6 (ebk)

Contents

Acknowledgements vi

Introduction 1

PART I : LAW ENFORCEMENT

1   Drug Enforcement Strategies 11
2   Under Pressure: Policing and Demand Management 29
3   Principle or Pragmatism? Debating Drug Legalisation 51

PART II: DRUG REFERRAL

4   Drug and Arrest Referral in Trafford, Merseyside and Southwark 67
5   Drug Referral Schemes: Local Case Studies 91

PART III: OFFICIAL AND MEDIA REACTIONS

6   Agony and Ecstasy: Drugs, Media and Moral Panic 121
7   High Anxiety: Crack and Social Reaction 139
8   In Living Colour? Representations of Yardies 159

Bibliography 179
Index 193

Acknowledgements

As well as the people named here I want to thank friends and colleagues, past and present, for advice and encouragement. My work on drugs began at the Institute for the Study of Drug Dependence. Jasper Woodcock, Nicholas Dorn and Nigel South gave me the opportunity to work there and the influence of the latter two will be apparent from a glance at the bibliography. Sheila Henderson and John Witton helped to make it an enjoyable place to be at. Geoff Pearson and Robert Reiner managed to be sympathetically critical. Steven Groarke, James Sheptycki, Kevin Stenson and Ross Coomber provided many helpful comments on some of the chapters here. Michael Keith and Eugene McLaughlin have done much else besides. Many or all of these people will not agree with my arguments in this book though none of them should be held responsible for any errors in it. Finally, I also want to acknowledge the support of all members of my family over the years.

Some parts of this book have appeared before and I thank the following for enabling me to include them here. Chapter 1 was first published in the *Howard Journal of Criminal Justice* (Basil Blackwell); chapter 3 in *Sociology Review*; chapter 6 in *The Control of Drugs and Drug Users*, edited by Ross Coomber (Harwood Academic Press); and chapter 7 in *Community Care* and in *Scare in the Community: Britain in a moral panic*, edited by Polly Neate (Reed Business Publishing). In all cases the papers have been revised, sometimes extensively so.

Introduction

The three sections that make up this book are based on research carried out over several years. In this introduction I provide a brief overview of the contents and indicate some of the ways in which the issues raised have been developed.

Part 1 investigates law enforcement. Drugs, or drug traffickers, have been one of the primary driving forces behind advances in the law and in policing since the 1980s. In recent years the pace of developments has not slowed, though the main legal provisions usually consolidated and updated legislation from the 1980s. In the realm of financial penalties for drug trafficking and other crimes, the 1993 Criminal Justice Act strengthened powers of asset confiscation, while the 1994 Drug Trafficking Act introduced powers to forfeit drug trafficking money being imported into or exported out of the UK. In dealing with offenders, the 1994 Criminal Justice and Public Order Act introduced powers for drug testing in prisons and, most recently, the Labour government's 1998 Crime and Disorder Act introduces provisions for a Drug Treatment and Testing Order. In between those two pieces of legislation the Crime (Sentences) Act, 1997 introduced mandatory minimum sentences for repeat drug offenders among others. In policing, the establishment of the National Criminal Intelligence Service has now been paralleled by an operational National Crime Squad, formed out of the previous Regional Crime Squads. Beyond Britain, the Europeanisation and transnationalisation of policing have been observed by Dorn (1996), Dorn *et al.* (1996) and Sheptcyki (1995). Also reaching beyond the borders, in 1997 the British Foreign Secretary promised that as well as the police and Customs, the secret intelligence services would be deployed to assist poorer countries in tackling and eradicating drug production and trafficking ('Spies and SAS join drugs war' and 'all-out war on drugs', *Evening Standard*, 28 August 1997).

Set against all of this, it may seem curious that the main thread of chapter 1 is a charting of the failings of high level enforcement and the grounds for low, or street, level drug enforcement. Low level enforcement or 'nuisance policing' has never, in either public or policing terms, achieved the status and importance that high level enforcement strategies and operators have commanded, though it was central to the well publicised Operation Welwyn in the area around Kings Cross station in London (Lee, 1996), as well as in disrupting established drug markets in particular areas (Fraser and George, 1996). It may be that set against the spectacular world of 'big traffickers' and organised crime, low level policing is regarded as simply too mundane to command much attention. If this correct, it still arguable that forms of low level enforcement have become a routine part of street clearance tactics when allied with local multi-agency initiatives. Dorn (1996) has argued that a single market in Europe may witness further developments in small scale, flexible trafficking, contrary to conventional views that it opens the door for organised crime and big traffickers. Hence the effects of European integration may be much more mundane than some have imagined. This argument indicates that low level policing may be more appropriate than conventional high level strategies. Furthermore, it can be noted that the stress upon demand reduction continues and while this is sometimes taken to mean prevention in a narrow sense, the argument in this book is that it has been conceived as a means of transcending and encompassing the standard distinctions between enforcement, prevention and treatment. Demand reduction was for instance one of the key elements of the United Nations Special Session on the World Drug Problem in New York in June 1998, as well part of the strategy of successive British governments (HM Government, 1995, 1998a).

Low level and local policing of a street drug market is also the issue that chapter 2 begins with, though it concentrates on demands on the police and the ways in which they might respond to and manage those demands, particularly in a period where the police have been reshaped or re-presented as efficient, responsive, consumer oriented organisations. In enforcement terms, I discuss reactive and proactive responses, arguing that from a demand management perspective, partnership through multi-agency social crime prevention strategies that spread or share demands among different agencies are probably the only way in which 'quality of life' concerns in urban areas can be addressed. Low level policing combined with longer term remedial action involving the local community is what Rengert (1996) calls 'weed and seed' tactics, which he sees as necessary for 'drug marts' which have taken over a neighbourhood. He argues that, 'The real victims of drugs are the law-abiding citizens who must try to survive the deterioration of their communities. Too much attention has been focused on the criminal aspects of drugs abuse and on the drug user as a victim. Too little attention has been focused on treatment and on neighborhood revitalization. We should no longer ask those who obey the law to suffer the brutal, dehumanizing effects of life in the drug marketplace' (Rengert, 1996: 132; for another perspective on the place of drug markets in urban life, see Ruggiero and South, 1997). Rengert's wider argument is that the success or failure of retail enforcement needs to take account of different types of street markets. My account of a street market does not conform with his description of a drug mart, though it could have been somewhere in-between what he calls a 'periodic market' (i.e. one with limited sales and to which buyers are only willing to travel limited distances) and a 'fixed site neighborhood sales point' where demand is sufficient to yield profitable sale volumes. However, the main issue in not the nature of the market but police responsiveness. The latter, as I argue in chapter 2, is likely to become more significant in a context that stresses localism and local partnerships. The trend to localism itself takes place within managerial reform of the police (McLaughlin and Murji, 1995, 1996, 1997; see also Morgan and Newburn, 1997). Localisation and managerialism in relation to drugs and policing strategies are evident in the White papers outlining Conservative and Labour government policies (HM Government, 1995, 1998a, b), as well as in the local indicators for drugs strategies developed by Chatterton *et al.* (1995) and the survey of Drug Action Teams by Duke and MacGregor (1997; see also some contributions in O'Connor *et al.*, 1998).

Chapter 3 is a review of the philosophical and practical arguments for and against drug legalisation. This hardy perennial in media and public debate attests to the degree of interest in the subject, even though the arguments are often tautological. In the past couple of years a raft of developments have helped to push the issue of the legal status of cannabis further into the public arena. In 1997 the British Medical Association (BMA) voted for cannabis products to be made legally available for medical use with conditions such as multiple sclerosis or cancer (*The Guardian*, 3 July 1997). A few months later the Lord Chief Justice called for 'detached, objective [and] independent consideration' of the case for legalisation, though the Home Secretary ruled out both a Royal Commission on drugs as well as decriminalisation of any drugs (*The Guardian*, 10 October 1997). The Police Foundation's establishment of an independent two-year inquiry to review the operation of the 1971 Misuse of Drugs Act was widely seen as a substitute for a Royal Commission ('New review of drug laws' and 'It's high time for a focus on drugs', *The Guardian*, 25 August 1997). Influenced by the BMA decision, the House of Lords Science and Technology Committee launched an inquiry into cannabis decriminalisation in 1998. Lord Perry, a member of the committee, said that the inquiry would 'call for factual scientific evidence and reject "sociological prejudice"' (in *The Guardian*, 11 February 1998). The Lords inquiry came about five months after the launch of a campaign for cannabis decriminalisation by the *Independent on Sunday*. Subsequently around 11,000 people took part in a demonstration through London on 28 March 1998 to support the newspaper's campaign (*The Independent*, 30 March 1998). It is of course inevitable that much of this has been contested. For instance, the Christian Institute's *Drugs Bulletin* (Winter, 1997/1998) questions the medical benefits of cannabis and provides an alternative reading of some of the scientific evidence that Lord Perry seems to imagine stands outside politics. Moreover, some supporters of a public health rather than criminal justice approach to drugs still rule out legalisation because they oppose the individualistic opposition to government regulation of any self-regarding actions that informs the latter perspective (Bertram *et al.*, 1996).

The election of a new Labour government in 1997 has led some MPs to voice arguments for legalisation (e.g. 'Blair told to rethink drugs ban', *The Guardian*, 11 August 1997) and prompted a hope by some fellow travellers that some drugs will be decriminalised, For Alan McGee, the head of Creation Records, no amount of sermonising by politicians changes the fact that many young people are taking drugs and that 'for many people, taking drugs *is* like getting up and having a cup of tea in the morning. Fact.' (In *The Guardian*, 14 March 1998). McGee believes that politicians are wildly out of step with youth culture and his general argument is akin to Parker *et al.*'s (1995) use of the term 'normalisation' to describe the ways in which drug use - particularly ecstasy (Coffield and Gofton, 1994; Henderson, 1997) - has become commonplace and taken-for-granted. Consequently for McGee and many others, the argument for decriminalisation is based upon a view that the law is out of step with popular sentiments because drug use is now so prosaic and extensive. However, Shiner and Newburn's (1997) critical evaluation of the normalisation thesis contends that it exaggerates the extent of drug use and over-simplifies the way in which drugs are perceived by young people.

In Part 2 I present research on drug referral schemes across the country, now more commonly known as arrest referral schemes. Chapter 4 lays out the context and describes the development and assessment of referral in three areas, Trafford, Southwark and Merseyside. Chapter 5 surveys some local referral schemes in action and identifies common problems that have recurred, as well as suggesting the scope and role of referral schemes within multi-agency collaboration. The latter forms an umbrella within which different types of schemes can be characterised, though the distinctions are not always clear in practice. Welfare schemes prioritise information provision, crime-control schemes aim to intervene in offending careers and perhaps to cultivate informants from arrestees, while efficiency concerns embrace the latter, as well as throughput (how many referrals are taken up? what effect does it have on the people referred? how much police time does it occupy and is it worthwhile?). Similarly, in a research review, Edmunds *et al.* (1998) portray referral schemes in terms of information, pro-active and incentive models: the defining feature of the first model is the provision of information by the police to some or all arrestees. In the pro-active model drugs workers work in close cooperation with the police, including in the police station itself, as a first port of call for people in custody who will then be offered advice about drug treatment and services. In the incentive model the coercive power of the criminal justice system is used to 'encourage' drug users - perhaps through caution plus schemes - to take up offers of help (Edmunds et al., 1998). The first fits in loosely with the welfare model, though the second and third cut across the crime-control and efficiency perspectives discussed in Part 2. For Edmunds et al., the weakness of the welfare/information model is that it leads to limited take-ups and is therefore of questionable utility. Referral schemes experience many problems as the examples discussed show, but whether low take-up should be regarded as one of these or not depends on how referral is conceived of. The view that a police service ought to ensure that the people it comes across have access to information about various forms of aid available to them (of which drugs services need only be one) envisions referral as a small intervention. This is akin to the view taken by the ACMD (1991), though, additionally, the work reported here suggests that there could be other pay offs in terms of multi-agency developments. But, returning to some of the concerns of chapter 2, a police service also exist in a climate where economy and effectiveness are significant, which is why the crime-control and efficiency (or pro-active and incentive models) have received greater attention.

The Get It While You Can (GIWYC) scheme in Brighton is a recent example of a pro-active approach. Drugs referral workers visited potential clients in the police station and provided them with information about drug services, as well as offering an appointment in an office based in the magistrates' court. The latter was designed to tie in with a court appearance and was seen as the place to carry out a detailed needs assessment and provide more specific information about drugs services. In the first six months of 1994, 250 monitoring forms were completed by GIWYC project workers. From the further appointment at the project office, 84 clients were referred to helping agencies; from information about 60 of these people, over half attended the agency to which they had been referred. It is reported that from information about 28 people, 14 had stopped taking drugs or alcohol, while six others had reduced their level of use. In relation to offending behaviour, drugs agencies reported that 14 out of 16 referrals had committed no further crimes (Turnbull et al., 1996; see also Hough, 1996). The *Evening Standard* (3 December 1997: 23) hailed this as a 'new drugs scheme [that] could save millions', recounting that, 'a revolutionary scheme....has succeeded in breaking their [addicts] dependence on drugs, leading to a drop in the number of crimes committed to pay for them'. Edmunds et al. (1998) argue that referral schemes based upon a pro-active model can be effective in reducing both drug use and drug-related crime. It is likely therefore that the weight given to referral schemes by the Home Office's Drug Prevention Initiative and within local anti-drugs strategies (Chatterton et al., 1995; Duke and MacGregor, 1997; HM Government, 1998a, b) carries some expectation of effective intervention in drug offending, not simply welfare and information service provision. The shortcomings of the latter from an efficiency perspective and the emphasis on crime-control both reflect a reliance upon criminal justice that reaffirms arguments about low level policing in chapters 1 and 2, particularly when combined with the proposed Drug Treatment and Testing Order as a way of targeting the most criminally active drug users.

Part 3 of this book moves away from a narrow focus on the police to examine official and media reaction to crack cocaine and yardies, and more recently, to ecstasy. The origins of this section date from an invitation by the publication *Community Care* to contribute a chapter on drugs for a series on moral panics in contemporary Britain. The other contributions looked at youth crime, mental illness and violence, lone parents and child abuse (Neate, 1995). My contribution reflects a degree of unhappiness about using moral panic as well as some critiques of it, though it was not possible to develop either of these points in that context. Chapter 6 fleshes out my argument against the term moral panic. In probing the counter-reaction to media reaction to the death of Leah Betts in 1995 that was commonly associated with an ecstasy tablet that she had taken, I outline some problems with counter-reaction and the **difficulties** in deciding what issues should be called a moral panic. My view follows and extends some earlier critiques, though it differs from Tester's (1994) view that the media is incapable of conveying moral value. Discussions of moral panics seem to have been undergoing something of a revival, perhaps because the 1990s have been characterised as anxious times, or even an age of moral panics, reflecting a 'dark-ages type millennial fear' (Dunant and Porter, 1996), or a 'culture of fear' (Furedi, 1997). For Dunant and Porter (1996) and Thompson (1998) the increasing quantity and scope of panics - AIDS, BSE, listeria and flesh-eating bugs come to mind as recent examples - may be an expression of the insecurities that result from the intensification of globalising economic and media processes combined with the loss of family and neighbourhood security. Others, including McRobbie and Thornton (1995), Hunt (1997) and some contributors to the journal *Media International Australia* (1997) arrive at more ambivalent conclusions about the usefulness of the term moral panic to describe and make sense of scares and fears.

One aspect of my critique of those who use the expression moral panic is the tendency to homogenise social reaction as part of an all-encompassing control culture. This perspective is extended in chapter 7 where I examine social reaction to crack cocaine. I suggest how the reaction to drugs and crack in particular can be conceived of as a symbolic crusade by politicians and as involving moral enterprise by the police. Allied beliefs include the views that both drugs and drug couriers have become modern folk devils (Sheptycki, 1995; Green, 1996). In reviewing Australian drug history, Manderson (1997) argues that the regulation of opium emerged from fears of Chinese immigration in which opium was a symbol conjoining race, sex and fear. While I mention and outline similar arguments, my contention is that the ideas about symbolic crusades and moral enterprise contain some defects that are also associated with the moral panics argument, in particular the question of what issues get called panics, what counts as moral enterprise, and unevenness and contradiction within social reaction. I suggest instead that the term problematisations can offer ways of exploring social reaction without the pejorative connotation attached to the expression moral panic. This is akin to Sumner's argument for a sociology of social censures, rather than a sociology of deviance (Sumner, 1990). A central aspect of the reaction to crack and a key site of problematisation is its association with a new group of black criminals, the yardies, which is the subject of chapter 8. Drawing on ideas about culturalism, racialisation and from post-colonial discourse analysis, I lay out some of the main themes in representations of yardies as Other, indicating the extent of overlap and repetition from different sources and, finally, I explore some contradictions within the images presented.

PART I

LAW ENFORCEMENT

1 Drug Enforcement Strategies

Karl Marx once wrote that 'the criminal produces the whole of the police and of criminal justice'.[1] In the 'age of the dealer' (Campbell, 1991) the drugs business has been one of the key sources of productivity for policing and criminal justice. Drugs have been at the forefront in making the case for far-reaching changes in law enforcement, producing legislative innovations such as the 1986 Drug Trafficking Offences Act, which brought into law powers of asset seizure and forfeiture. Drugs have helped to nationalise and transnationalise policing in the shape of the National Criminal Intelligence Service (which incorporated the former National Drugs Intelligence Unit), the National Crime Squad (constructed from the former Regional Crime Squads) and Europol. Furthermore, drugs have also been a major reason for the ever increasing array of International Mutual Legal Assistance Treaties between many governments, authorising mutual powers of search, seizure and mutual assistance between law enforcement agencies. In the post-cold war 1990s, the Secret Intelligence Services have also been playing a role in drug enforcement. Drugs therefore stand second only to terrorism as a major stimulus to developments in law enforcement (Dorn and South, 1991; Dorn et al., 1991, 1992).

Throughout this period the focus of enforcement has been almost entirely on the search for the 'big trafficker' and weighty drug seizures. The value of 'high level' enforcement strategies has however been called into question. A common response to the perceived or actual shortcomings of drug enforcement is the call for some form of decriminalisation or legalisation of drugs. Another response is an interest in 'low level' enforcement aimed at street or retail drug markets. This is not to say that street-level enforcement as such is new. More significant is the attention that has been paid to it and the support for it from particular individuals from across the political spectrum. In this chapter I examine four approaches to drug enforcement. Three of these are high level approaches that are dominant in thinking about drug enforcement. In reviewing the arguments for and the limitations of each of these, I argue that their shortcomings have led to arguments for a fourth way, low level enforcement. The four approaches are presented in a logical order from crop programmes to interdiction to organised criminal networks.

Greatest attention is paid to the theory and practice of interdiction because of its significance for the subsequent argument. Drawing on economic models of the drug market and the behaviour of drug buyers, the arguments for low level drug enforcement are described and some concerns are raised.

Two qualifications should be noted at the outset. First, this discussion is mostly based on literature looking at drug enforcement in the United States, though parallels are drawn with developments in Britain, where similar trends have been identified (Pearson, 1989, 1992; Dorn et al., 1992; Dorn and Murji, 1992a, b; Collison, 1995). Secondly, while law enforcement is tiered at three levels - the upper, middle and level lower levels of enforcement, corresponding in Britain to national/regional crime squads, county drug squads and local CID/uniformed policing (see ACPO, 1985) - this does not necessarily mean that the drug market is tiered or structured in any corresponding way. Indeed even the notion of a tiered drug market should be regarded as problematic (Dorn and South, 1990; Dorn et al., 1991).

High level enforcement

Enforcement agencies tackle drug importation, distribution and the crime networks associated with both of these using a variety of methods. Drug enforcement can aim to interrupt and disrupt the supply of illicit drugs to the market, mainly through crop programmes in source countries, interdiction at the borders or by targeting key individuals in trafficking organisations as part of an organised crime approach. Together these constitute the three conventional approaches guiding supply reduction efforts (Moore, 1988, 1990).

Crop programmes

The first approach is based on the idea that the most effective method of enforcement is to 'strike at the source' of the problem (Moore, 1988, 1990). This strategy has a simple and straightforward appeal. It offers a clear solution to the problem of how to reduce the supply of drugs. But its simplicity is also part of the problem. The 'source' could be seen as any one of a number of places, from the point at which plants are grown, or at the borders where drugs come in, or the trafficking organisation that distribute drugs. Since the late 1980s, a process of re-imagining has seen drugs users and buyers as 'the source'. In a 'zero tolerance' climate, terms such as 'demand reduction' and 'user accountability' have meant measures targeted at drug users and buyers since, in this view, it is the demand for illicit drugs that ultimately enables, supports and maintains the existence of illicit drug markets. As

Inciardi points out, this position rests on a number of premises including: 'that if there were no drug abusers there would be no drug problem...that drug abuse starts with a willful act...[and] that most illegal drug users can choose to stop their drug-taking behaviors and must be held accountable if they do not' (Inciardi, 1991: 11). Demand reduction is therefore only a partial counterweight to the prevailing emphasis on supply side policies, though it does include more of an emphasis on the need for education and prevention programmes rather than just law enforcement. In practice, demand reduction not only operates alongside law enforcement but can also be seen as an enforcement tool. For example, the police department in Los Angeles have made use of the demand reducing DARE (Drug Abuse Resistance Education) programme and even said that it is their only hope for future generations, since the current generation of drug users is considered to be 'already lost' (Kleiman and Smith, 1990; for a discussion of demand reduction, and its relationship to US drug control policies under the former 'drugs czar' William Bennett, see Dorn and Murji, 1992a; Dorn and South, 1993).

Locating the 'source' as the point at which the 'raw material' is produced does not solve the definitional problem. Although crop eradication and substitution programmes have been heavily promoted by successive US governments and under the aegis of United Nations agencies, their success has been mixed at best. Farmers in so-called 'source' countries have been encouraged in various ways to substitute coca leaf, opium or marijuana plantations with other crops. Where farmers are recalcitrant, drugs crops are simply destroyed through aerial spraying of defoliating chemicals. An immediate problem with this approach is displacement and replacement. Crops eradicated or substituted in one area can easily be grown elsewhere. One consequence of such replacement has been that, in the case of marijuana in the US, the 'home grown' replacement is more potent than the imported variety (Kleiman, 1989). A second problem is that spraying from the air causes what is euphemistically referred to as 'collateral damage' to other crops, hence raising environmental questions that at least cut-across, or possibly go well beyond, drug policy concerns (del Olmo, 1987). The alternative - clearing plantations at ground level - is cumbersome because plans for ground-level clearance programmes are obvious long before any action can take place. That leaves plenty of time for counter-measures (Moore, 1988).

Another problem is that governments in 'source' countries may not be able to carry through substitution and eradication policies, perhaps because of relatively weak control of some regional areas and/or guerilla warfare, or corruption. The contradictory demands of US drugs and foreign policy concerns have also confused the picture, and the latter have often been seen to win out over the former (Moore, 1988; see also Reuter and Kleiman, 1986;

Reuter, 1992). Finally, crop programmes do not of course apply to synthetically manufactured drugs such as ecstasy, amphetamines and LSD. In these cases, the 'source' becomes the laboratory and this has stimulated policing methods based on 'chasing the chemicals', that is, monitoring the sales of precursor chemicals that can be used in drug manufacture (see Dorn et al., 1992, chapter 9).

Interdiction

A second conventional method is the reliance on interdiction as the principal means of stopping drugs at the border. Public announcements about the seizures of large quantities of drugs are fairly commonplace and the weight of drugs captured acts as a rough and ready indicator of enforcement success. But whatever the quantity of drugs interdicted, an unknown percentage still gets through. Two more substantial problems with interdiction have been identified by Reuter et al. (1988). One is the process of 'modelling adaptations'. Drug smugglers always seek to utilise forms of importation that carry least risk. As enforcement pressure bears down on particular routes, amounts or methods of importation, drug importers are likely to change or modify their methods. This process of 'learning by doing' is not unique to this level of the market since law enforcement and drug markets continuously interact and shape one another (Dorn and South, 1990; Dorn et al., 1992). A second problem is that the economics of drug production and smuggling mean that the 'replacement cost' of drugs seized is low and adds little to costs at the retail level. Reuter et al.'s (1988) explanation for this is that interdiction primarily effects the smuggling costs of drug distribution. Because replacement costs to traffickers are a relatively minor part of the total cost to the distribution system, successful interdiction can make only modest contributions to overall consumption. In the case of cocaine for example, only a small part of the final price of the drug (perhaps around 10 per cent) is accounted for by the costs of smuggling (see also Reuter and Kleiman, 1986; Moore, 1990; Wagstaff and Maynard, 1988).

A key justification for interdiction is that seizures will induce shortages in the market, driving up prices at the retail level and so lead to reduced consumption. Interdiction is expected to raise retail prices by imposing costs on those who have to replace the seized drugs, by increasing both the risks associated with smuggling drugs and the uncertainty about income and supplies for dealers at the retail level (Reuter and Kleiman, 1986; Reuter et al., 1988; Reuter, 1992). It is the role of prices that I want to focus on here. Their significance as a means for evaluating enforcement efforts is clear: 'The single most important bit of empirical evidence on the effectiveness of supply-reduction efforts is data on price and availability of drugs in illicit markets' (Moore, 1990: 121). There are however considerable difficulties with using price data as a measure of the effectiveness of supply reduction. First, the reliability of the data on prices is questionable. Secondly, there is the question of whether the purchase price is a sufficient measure of the impact of supply reduction measures. What the street price does not measure (except perhaps indirectly) is what is called the 'search time', which includes time spent searching for a 'connection', and the difficulties and dangers for consumers in making the deal. Thirdly, there is the problem of separating the effects of supply reduction efforts on price from the other multiple factors which effect price, such as demand. Movements in demand in relation to supply can cause prices to rise or fall even if the effectiveness of enforcement efforts remains constant or declines (Moore, 1990). Nevertheless, Moore points out that 'the price of drugs in illicit markets remains one of the principal empirical measures available for assessing the effectiveness of supply-reduction efforts' (Moore, 1990: 123). For present purposes it may be sufficient to note that the continuing reliance on prices as measures of supply-reduction efforts tend to be heavily hedged with qualifications about their reliability (for example, see Wagstaff and Maynard, 1988; Moore, 1990). This makes them rather less revealing than they might at first sight seem. A linked point is that the use of data on arrests and seizures as a measure of organisational productivity is also subject to qualifications which significantly reduce their usefulness (Polich *et al.*, 1984; Wagstaff and Maynard, 1988).[2] Setting aside some of these problems, we can turn to consider the role that prices are *expected* to play at the retail level by drawing upon simple supply and demand economics. As the supply of a commodity becomes scarcer while demand remains the same or increases, its price will rise. That price rise will consequently sap some of the demand as those unable to afford a particular commodity adapt their economic behaviour accordingly. As far as drugs are concerned, supply reduction efforts should raise the prices of drugs and consequently drive some users out of the market, though the effectiveness of interdiction as a means for achieving that has been questioned.[3] Minimising supply and availability and increasing the price of drugs is a cornerstone of what Moore (1990) calls the 'drug policy perspective' (see also Moore, 1979; Reuter and Kleiman, 1986).

There is an obvious line of counter-argument, which sees the attempt to force up prices as being both limited and counter-productive. Limited because of the view that demand for drugs is not particularly responsive to price increases, and counter-productive because price increases might result in the commission of greater amounts of drug related crime (Wagstaff and Maynard, 1988). But:

> This conclusion has recently been challenged on the grounds that the price

> elasticity of demand for drugs may not be so low as previously thought. One reason is that users of drugs such as heroin tend (or are at least able) to switch to other drugs as the price of heroin (or whatever) rises. The existence of substitutes means that the demand for hard drugs may not be so price-inelastic. Other writers suggests that demand may be price-elastic at least over some price ranges. At low prices some of the market demand will be from occasional users, whose use may be expected to drop (or even cease) as the price rises. Thus, even if addicts' demand may be price-inelastic at low prices, the market demand need not be. At high prices addicts' demand may be price-elastic, since as prices become very high they will find it harder and harder to fund their habit. They will be more likely to be detected when engaging in theft and therefore more likely to be arrested. They may also be more likely to enter treatment programmes voluntarily as supporting their habit becomes more difficult. The upshot of all this is that supply-side law enforcement may, after all, have a role to play (Wagstaff and Maynard, 1988: 55).

As this quote indicates a key point around which differing positions are constructed is the elasticity of demand by users. Any claim that demand is perfectly inelastic (i.e. not at all responsive to price changes) is clearly untenable since, as Moore points out, there is no good which is perfectly inelastic: 'Everything seems to respond to price' (Moore, 1990: 114). But what of the lesser claim that demand for drugs is somewhat inelastic though not perfectly inelastic? Under such conditions, usage must decline, or at least patterns of usage must change in relation to price increases and availability (for an example, see George and Fraser, 1989).

Supply reduction efforts do contribute something to increasing prices, where these are taken to be of a money or non-money kind, as we will see in the 'risks and prices' model. Enforcement measures which disrupt the market can, indirectly, lead to a reduction in the volume of drugs which pass through the market by creating increased uncertainty for sellers and buyers, as we will see in the 'market constriction' model. Here then are two embryonic arguments for policing 'down market', or low level drug enforcement. One is that price increases might play a role in persuading 'heavy', perhaps addicted, users to enter drug treatment ('taking early retirement' as it has been described by Gilman and Pearson, 1991). A second is the discouragement of novice or newer users from entering the market, or at least to consume less often, both leading to an overall decline in market turnover (cf Wilson, 1985; Pearson, 1989). I return to this in the discussion of low level enforcement below.

Tackling organised crime

The third conventional approach is based upon the attempt to arrest and imprison the main individuals at the top of drug trafficking organisations. This 'Mr Big' approach suffers from weaknesses in principle and in practice. In principle, the assumption that there are highly centralised organisations with key players who are at the centre of everything it does has increasingly come into question (Reuter, 1983; Moore, 1988; Moore and Kleiman, 1989; Dorn and South, 1990). The image of a 'Mr Big' is close to the demonology of the mafia and its 'Godfather' as portrayed in various books, films and on television. But it is worth recalling that, even there, there is always a new Godfather ready to succeed one who has become indisposed. So one limitation of this approach is that, 'the "big connections" and "top dealers" who indeed exist and who generally are not users, are in many ways the least important part of the heroin market system, because they are the most easily replaced. A new "connection" arises for everyone put out of business' (Wilson, 1985: 212).

In practice, targeting 'Mr Big' has quite simply not been a very effective method of law enforcement as an evaluation by the US General Accounting Office (1984) showed. Criminal organisations are durable enough to withstand the arrest of one, or several, individual(s). One reason for this is because ascendance within the hierarchy is rapid, as Wilson points out above, and arrests can create a vacuum or space to be filled. Thus, over time this enforcement strategy may have the ironic consequence of making criminal organisations more sophisticated and therefore more difficult to break (Reuter and Haaga, 1989; Kleiman and Smith, 1990). As Reuter and Haaga conclude:

> Ease of entry [to drug trafficking as a profession]... lessens any hope one might have that the removal of the more experienced individuals could make a significant difference. Lower-level dealers are higher-level dealers in training. This lack of differentiation in the population suggests that incarcerating or otherwise incapacitating even a large number of experienced higher-level dealers would not seriously disrupt the markets (Reuter and Haaga, 1989: 56).

The limitations of conventional supply reduction efforts does not mean that they have been discontinued or replaced. Indeed it is clear that these 'high level' approaches have continued to expand, for instance through intelligence sharing across Europe and beyond (McLaughlin, 1992; Bunyan, 1993). But as the limitations and shortcomings of conventional supply reduction methods have become manifest, some influential academics and commentators have been advocating retail level enforcement (Moore, 1979; Moore and Kleiman, 1989; Reuter and Kleiman, 1986; Wilson, 1985; Pearson, 1989; Hayeslip, 1989).[4] I now turn to consider two approaches that seek to theorise the impact of retail level enforcement on drug markets. One is the 'risks and prices' model developed by Reuter and Kleiman (1986; see also Reuter *et al.*, 1988; Kleiman and Smith, 1990; Reuter, 1992). The other is to seek to constrict the market by targeting its key point of vulnerability, the point of transactions or 'connections' (Moore, 1979, 1990). Both approaches are based on economic models of the markets and there are assumptions built into these models that are not discussed here (but see Reuter and Kleiman, 1986; Moore, 1979, 1990). Some examples are given of enforcement operations which can flow from the application of both approaches. That there are similarities and overlaps between the two approaches will become apparent, especially when looking at their applications. But they are considered separately here in an attempt to clarify their different starting points.

Low level enforcement

Risks and prices

In his seminal work *Buy and Bust*, Moore (1977) compared prices in licit and illicit markets and concluded that the higher prices to be found in the latter can, to some extent, be attributed to the impact of enforcement pressure on markets. Building upon this, Reuter and Kleiman's (1986) 'risks and prices' model regards enforcement rather like a tax in that it imposes costs on dealers in illicit markets. Increased costs can be of both a money and non-money kind (including drug seizures and prison terms) and, as argued earlier, the imposition of such costs should lead to increased prices which could lead to decreased throughput. But unlike interdiction, low level enforcement benefits from the advantage that non-money transactions are important as a cost to buyers and sellers in retail markets (Kleiman and Smith, 1990). The effects will obviously depend on the extent of the costs involved and the behaviour of consumers. If drug markets are large then the model predicts that local or low level enforcement can produce only limited effects. For example, an estimate for New York City is that the seizure of an additional 500 kilograms of cocaine per year or the imprisonment of another 200 cocaine dealers would produce only a 1 per cent increase in price (Kleiman and Smith, 1990). But the model also predicts that early intervention and *concentrated* retail level enforcement activity would produce shrinkage of the retail drug market. Market inertia might make this shrinkage self-sustaining, leading to a collapse of the market (Kleiman and Smith, 1990). One example of focused or concentrated enforcement activity cited as a successful application of the risks and prices approach is Operation Pressure Point.[5]

Operation Pressure Point (OPP) on the Lower East Side of New York City was a concentrated 2-year disruptive policing operation, or 'crackdown'.

In this area the trade had become sufficiently open for descriptions such as 'drugs supermarket' and 'the most open heroin market in the nation' to be applied (Zimmer, 1987: 1; see also Sherman, 1990). A combination of reasons made the area attractive to drug users and a difficult area to police. As the drug trade expanded it passed beyond the capacity of the local police to contain it. The assignment of Special Narcotic Enforcement Units was described as 'too little, too late' (Zimmer, 1987: 3). Media and political interests focused attention on this drug 'hotspot' and in 1984 Operation Pressure Point was launched as a response. At a cost of $12 million per year, it used more than 150 uniformed officers. It entailed police foot patrols 'sweeping'[6] the streets, dispersing crowds, issuing parking tickets, and searching and arresting people. In addition, operations were carried out on public housing projects, mounted police rode through the area, police dogs were used to search out empty and abandoned buildings. Hidden surveillance and 'buy and bust' operations were carried out by the Organised Crime Control Bureau while helicopters hovered above watching for any attacks on the police. The courts contributed by handing out harsher penalties.

> Even when unable to make arrests, OPP forces tried to discourage involvement in the drug trade by acting as what Sagarin and McNamara (1972) call a "judicial punitive body". This is a euphemism for harassing suspicious people in "known drug areas" by stopping them, questioning them, perhaps searching them and telling them to "move on". From the police perspective, the advantage of this type of intervention is that it does not take officers off the street. The cost to the suspect is substantially less than with an arrest but a greater number of interventions per officer becomes possible (Zimmer, 1987: 6).

By increasing the risk of arrest for buyers and sellers, OPP led to changes in the pattern of trade. Buyers responded by spending less time on the streets and sellers varied the place and time of their sales, dealt in larger quantities and employed more helpers. 'Steerers' notified buyers where and when sales would take place, 'lookouts' sent out warning signals when the police appeared (Zimmer, 1987; cf Dorn et al., 1992, chapter 7). Because OPP led to reduced drug dealing in the area, a change to less overt dealing, a displacement of some drug sales to other areas and a decrease in drug-related acquisitive crime - as well as reductions in robberies and homicides - it was regarded as a successful operation for the NY police.[7] Sherman (1990) states that the deterrent effect of the operation was maintained for at least two years. However, Zimmer points out that the operation was more successful because the area was already undergoing gentrification, that sustained police pressure was required, without which the trade would rapidly re-emerge (the 'push-down/pop-up' factor - Nadelmann, 1991) and that a similar police operation in Harlem had little impact. Furthermore, the 'early success occurred primarily because the drug traffic had become so blatant; now that buyers and sellers have had time to adjust to the police presence, law enforcement has become more difficult' (Zimmer, 1987: 15).

OPP led to rising public expectations because residents in other areas demanded similar operations by the police. The organisational dilemma is that seemingly successful operations can create or increase public demands for law enforcement. Seeking to address those expectations may mean diminishing the resource commitment to the operation which initially raised expectations, thereby putting at risk the gains made, as enforcement pressure elsewhere leads to a displacement back into an area which has previously been cleared. But displacement does not have to mean a simple one for one substitution; indeed it could even be conceived of a means by which enforcement helps to re-model drug hotpsots, or even to re-shape the form of drug markets in the direction of harm reduction (Dorn and Murji, 1992b; Pearson, 1992; ACMD, 1994).[8] Returning to the model, it appears that in OPP the disruption of 'connections' between buyers and sellers and adding to the 'search time' for buyers did act to squeeze or constrict the market. This outcome is the basis of the next model to be described.

Constricting the market

Moore (1979) and Wilson (1985) have advocated law enforcement aimed at constricting drug markets. The means to this end is *disruptive policing*, which aims to make markets less predictable in various ways, chiefly by introducing greater uncertainty into them.[9] Two examples of police operations directed towards this end will be considered: (i) selective policing against 'heavy' users; and (ii) inconvenience policing aimed at deterring new or novice users. These ideas are drawn from work by Moore (1977, 1979). Moore's approach is based on an attempt to identify the weak points in the supply system, which he calls the optimal points of attack by supply reduction enforcement: 'The basic objective of supply reduction efforts is to reduce the throughput capacity of the systems that supply drugs to illicit markets. The strategic problem is to find the specific points in the system which can be attacked, and which, if effectively attacked would result in large, durable reductions in the rate at which drugs move to illicit markets' (Moore, 1979: 188-9). Moore argues that *transaction* points are the specific point of vulnerability for dealers, not just because of possible intervention by undercover police officers, but also because of the threat of 'rip-offs' by other dealers and buyers. So drug dealers have to build in 'defensive strategies' to prevent 'rip-offs'. This necessitates the investment of time and effort and makes them more cautious about who they are selling to. The effect of this dual constraint is, Moore argues, to 'make dealers less efficient distributors of drugs, and constrain the aggregate throughput capacity of the system' (Moore, 1979: 191). As with the risks and prices model, both direct and indirect measures of enforcement activity are pertinent. The direct (arrests, seizures, etc) and indirect (increased use of defensive strategies by sellers making them less efficient distributors) effects of law enforcement can, metaphorically, be thought of as dismantling some sections of a pipeline, and as constricting other sections of the pipeline that remain in existence (Moore, 1979). Thus, indirect consequences are as important as direct ones:

> To the extent that the police use undercover police and informants, they contaminate the pool of potential associates and force dealers to be surreptitious in executing transactions. Since transactions are difficult even without active police interference and since threats of interference makes the transactions still more complicated, the indirect effects of enforcement efforts are likely to be significant (Moore, 1979: 305).

The principal aim of disruptive policing at the retail level is to make life a good deal less predictable for dealers by increasing the difficulty associated with completing transactions.[10] Moving from theory to practice, there are two applications of this approach.

Selective policing - arrest 'heavy' users   In a selective policing operation the focus would be the arrest of large numbers of established users and minor user-dealers on the streets. Such street level operations are said to have been commoner in the past (Moore, 1988), though perhaps fell out of favour in the rush to make big seizures and capture 'top' individuals. Wilson mentions two reasons why targeting users has not been a consistent policy. One is the belief that detaining addicts merely for their addiction is a violation of their civil rights. Another is the view that the resources of 'law enforcement should concentrate on the "pushers" and the "big connections" and not the innocent user' (Wilson, 1985: 212). Similarly, Pearson (1989) points out that street level enforcement is regarded as unsavoury by many people because it targets the user and not the 'top level' suppliers. However, in an interesting convergence between commentators from opposed ends of the political spectrum, both Wilson (1985) and Pearson (1989) have argued for street enforcement as a means of arresting users with the aim of diverting them into treatment programmes (see also Johnson, 1989; Gilman and Pearson, 1991).[11]

> One can imagine a variety of law-enforcement strategies that could have a powerful effect on the number of addicts on the street, and thus on the number of street crimes that they might commit and other harm that they might do to others and themselves. One could arrest every known addict and send him to a "heroin quarantine center" with...intensive care programs. Or one could arrest every known

addict and send him back onto the street under a "pledge" system requiring him to submit to frequent urine tests which, if omitted or failed, would then lead to confinement in either center or jail (Wilson, 1985: 211).

This 'sentenced to treatment' approach has already been operating in various parts of the US for a number of years. It has been slower to develop in Britain. But the 1991 Criminal Justice Act did encourage the imposition of treatment conditions as an alternative to custodial penalties, where drug use is shown to be a significant factor in a person's offending pattern. Subsequently, the Advisory Council on the Misuse of Drugs (ACMD) encouraged drug agencies to comply with the Act in providing treatment alternatives to custodial penalties (ACMD, 1991; *Druglink*, 1992). While the ACMD recognised that the different cultures of drugs agencies and the police are considerable obstacles to 'meshing' approaches to drug offenders, its encouragement for this method and the possible cooperation of drug agencies could mean that the existence of treatment alternatives could actually encourage low level policing as users are swept up with the ultimate aim of diverting them into treatment (see ACMD, 1991, 1994; cf Pearson, 1992; Collison, 1993).[12]

There are other arguments for selective policing. One is that dislodging 'heavy' user-dealers from the street would remove the most regular customers that dealers have. The reduction of demand might be linked to a reduction in the price of a drug, but it would force dealers to deal with more novice users, consuming smaller amounts thereby reducing overall consumption of the drug (Wilson, 1985). This could lead to further reductions in the price of the drug and the profits to be made, unless dealers are able to attract large numbers of new buyers. A second claim for this type of enforcement is that it could have effects on the overall crime rate in an area.[13] 'Controlling user crime' as Kleiman and Smith (1990) call it, is premised on the idea of a strong drugs-crime link, i.e. that drug users engage in acquisitive crime to be able to pay for drugs. Kleiman and Smith argue that this is an example of a positive congruence between drug control policy - reducing the level of drug misuse - and crime control policy - reducing crime rates in a given neighbourhood or area. But the effects are far from straightforward. Price increases might lead to the commission of greater amounts of acquisitive crime by users. Here we are again in the land of suppositions about demand elasticity. Kleiman and Smith (1990) estimate that if demand is relatively inelastic, a 10 per cent increase in the price of heroin which produces a 5 per cent decrease in consumption would require an additional 4.5 per cent of income to pay for drugs, presumably to be financed by extra income-producing crime by heroin users. Conversely, if demand is relatively elastic and the same price increase produces a 20 per cent decrease in consumption, then total amounts expended on drugs would fall by 12 per cent and so, presumably, would the extent of income-producing crime by heroin users.

Inconvenience policing - deter novice users   The other side of the coin to selective policing is inconvenience policing, targeted at inexperienced or novice drug buyers (Moore, 1977, 1979). Based on studies of the economic behaviour of potential drug buyers, its rationale is that novice heroin users are:

> quite vulnerable to changes, even small ones, in the availability of heroin...a person who has not yet become a heavy user will not conduct an intensive search for a supply. Some studies have suggested that a "dabbler" may use heroin if it is immediately available, but will not use it if it requires two, three, or four hours of searching. Extending the search time for novices may discourage or reduce the frequency of their use of heroin (Wilson, 1985: 214).

Under these conditions intensified policing could lead dealers to abandon their traditional areas of supply or make them more cautious about dealing to unfamiliar buyers, on the grounds that the new buyers may be undercover police working to a 'buy-bust' policy (Moore, 1977).[14] In either case the effect of police activity is, again, to make life considerably more difficult for dealers and in particular for casual or novice buyers: 'Heroin customers can be thought of as a "queue" with the heaviest users at the head of the line and the casual ones at the end; how far down the queue the dealer will do business depends on the perceived level of risk associated with each additional customer, and that in turn depends on how strongly "the heat is on"' (Wilson, 1985: 214).

The argument for inconvenience policing - aiming to deter the casual buyer by increasing the 'search time' which it will take her/him to find heroin - has been most clearly articulated by Moore (1977) and Wilson (1985). Pearson (1989, 1992) has argued for this approach in Britain.[15] An important basis for it is the realisation that the effects of law enforcement may drive up the street price of a drug over the long term, but that this is not the only way in which enforcement can impact on drug markets. As Wilson concludes - 'in the short term, antidealer law enforcement probably affects access (finding a "connection") more than price' (Wilson, 1985: 214). Both selective and inconvenience policing contribute to greater uncertainty in drug markets. The removal of regular buyers forces sellers (or at least those who wish to continue selling) to deal with more unfamiliar purchasers, which means more potential hazards for them in their dealings. Inconveniencing novice buyers constricts the market by deterring some would-be buyers and forcing sellers to invest more in defensive strategies. Both reduce what Moore (1979) calls the 'throughput capacity' of the system.

Conclusion

The application of economic models to drug enforcement has been relatively under-considered within criminology.[16] Naturally theory and practice will not always match up. There are problems with the models of low level enforcement and with their applications. First, the models suffer from a lack of data which means assumptions have to be made (Kleiman, 1991). The reliability of the assumptions is a matter for empirical investigation and subject to the usual qualifications about price data. Second, the application of these approaches to drugs other than heroin has been questioned (Reuter and Kleiman, 1986). Third, the character and form of US drug markets is likely to be distinctive from those to be found elsewhere. It is probably un-wise even to generalise about US drug markets as if they were all of a single type. The lesson for low level drug enforcement is that particular attention may need to be paid to the nature of localities in which enforcement action takes place. Fourth, market separation by drug type may be a desirable policy objective, if it separates more from less harmful cultures of drug use (for example, an environment where injecting heroin is common from one where only smoking the drug is accepted). But there are considerable problems in the face of poly-drug using cultures and of substitution of drugs, when there are shortages of the primary drug of choice (George and Fraser, 1989; see also Pearson, 1992).

Nonetheless, in the wake of the disappointment with conventional high level enforcement strategies it may be that the arguments for low level enforcement can be persuasive, especially when allied with demand reduction in the form of treatment for addicts and prevention for less regular users (Dorn and Murji, 1992a; Dorn and South, 1993). Street level enforcement itself is clearly not new, but what is significant is the emphasis it has received from academics, policy makers and the police in recent times and the fact that it can draw on support from both right and left wing perspectives.[17] The prospect of picking-up large numbers of users and dealers may fail to excite many officers, some of whom see low level enforcement as a diversion from their 'real job' of catching people 'at the top' (Kleiman and Smith, 1990). One concern about low level policing is that it may achieve little beyond mass criminalisation of minor users and dealers. Another is that the effect of street or low level enforcement may mean that black people and/or ethnic minorities are disproportionately targeted and swept up into the criminal justice net, a concern that led the ACMD (1994) to call for ethnic monitoring to accompany such police operations (see also Manning, 1980; Davis, 1990;

Kraska, 1990).[18] These are just some reasons why developments in low level policing are contingent and likely to vary considerably according to the inclinations of the police, of local community demands, of the character of local drug problems and the extent of broader public and media support for such actions (Dorn and Murji, 1992b).

Finally, it would be as well to note two practical difficulties that have been linked with low level policing. The first is a pragmatic one concerning the effects of different levels of policing. That there are such difficulties is apparent from Kleiman and Smith's (1990) instructive discussion of the difficulties involved in planning the allocation of resources to state and local levels in the US. A reason for such problems is that enforcement at different levels can produce contradictory effects. 'Tough' enforcement can lead to 'the survival of the fittest', in which removal of some weaker players in the market leaves the hardiest and most arrest-resistant surviving. Hence, ironically, enforcement can increase the tendency towards monopolisation of the market. A second point is about the ability of the criminal justice system to respond to and absorb the effects of low level policing. Both the courts and prisons have to deal with the volume of work created by mass arrest programmes (Belenko, 1990), and for those 'sentenced to treatment', services have to exist and be capable of dealing with them. In this situation the bureaucratic imperatives of different strands of the criminal justice system can produce contradictory results:

> Press (1987) compares the New York City criminal justice system to a person with bulimia, gorging itself on masses of arrests only to vomit them back up in plea negotiation. Press makes it clear both that the police can easily swamp the courts with drug cases, and that the courts will respond to control their own workloads in ways that may largely neutralize the value of mass-arrest programs (Kleiman and Smith, 1990: 81).

The 'war on drugs' can easily be characterised as a gung-ho exercise, especially when, after the Gulf War, President George Bush could be heard calling for a 'domestic Operation Desert Storm' to combat drugs. Low level policing cannot be seen as any sort of counter-weight to such trends, indeed for those who find the 'war' theme useful, it is probably better viewed as the 'war on drugs comes home' (see Bennett, 1989; Meese and Carrico, 1990). That view certainly underlies the interest in reducing the demand for drugs as a response to the limitations of supply side enforcement, though many have argued that it can mean a 'civil war' on the population (Weisheit, 1991). Nevertheless, within a new broader conception of demand reduction, supply reduction need not be confined to the conventional, high level approaches. This development may mean that some of the distinctions between enforcement, prevention and treatment may be blurred or break down as new forms of inter-agency strategies are brought to the forefront of drugs policy.[19]

Notes

1. In *Theories of Surplus Value*.

2. Wagstaff and Maynard suggest that there would be a differential impact of supply side enforcement depending on whether it is targeted at the importation or distribution and wholesale or retail level of the market. They conclude that various factors produce contradictory effects, hence 'it is impossible to say *a priori* whether law enforcement aimed at the import level (or indeed distribution level) yields higher or lower benefits than enforcement aimed at street level' (Wagstaff and Maynard, 1988: 49; cf Reuter *et al.*, 1988).

3. The extent of the effect of interdiction on retail prices has been called into question by Polich *et al.* (1984) and Reuter *et al.* (1988). Calculations by the former predicted that even if the interdiction rate could be doubled, retail prices would rise by only about 12 per cent at most. Expanded investigative efforts would be disproportionately costly and also produce only marginal changes in the retail price (Polich *et al.*, 1984: viii-xii and 45-82).

4. Moore, Kleiman and Wilson were singled out for praise by William Bennett during his period as 'drugs czar' as noteworthy examples of intellectuals making a distinguished contribution to drug policy (see Bennett, 1990).

5. Both Reuter and Kleiman (1986) and Kleiman and Smith (1990) make qualifications about the model and its successful application to drugs other than heroin.

6. Eck (1989a) describes sweeps as one of the methods which can be used by the police in targeting mid to low level dealers, including street dealers. An overtly disruptive method, it entails the police 'sweeping' areas said to have become synonymous with drug dealing. Who gets 'swept up' is essentially unselective - 'everything that moves on two feet, and some on four, is arrested' (Eck, 1989a: 8).

7. Kaplan has recommended selective enforcement as a means to force drug dealing indoors, on the grounds that, 'a large percentage of potential customers are afraid to go [in there]' (Kaplan, 1988: 45).

8. Barr and Pease (1992) suggest that displacement effects can be spatial, temporal, tactical or in terms of target.

9. For an elaboration of this idea at the level of interdiction strategies see Reuter *et al.*, 1988.

10. Market disruption carries other dangers which are more evident in the notion of 'turf wars' between rival dealers competing to fill a vacuum created by enforcement actions. There have been reports of what is said to be increasing drug-related violence in the city of Manchester. What may be an example of this was featured on the Granada Television

programme, 'Open Eye'. It reported that in Operation Popeye in February 1990 the Greater Manchester Police arrested two men with around 1.5 kilos of heroin. These two men were said to be working for someone with a near monopoly of the heroin market in the area. The seizure lead to a temporary drought, during which there was a three-fold increase in reported shootings in the area (the actual numbers were not reported). This violence is said to be linked to rival organisations fighting it out to 'fill the drugs vacuum' (Open Eye, 1990).

11. Gilman and Pearson (1991) have derided the 'myth of voluntarism' in explaining how people come to enter into drug treatment. They describe ways in which law enforcement activity can persuade drug users to take 'early retirement' from their drug using careers. Arrests of users can then be justified on law enforcement or health and welfare criteria, or both. For Johnson, 'Compulsory treatment is probably the most effective way to control the largest number of criminally active heroin users... people tend to reduce their criminality substantially while in treatment but not necessarily after release from prison or after treatment (Johnson, 1989: 12).

12. This represents a clear concordance between 'welfare' and 'criminal justice' objectives. Another example of this may be found in the existing cooperation between police forces and drug agencies in drug (or arrest) referral schemes, in which the police seek to encourage diversion into helping agencies. The difference between the US and the UK in the availability of drug services may then itself be a spur to selective policing operations in this country. However, Collison's research suggested that 'many individuals drawn into the criminal justice system as the result of low-level polic[ing]...were problem users and, once in the system, were likely to rapidly lose their victim status and be dealt with via the logics of punishment and deterrence ideally reserved for the villains' (Collison, 1993: 384).

13. Kleiman and Smith (1990) cite evidence that interventions directed at reducing drug use by offenders do lead to a decrease in offending rates and that periods in drug treatment are correlated with reduced criminal activity (cf Johnson, 1989).

14. While both 'buy' and 'sell' operations by police officers are well known as enforcement techniques in the US, their role is less clear in the UK. Generally, 'buy-bust' is routine (especially in undercover operations), while 'sell-bust' is frowned upon, since it can be seen as the police acting as 'agent provocateurs'. For a fuller discussion see Dorn *et al.*, 1992, chapters 6 and 8.

15. Reiner (1991: 153) cites this observation by a Chief Constable: 'The policeman's biggest weapon is inconvenience, not arresting people. Some people call it harassing. But there is no way we could do our job without occasionally having to inconvenience people. If it's just to stop them and ask questions, that's an inconvenience'.

16. But see Wagstaff and Maynard (1988). Cost-benefit arguments from economics are more commonly used to present the consequences of, and usually also the case for, drug legalisation.

17. For an expression of police interest see 'Police urged to hit local drug markets', *The Guardian*, 15 October 1992.

18. The element of racial hygiene in police crackdowns has been observed by Manning in a passage on the ritual meanings which underpin drugs policing: 'Officers may focus on black street dealers in an attempt to clean up a street scene....This is an instrumental act and intended as a means of "cleaning up" a street scene (an end). It also has ceremonial or expressive aspects because it differentiates a group for pressure and makes a strong statement about its character; it emphasises the dominance of the police (who are predominantly white).... Thus, any enforcement of drug laws always...contains a political...and a ceremonial component, a set of messages about the groups, selves, and identities of participants' (Manning 1980: 95-6).

19. Cf: 'The boundaries of what constitutes enforcement and what constitutes prevention, treatment and care are being redrawn' (Howard et al., 1993: 9).

2 Under Pressure: Policing and Demand Management

> Quality of service in the police force must not be just an empty slogan. It has to be seen as a sustained commitment to improve performance in ways that can be noticed by the public and welcomed by those who come into contact with the police.[1]

Low level drug enforcement, discussed in chapter 1, represents one form of the 'localisation' of drugs policing. This chapter is also concerned with local policing, though in the somewhat different context of demands on the police, consumerism and performance evaluation. The two main aspects to this context both point to the significance of the locale as the focus of drug policy efforts. First, the Conservative government's five-pronged anti-drugs strategy (Home Office, 1990) identified national, regional and local levels of response. Enforcement has to some extent taken on much more of a national and regional character (see Dorn et al., 1991, 1992) but prevention and treatment efforts are mostly regional and local.[2] I will briefly trace some pressures on the police which are leading to localisation. Drugs appear episodically as an object of media, political and public attention. Drug enforcement has received the lion's share of drug policy resources in the US and in Britain. The focus of much of this is on the spectacular - the 'big trafficker' and weighty seizures, the breaking up of criminal gangs, cartels and the mafia, all of which has spurred developments in policing and the law (Dorn et al., 1992). While drug policy responses are likely to involve a variety of agencies, it is still the case that enforcement remains the primary element. The police are frequently regarded as the first port of call in demands to take action against drugs. Having benefitted from 'talking up' the threat of drugs in the 1980s, it is hardly surprising that they should be seen in this way. But, locally, there are various problems with the spectacular representation of the drugs world. First, it has very little to do with the everyday world of policing. Not only does it not fit in with what almost all uniformed and non-specialist officers do, it is questionable how much relevance it has to the work of most drug squads outside of the big metropolitan forces. Secondly, the focus on the spectacular inevitably masks the mundane reality of everyday drug use, dealing and enforcement. Most drug use and dealing is local, indeed one commentator has stated that 'ultimately, all drug dealing is retail' (Kleiman, 1991). Thirdly, the spectacular has little to do with the ways in which most people perceive drug problems in their areas. Media parades may lead to increased public fear, or scares about particular drugs. But these fears are realised at the local level. People may have concerns about the availability of drugs to young people and school-children and the 'problems' attached to an area, street or locale identified as a site of regular drug availability (Leitner et al., 1993).[3]

A second contextual aspect is that since the early 1980s the police have been faced with government requirements for economy, efficiency and effectiveness (Reiner, 1992). This theme has been consistently developed from various Home Office circulars through to reports from the Audit Commission and the Inspectorate of Constabulary (HMIC). One outcome has been the advancement of police managerialism, realised in the form of policing by objectives for example. Other developments also approximate to some of the generic, private or public sector, language of management, through ideas about consumerism and quality of service.[4] From this has emerged a set of evaluations of police performance based on previously unfamiliar criteria, in which terms such as total quality management and 'more for less' efficiency requirements are articulated (Beckett, 1991). Critics of 'new managerial' reform have usually claimed that it leads to increasing centralisation. Such a view pays insufficient attention to the decentralisation (or localisation) that reform has entailed in the form of devolution of budgets and operational control to middle management. The Leicestershire and Surrey police forces pioneered this approach, though its scope has spread, especially after the Police and Magistrates Courts Act, 1994. Hence, rather than contrasting nationalisation and localisation, or centralisation and decentralisation - and, for that matter, force and service - it makes more sense to see all these things occurring simultaneously, though unevenly.

The significance of this is that police responsiveness to public demands takes on added importance. Consumerism, a service ethos and being 'closer to the ground' should mean that police officers and managers have a clearer idea about the priorities and expectations of local communities. With financial and managerial control, a local chief officer ought to have more flexibility about the deployment of resources. Since there will continue to be more calls on police time than available resources to deal with them, issues about priorities and accountability arise. As well as demand *responsiveness*, there are questions about demand *management* and even demand *reduction* (Beckett, 1991). This introduces another conception of demand reduction to that raised in chapter 1. Here the demand to be reduced (or managed) is that for police time and resources. Beckett (1991) argues that the consequence of not managing demands is that the police can get locked into a 'reactive demand spiral' in which resources can never keep up with public expectations and calls upon police time. In what follows, I explore whether particular responses contain or reduce demand, as well as various aspects of management. These concerns foreground the 'rational-technical' model of police management (see Jefferson and Grimshaw, 1987) that underlies the work of the Audit Commission (1993) and Beckett (1991) for example, though Reiner (1992) and Waddington (1993) among others are sceptical about the applicability of such models. Whether the instrumentalist preoccupation with efficiency and effectiveness is seen as an aspect of 'new managerialism', a fad, or as a symptom of a post-modern society, it clearly chimes with the emphasis on 'what works' in law enforcement and crime prevention (cf Wilson, 1985).

Street scene

Before moving on, I furnish a brief sketch of a particular locality in an English city, drawn from some research that I carried out in the early 1990s. Within that city, an area just outside the city centre has over some years acquired a 'reputation' for various things.[5] Socio-economic indicators show that it has the highest rate of unemployment and social deprivation in the city. It also has one of the highest concentrations of black people in the region, predominantly a population of African-Caribbean descent. Given the unemployment rate and the make-up of the local population it is not surprising to see a number of black people (all or mostly men) 'hanging around' in the street or inside a cafe in a particular road, which I will call 'Empire Road'.[6] It is apparent that, over the course of many years, Empire Road has become known as the local 'front line', meaning both an area where drugs are said to be commonly available, as well as a place that has come to be regarded as a policing problem, or what might be termed a 'hostile, high demand environment' (Beckett, 1991).

Empire Road is a busy shopping area containing many small to medium sized shops. In a private meeting, the shopkeepers have complained to the police that the men hanging around are engaged in drug dealing. This, they say, is having the dual effect of filling-up the road with 'undesirables', and driving other members of the public away from shopping there. The traders are concerned and claim that it has had a direct effect on their businesses and livelihood. They want action and suspect that policing has been scaled-down (it is not clear when they think this started) because the police are worried about the 'volatility' of the local population, or because they like the idea of keeping the main site of drug dealing contained within a known area, to stop it spreading to other parts of the city.[7] Empire Road's reputation is taken-for-granted by local players. A local drugs agency and some researchers say that crack cocaine, among other drugs, is available in the road and the cafe, a finding picked-up and reported in some national newspapers (though a few months after the time period I am discussing). The head of a local task force agrees that this is the case. He believes that the police are reluctant to take action because they are wary of charges of racism following earlier conflicts with the black community, and/or worried about provoking public disorder.

In another version of the story, I was told that the people 'milling about' consisted of two distinct groups. One, the unemployed, have little else to do apart from 'hang around'; the other group are the drug dealers using the unemployed as 'cover' for their activities. It was suggested that the dealers wanted to maintain harmonious and stable relations with the traders, because otherwise greater police attention might result. The unemployed men are unconcerned about these niceties. Thus, in this version, it is the latter who are causing problems, perhaps by making the street seem and feel 'crowded' and 'unwelcoming' to the public, while it is the former who - even though they have the same goals as the shopkeepers - are the object of complaints.

In any case, the police appear to be unconcerned about the claims, which do not accord with their perception of the road or their statistics. Their view is that while drug dealing does go on in the road, it is not exceptional. Moreover, the police and the secretary of the local police consultative committee (PCC) say that environmental improvements in the 1980s have led to a substantial change in the character of the area in general and of Empire Road in particular, to the extent that the latter is said to be an 'oasis' compared to its previous incarnation. The PCC secretary describes the area as 'deader than last week's supper'; he says that the shopkeepers claims are a 'hangover' from its earlier 'problem' image. Moreover their complaints are a symptom of wider ills. As one sceptical police officer put it: 'of course the recession's got nothing to do with it', i.e. the decline in custom, which is also attributed to the recent opening of a large superstore in the vicinity. Nonetheless, the police are under pressure to take action, albeit 'off the record' in private meetings with the traders. All sides are worried in case the local press gets involved; the traders because it would further confirm that they are in a road which is 'well known' for drug dealing and the police because it will lead to increased pressure on them to respond in some way. The traders want high-profile symbolic policing to deter the dealers from hanging around, the police apparently just want to 'keep an eye on things', while refusing to discuss any current operations they are mounting. Filling in for the reticence of the police, the PCC secretary argues that the police strategy is to target suppliers only, and not buyers and petty dealers. The police, he says, are maintaining surveillance and keeping the problem contained, the latter matching what the traders maintain. There is therefore a substantial mismatch in the perceptions of what is going on between the police and the public (in this case, local traders) and a gap in their views of what should be done about it.

One of the barely submerged issues in all of this is the racialised character of the discussion, either through a linking of social deprivation, 'race' and drugs, which some see as an expression of 'ghetto culture', or in coded terminology about reputation, or the need for 'sensitivity' (see Keith, 1993). Another is the issue of contested public space and the 'appearance' of a locale or street which, according to differing interpretations, makes it seem less or more welcoming to particular kinds of people. A third issue is about police responsiveness and managing demands for enforcement action. Empire Road was, according to the police, being policed normally, but whatever that level is, it did not appear to register with local traders who believed that the police were doing little or nothing. While the police asserted that drug dealing was not a particular problem in the road, some local people and others said it was. At one level this is a question of whose perception counts. If one takes the view that proximity is closer to reliability, then the traders were closer to the action, though the possibly of establishing the 'truth' of competing perceptions and explanations is likely to prove elusive.[8] The problems are multiplied by the fact that drug dealing was identified as the problem, since it is by nature an activity in which people utilise secrecy and security. But let us concentrate on public demands on the police and their attempts to address, constrain or deflect those demands.

Sources and forms of demand

With regard to the local and day-to-day level it seems to me that we can speak of demands on the police as realised through various levels. Some typical means are through emergency 999 calls (though Audit Commission research has revealed that a proportion of these are not urgent, and indeed that some are trivial) through to non-urgent calls, personal communication with officers, visits to the police station and letters (Beckett, 1991). While these are mostly based on direct contact there are also indirect channels of communication: 'information received' by the police could include 'tip offs' from informants; from anonymous calls and through information solicited by police and Customs and Excise telephone 'hotlines'. Anonymous messages are said to make up a significant number of the calls made to lines such as Crimestoppers, often containing allegations about drug dealing.[9] There is a further level and source of demand which arises from police contact - initiated by either side - with voluntary associations. Police consultation with residents and tenants associations and community groups may also lead to expressions of public pressure for police action about some problem. A third source of demands may arise from police contact with professional or other public sector bodies, for example a local chamber of commerce and local authorities.[10]

What is the nature of these demands? Despite their ostensible law enforcement orientation, empirical research has found that a good deal of what the police are asked to do is not directly related to crime (Ekblom and Heal, 1982; Shapland and Vagg, 1988; Waddington, 1993). Beckett (1991) says that 80 per cent of demands are of a service nature, while 20 per cent are directly related to crime, though other sources, such as the British Crime Survey, estimate the latter as making up to a third of calls on police time. However, the dividing line is not quite so neat, since a proportion of the 'service' calls turn out to be conflictual where the police are asked to intervene in and resolve conflict. From Beckett's qualitative demand analysis it emerges that the majority (60 per cent) of 'service' calls are in fact of a 'conflict' nature, or 'potential crime' (Shapland and Vagg, 1988).[11] Policing by objectives and its variants is one attempt to rationally plan the allocation of police resources to public demands. In contrast, Waddington (1993) views the police as a demand-determined agency, not one that can be driven by policy 'from the top'. The public initiates police action by (a) choosing which crimes to report and which not; (b) as an influence on what type of action the police will take at an incident; and (c) in turning to the police to resolve a variety of emergency situations (Waddington, 1993; Reiner, 1992). This reactive view stresses the structural determinants of police actions and responses, and diminishes the role of police agency that is stressed by other perspectives, often radical ones. While there is a danger of going too far in one direction or another, the concept of 'duality of structure' (Giddens, 1987) would suggest that this is not an either/or issue; rather, the police could be seen as both shaped by the external environment, as well as actively shaping their workload.

Even when called upon to intervene in conflict situations, the police's prime aim is to maintain order rather than enforce the law. For Waddington (1993) and others, the 'craft' of police work is to restore order through informal rather than formal (legal) controls. This could include 'winning by appearing to lose' when withdrawing from contested spaces (Waddington, 1994). But in Empire Road the police were not one of the contestants, but apparently positioned somewhere in-between, and under pressure from one side to take action against another (cf Stenson, 1993). In Empire Road the issue was one of a perceived lack of police action, a point probably clouded by conflicting perceptions of the extent of 'the problem'. The response in such situations may be one that requires intelligence gathering through covert surveillance, which could appear as if 'nothing is happening' to complainants.

This suggests that public relations must also play a role in demand management as the police have to simultaneously manage the impression of taking public concerns seriously, of not 'over-reacting' and of maintaining an overall balance between different crimes and areas that are deemed to require more or less attention. Before returning to issues of public relations and conflicting community demands, I want to consider two main forms of police response and assess them in terms of their capacity to manage or reduce demand.

Three types of police activity

Chapter 1 examined four types of enforcement strategies targeted at different 'levels' of the market. Here, in contrast, I want to focus more on policing methods following a hybrid structure derived from accounts by Moore (1977) and Wilson (1978). In considering the range of methods of policing drugs, Moore (1977) describes three types of police activity, while Wilson, looking more specifically at detective work, describes four methods of crime investigation (Wilson, 1978; see also Manning, 1980).[12]

First, Moore (1977) says that patrol work is 'an effort to monitor more or less superficially and more or less indiscriminately the entire "space" of possible offenses. The objective of patrol is to "happen across" offenses as they are occurring...typically [it] relies on large numbers of men, rapid mobility, and rapid communication'. Secondly, retrospective investigation is: 'an effort to reconstruct offenses that have already occurred, and to corroborate each element of the reconstruction with physical evidence, or the testimony of credible witnesses. [This] allows the police to focus their surveillance and investigative efforts on relatively small nooks of the space of possible offenses' (Moore, 1977: 129). Wilson (1978) describes two forms of retrospective investigation. Where a suspect has been apprehended and there is adequate information about his/her behaviour, no actual investigation is required and the only real issue for the police is one of administrative case management and prosecution. Alternatively, where there is reliable information after a crime has been committed but no suspect has been identified or apprehended, the police would be required to employ detective skills to pursue the case.

Thirdly, Moore (1977: 129-30) says that prospective investigation is:

> an effort to solicit specific information about offenses likely to be committed in the future. Like retrospective investigation, prospective investigation seeks to focus police attention on relatively small nooks of the total space of possible offenses... the objective is....to anticipate the offense so that the police can observe the offense

directly.

Similarly, Wilson (1978) describes two variants of prospective police investigations. Where the suspect is known and under observation, but there is inadequate information about current behaviour, the police would need to use observational or surveillance techniques in order to observe a crime being committed. The other is a situation where there is an absence of both a subject or suspect and of adequate information. Here police action is based on 'hunches' or tips which lead to exploratory inquiries and intelligence gathering.[13]

In Empire Road the police could presumably have responded through either retrospective or prospective methods. The former could have entailed increased and visible patrolling - which Leishman and Savage (1993) call 'waiting for something to happen' - or surveillance through CCTV cameras. The latter might include 'buy bust' and other forms of undercover work, as well as surveillance. Low level drug enforcement (Dorn and Murji, 1992b; Pearson, 1989, 1992) could be a component of either approach. Each strategy impacts differently on the market's distribution systems (Moore, 1979, 1990; Dorn and South, 1990). Faced with public demand to take action against retail markets, police forces might pursue any of these approaches. I now want to apply the reactive/proactive dichotomy in order to consider demand management.

Reactive enforcement

Reactive enforcement has been likened to a 'fire brigade' approach to policing. Some of its most visible and spectacular manifestations include 'sweeps' and 'crackdowns' (Eck, 1989a; Kaplan, 1988; Meese and Carrico, 1990; Sherman, 1990), or saturation policing (on Operation Hammer in Los Angeles, see Davis, 1990), as well as raids (see Waddington, 1992; Dorn et al., 1992; Silverman, 1993, 1994). Another example of reactive enforcement is Operation Pressure Point (OPP), a police operation in New York City (discussed in the previous chapter) when police actions did lead to reduced drug dealing, as well as less overt dealing and displacement of the drug market. However, Zimmer (1987) points out that the success of the operation depended upon sustained police pressure, without which the drug trade would have rapidly re-emerged. Most importantly for this discussion, OPP led to rising public expectations. Residents in other areas demanded similar operations of the police. The organisational dilemma then becomes (a) how to address those demands, and (b) how to avoid a position where shifting resources to another area thereby creates the conditions for a revival of the drug trade in an area which has already been 'cleared'. This is what has been called the 'pop up' effect following the 'push down' (Nadelmann, 1991).[14] Reactive enforcement therefore highlights the limits of a purely law enforcement approach. It is now commonplace to suggest that the effect of enforcement pressure may be likened to a balloon: as one part is squeezed, another part bulges out elsewhere. Enforcement on its own, without other measures to improve and change a street or an area, may turn out to be futile, a point reaffirmed by the ACMD (1994).

If OPP is judged by public expectations criteria then its success is questionable. Clearly it did not reduce demand since it led to new and extra demands on police resources. Resources either become spread very thinly or the police spend their time chasing the next 'fire'. Media and political pressures led the police into the operation and these interests alone would have meant that its results were closely monitored. It would not be unreasonable to assume that some of these interests, as well as the police, needed to publicise success as a sign that the crackdown had proved to be effective. But that same publicity may well be the cause of rising expectations which are beyond the capacity of the police to manage, at least on their own. Reactive approaches can be good for short-term 'effect', they help to douse the 'fire'.[15] Their appeal at a managerial appeal is in giving the impression of organisational control and a firm, decisive police response, especially in a situation where there has been public and media attention on a particular street or location. But beyond that the consequences are more problematic, leading to the reactive 'demand spiral' discussed previously. Hence Beckett (1991) argues that police managers should seek to anticipate and negate demands before they lead to this position. In other words, this implies a proactive approach.

Proactive enforcement

Preventing crime before it occurs is part of the police's historical mandate, even if it has been a poor relation to crime detection. Moore and Wilson's discussion of prospective investigation included the possibility that the police will 'seek out' the commission of offences before, or perhaps as, they occur. Such techniques have led to concerns about whether the police might actually be encouraging, or even initiating, crime. Hence the effectiveness and probity of such methods are contested (Dorn *et al.*, 1992, chapter 8). It is possible that the police were undertaking undercover and surveillance work in Empire Road though there was, perhaps inevitably, no sign of this. Whether such activities can reduce demand for police action is not clear. Successful enforcement in one location could lead to displacement and sustained pressure may be required, so it is possible that the same problems that arise from reactive enforcement could occur.

A different aspect of proactive policing is in the form of multi- or inter-agency practice. The limitations of reactive policing, and an acknowledgement that longer-term remedial action depends on more than police action alone, have both led to the police routinely working with other agencies in joint approaches to crime and crime prevention (Sampson et al., 1988; Blagg et al., 1988). The range of activities is large, including juvenile diversion, leisure schemes, environmental improvements, licensing, domestic violence and racial attacks, as well as drugs. In the case of action targeted at a particular neighbourhood or street or estate, 'quality of life' considerations arise. These concerns do not rule out reactive enforcement which - in the form of a 'blitz' as in OPP - may be seen as 'opening the door' for other agencies to come in and play their part.[16] It is arguable that demand management concerns inevitably require public pressures to be spread or shared among different agencies. The fullest expression of that is social crime prevention. This conception of multi-agency work corresponds to several categories identified by Bayley (1994), including 'honest law enforcement' in which the police role is limited and minimalist (cf Kinsey et al., 1986); 'efficient law enforcement' which entails more emphasis on community and problem solving policing; and, to a lesser extent, 'stratified crime prevention', in which those officers closest to communities take the lead in developing crime prevention. It does not correspond to what Bayley calls 'determined crime prevention', wherein the police take the lead in defining problems as well as solutions, which include the activity of diverse agencies. The latter would fit in with a 'conspiratorial' view (Sampson et al., 1988) of multi-agency relations as dominated by the police and a narrow conception of crime prevention.

Social prevention - 'treat the underlying causes'

An increasingly influential aspect of inter-agency approaches is to treat drug problems as social 'symptoms' and to tackle the presumed underlying causes on a local or neighbourhood level. Building on the influential 'broken windows' thesis (Wilson and Kelling, 1982), this may entail the formation of agency partnerships in the attempt to 'clean-up' streets, estates and neighbourhoods which have become known as locales for drug dealing and use (Hayeslip, 1989; Meese and Carrico, 1990). More specifically, local authorities, private sector firms, voluntary agencies and the police work together to tackle local social and economic problems, to reduce unemployment, to improve housing and amenities, to brighten streets and enhance lighting, and to induce more community beat policing. Some of this goes under the name of 'problem-oriented policing' (see Eck, 1989b). Social prevention is supported from across the political spectrum and within the police. It has been extensively used by NACRO's Safe Neighbourhoods Unit (Bright, 1987, 1991). Government departments have also travelled along this road. The Home Office Safer Cities Projects sought to develop and support inter-agency approaches to local problems (Tilley, 1993) as do the Department of the Environment funded City Challenge/Inner City Task Force initiatives. The similarly constituted local Drug Prevention/Action Teams also adopt elements of this approach, which has been advocated by the ACMD (1994) among many others.

Social prevention does not exclude situational prevention, which it can encompass as suggested above. The police contribution to this could include community policing through symbolic street patrols, backed up with measures to ensure that the local community are kept informed about what the police are doing. Another aspect could be low level policing and demand reduction, involving disruptive and inconvenience policing (Moore, 1977, 1979; Dorn and Murji, 1992b).[17] Its inter-agency aspects might include any or all of the following: (a) encouraging drug users to seek help from drug services, perhaps by linking this to a liberal cautioning policy; (b) working with local agencies to provide 'treatment packages' for problematic drug users, especially where they have become regular 'police property'; and (c) working with local authorities and other organisations, including the private sector, to improve the environment to 'design out' crime (Dorn and Murji, 1992a, b; Gilman and Pearson, 1991; Pearson, 1989, 1992).

On the face of it, this approach has greater potential for meeting public demands since it can encompass the 'blitz' as well as longer term preventive action. It does not focus narrowly on enforcement but draws in other public agencies as well. For the police, the advantage is that it de-emphasises their role and diffuses responsibility among different agencies and sectors. Whether it works (or not) depends on a host of factors which may be specific to the strategy adopted, the mix of approaches and other local ingredients. But two cautionary points might be raised. First, social and environmental improvements are policies which ought not to have to carry the burden of crime prevention and social amelioration; otherwise, the 'failure' of the former to impact on the latter can lead to the pessimism that 'nothing works'. Areas have been improved and transformed, but perhaps at the cost of furthering the residualisation of the poorest areas. Secondly, there is also a note of caution about amelioration. It may well be that some young people would see employment as a means of escaping from crime, but it could also be that gainful employment is not quite as appealing as is sometimes assumed; crime and drugs may well offer excitements (and risk) which the mundane world cannot match (Katz, 1988). The potential of low level policing and demand reduction within a multi-agency strategy is therefore open to debate, though there is no general reason to believe that they offer a panacea. Rather they might simply be better ways of achieving certain limited policy objectives. Whether all or any of these reduce public demands can not be answered generally. They have the potential to, but the outcomes need to evaluated empirically (see also Dorn and Murji, 1992b; Collison, 1995).

Activating communities

The discussion so far has focused on the police and other public agencies. But there is a further aspect to be considered. Proactive engagement in social prevention helps to de-emphasise the role of the police and the 'sharing' of responsibilities with other agencies. In what has been called a 'responsibilization' strategy, the state increasingly withdraws from public safety and requires individuals and communities to do more for themselves. Couched in these terms it sounds like a neo-liberal approach, but since there is, or can be, an emphasis on strong communities, left communitarians can also be advocates of these tactics.

Encouraging active citizens - 'have a go'

There is no reason in principle why neighbourhood watch - and its close relative, business watch - could not be applied to drugs as well. In practice it already is the case that such schemes do take a keen interest in drug dealing in their areas.[18] Promoting active citizenship has however raised issues about what the limits on legitimate community action should be. The official view seems to be that as long as the public acts as the 'eyes and ears' of the police that is fine, but there is a problem when and if that boundary is breached. A problem with the representation of drugs as 'out of control' and beyond the capacity of the police to contain it - leading some police officers to call for legalisation and/or decriminalisation - is that this rhetoric may well lead some people to believe that the police cannot cope. One response might be to employ private security personnel to patrol streets and estates, though this has been for crime in general rather than drugs in particular to date. Or of course it may lead to more active citizenship and/or vigilantism. In the early to mid-1990s there have been a number of cases of this in the press and while the earlier examples were not drug specific, later ones certainly were.[19]

An intermediate position can be found in parts of the US where parents groups, apparently sanctioned by the police, have banded together to be present on the streets to dissuade 'drive through' drug buyers and sellers from operating in their neighbourhoods (see Dorn and Murji, 1992a). This is not unheard of in Britain. In Merseyside in the 1980s, parents joined forces to actively oppose drug dealers, arguing that the police had failed to do so.[20] Thus, the boundary between legitimate community action and vigilantism is likely to prove problematic. Police attempts to organise self-policing networks such as neighbourhood and business watch have thrown-up such problems. If the police argue that they are too hard-pressed to take action, then some individuals and communities have sometimes decided to make it their own business to do so. If there had been a business watch in Empire Road what would or should it have done? The shopkeepers were already passing on information to the police; their complaint was that nothing was being done about it. Thus, where the police articulate the rhetoric of responsiveness to local communities, one consequence may be that a lack of responsiveness leads to an unravelling of police legitimacy, when they are seen as being unwilling to take action. This therefore throws-up a further issue for consideration, the management of public relations.

Public relations/legitimation - building support

When under pressure to take action about a matter of public concern, the easiest thing to do would, presumably, be to take action. The complaint from shopkeepers in Empire Road was that no police activity was apparent. While nascent backing for enforcement action already existed, it is likely that support was not forthcoming from at least some other sections of the local community. In such circumstances, it may be that police public relations tactics are to avoid being pulled on to either side. A different aspect of public relations has been noted at times when the police need to mobilise public backing before a particular operation. One purpose served by this could be to generate support for 'tough' enforcement operations where the police can go in 'hard' without the fear that they would face a backlash about their tactics; a form of 'community policing with the gloves off' (see Moore and Kleiman, 1989; Hayeslip, 1989; Meese and Carrico, 1990). Something like this seems to have occurred before high-profile raids such as Operation Kingfisher on the Broadwater Farm estate (Waddington, 1992; Silverman, 1993). Thus appeals that emphasise the scale of the problem that the police face set the ground for a view that the ends justify the means and the rhetoric of the 'war on drugs' in the USA, expressed in Britain and Europe through the threat of the 'big trafficker', has helped to serve such a purpose (Dorn *et al.*, 1991, 1992).

One consequence of such rhetoric may be to serve as an important back-drop to the building of consensus at a local level. For instance, the representation of crack as a new 'worse than ever, instantly addictive' drug has been an important factor in the partial mobilisation of black communities behind some police operations. In the All Saints Road in Notting Hill, members of the black community, as well as the main black newspaper *The Voice*, called on the police to take action against dealers supplying crack to young people. They argued that the police should be taking action against the suppliers of such drugs instead of harassing young black men who are only 'hanging about' and/or involved with nothing more than cannabis. Such neat 'them and us' divisions in the market may be rather too simple, as well as too subtle for policing to operationalise. And of course they reproduce the simple dichotomy between 'evil' suppliers and innocent 'victims' in the shape of drug users or, in this case, between sellers of soft and hard drugs. In any case, the racialised constructions of crack are no less invidious when deployed against an enemy within the enemy within.

What occurs when the police do not take action and indeed appear to resist pressure on them to do so, is open to speculation. In the case of Empire Road, we have seen that a number of local figures explained the police's reluctance by recourse to past events such as difficulties with some sections of the local community; alternatively, the PCC secretary maintained that they were taking action but keeping it quiet. Since this debate was not occurring in public, there was no media discussion of it and therefore no call upon the police to justify their position publicly. With regard to the discursive strategies employed by the police, it would be interesting to note ways in which public relations are managed when the police are not doing something that they are being asked to do. Consideration of police discourses and rhetoric is significant because it may be that the ways in which drugs and crime problems are spoken about that helps to create or enhance public demands for police action. Thus, rather than seeking the police as led by multiple demands from the external environment, this perspective suggests that they may actually be initiating or inciting the very demands that they see themselves as being too-hard pressed to meet.

Management, demands and local drug markets

The discussion so far has centred on police responses and their capacity to address public demands. I now want to look at some aspects of management. In Empire Road the police were un-willing to provide any more details than I have reported, making it difficult to say anything about what action, if any, they did take. A need for secrecy is sometimes justified on operational grounds, which may mean that matters cannot be made known to the public; indeed one officer commented that the nature of drugs work meant that the police would find it difficult to discuss what methods were being used at any particular time. The recourse to operational confidentiality could be regarded as a 'traditional' form of management that seeks to circumscribe police authority to oversee and respond to particular problems, even when it leads to external complaints about whether they are doing anything at all. It is likely to be inimical to performance evaluation, perhaps because that would be seen as interference with the independence of the police. Observations of Empire Road indicated no visible increase in police patrols, or any other signs of activity. It is possible that the police were striving to keep the shopkeepers informed and aware of what they were doing, but otherwise the police response had the appearance of 'masterly inaction' in managing public demand.

Understanding police responsiveness within a demand management perspective has, for Beckett (1991), to predict as well as contain demands on the police. Such managerial speak is sometimes criticised for attempting to shield essentially political decisions about resource allocation and organisational decision-making behind a de-politicised, technocratic image of a rational bureaucracy at work. Detectives work within an organisational context which sets administrative limits on their actions. Whether bureaucratic rules determine, shape or have a marginal influence on their modes of working is open to debate, though the common view is that policing can not be 'done by the book', and can only be understood by paying attention to the actions and beliefs of those at the bottom of the hierarchy (Waddington, 1993; Reiner, 1992). Manning's analysis of narcotics officers in a southeastern part of the US supports the 'bottom up' view (cf Wilson, 1978).[21]

> decisions made by the agent in line with his or her own interests substantially set the direction of police drug enforcement. Even when policy is set, articulated and flows down the line to agents, it rarely actually constrains them, and they continue to act in line with their own perception of the practical problems of drug enforcement...Administrative aims and rhetoric differ from agents' praxis and perspectives, and an organizationally induced tension results (Manning, 1980: 16-17).

If policy has little or marginal influence on the ways in which detectives construct their daily work, there is a problem for management. How, in a climate based upon economy and efficiency, can drugs work be managed when it has been stated that 'drug squad work is possibly the least disciplined type of police work' (Collison, 1995: 104)? Appeals to the sensitivity and difficulty of the work are unlikely to mollify managers faced with internal and external pressures to demonstrate effective action. The tension that Manning noted is evident from a long-term undercover policing operation.[22] One officer said that 'every three days some civilian from Scotland Yard is ringing up and saying this is costing a fortune, you can't have it any more.

Then you have to go one jump up the ladder to get authorization to keep it'. The underlying point here is not that detective work can not be managed in a framework stressing the three e's. Rather, it is a question of which measures matter. What was being argued for by this officer is the relative importance of 'quality' versus 'quantity' criteria. In other words, the cost of the operation was said to be justified by its aim of 'removing' one or several middle-level dealer(s), ultimately producing a greater impact on the local drug market than the arrest of a larger number of minor user-dealers. This could be characterised as an 'expert model' of management since it is based on a trust or faith that detectives know what they are doing, that the person(s) 'taken out' are indeed of the stature ascribed to them and that there will be a noticeable impact on local markets. But because the expertise relied upon is as much, or perhaps more, to do with front-line officers than with managers, it could also be regarded as a 'strategy by default', because key decisions are made by the lowest ranks. In either guise, this approach could be somewhat more open to performance evaluation than the 'traditional' view, though both would be resistant to the use of quantitative indicators of effectiveness, a position supported by Collison (1995).

Management could also allude to managing drug markets. For some, the word management could be something of a misnomer here, though a couple of aspects can be speculated upon. First, successful management might mean containment of a market, so that its size, location, nature and other characteristics are reasonably well known, and some of this overlaps with the 'expert' model mentioned above. For this to count as effective demand management there would have to be an absence of any significant public criticism, i.e. it would not be successful if significant numbers of people though that the police were 'not doing anything'. Empire Road might conform to the first part of this (containment) but not the second part (effective demand management), since there were some complaints about police inaction. Even if the 'real' problem lies elsewhere (unemployment, economic recession) this does not seem to help the police very much. Second, management could refer to 'shaping' the form of drug markets. If law enforcement and drug markets are in continuous interaction (Moore, 1977; Reuter, 1983; Dorn and South, 1990; Dorn et al., 1992) then the former does have a potential to influence market structure and content. In the context of an inter-agency harm reduction strategy, a market where there are few 'casualties' and the level of danger is reduced, would be one that has been relatively successfully managed. In this scenario, policing may aim to 'shape' market characteristics towards some drugs rather than others (also entailing different methods of use) and modes of selling that attract least public 'fallout'. This could be regarded as a 'consequentialist' model of management where harm reduction is as significant as crime reduction, or perhaps more so, and all agencies seek to manage any public and/or media criticism from pursuing such policies (cf Dorn, 1992; Pearson, 1992). There are however few examples of the practicality of these ideas. In any event, if the policy is not well explained it still has the potential to raise some public ire. Inhabitants in parts of Amsterdam have raised concerns about the impact of the city's drug policy on their neighbourhoods (Inciardi and McBride, 1991); elsewhere, residents have complained about finding used syringes in public places, while acknowledging that the spread of HIV is being contained. This approach could therefore be regarded as the most 'open' of the three perspectives delineated, as well as one where public relations are as significant as whatever action is taken.

The position adopted in this chapter is that managerialism, combined with localism and consumerism, can actually politicise decision-making processes by making them more explicit and therefore more open to scrutiny and contestation. Demand management must include some greater or lesser emphasis on demand sharing between different agencies. In actuality, this could imply overall joint responsibility between different agencies, or it could amount to 'passing the buck'. In either case it can not be expected that the process will be smooth or unproblematic. Hence, I have added sections on community action and on public relations, whether in the form of keeping particular constituencies 'on side', or in terms of assuaging their complaints. For Waddington (1993) the only choice for the police is between responding effectively and responding poorly. A responsive police service would respect public definitions and concerns, while recurring demands indicate the need for more sustained treatment for social injuries (Waddington, 1993).

Public demands are of course not undifferentiated and it would be more accurate to refer to publics rather than the public. The situation in Empire Road encompassed a conflict between more and less organised sections of the public, with differing views of the 'problem' and what, if anything, should be done about it, and what would count as a successful result. The former, shopkeepers, are an 'owning community' who belong to a local forum that seeks to protect and advance their interests. It exists at the more 'professional' end of community groups that meet with, and in this case, seek to exert pressure on the police. The latter, the men 'hanging around' can only be described as a group in the loosest sense. Apart from secondary outlets - such as police consultation forums - they have no direct access to the police at all and little other way of making their views known. In a situation of competing demands for public space and community conflict, the police priority in Empire Road may have been to keep the situation under observation and success may equal the absence of disorder and overt conflict. For the traders the judgement of both priorities and success were likely to be rather different. In this situation the police could have appealed to any or all of the management models sketched here, as well to two further methods. One, to portray themselves as being 'stuck in the middle' and in the 'no win' situation of being asked to broker community conflict (see Stenson, 1993). The other is to provide authoritative, legal intervention in the name of 'neutral' enforcement of breaches of the law. But calls by some on a responsive police service to take action is likely to be experienced as a police force by others, raising the familiar dilemma of whose 'side' the police appear to be on. Non-enforcement raises questions about just what police resources are being used for. For Waddington (1993: 173) the key question is not how much policing is required but how much can be afforded. He notes that 'since police might do almost anything, the resources they might need are virtually infinite....since calling the police is relatively cost-free, demand tends to be insatiable'. Thus, perhaps, either the task has to be de-limited, or costs have to be made more explicit. Responsive policing, quality of service, consumerism and demand management therefore raise issues that go the heart of what the role and responsibilities of the police are. As the 'traditional' route declines and the 'expert' and 'consequentialist' models suffer from increasing scrutiny, while the police's omnibus mandate and continuing tensions about what their task really is push back a vision of minimal policing, such considerations may over time lead to an unravelling of police organisation and practice.

Notes

1. From an article by the then Home Secretary, Kenneth Clarke, in *The Independent*, 9 December 1992.

2. For example, prevention through national anti-drugs advertising campaigns have receded and, from the late 1980s onwards, the Home Office has invested in around 20 local Drug Prevention Teams to develop and support local approaches to drug prevention.

3. People's perceptions and fears of drug-related crime has been used as an indicator in Home Office research.

4. For Reiner (1992), the drive towards this re-conceptualisation of the police has its immediate origins in the controversy that has over-taken the police since the 1970s. From this three strands emerged, leading the police explicitly down the service road. First, the Scarman report prioritised peace-keeping over law enforcement, downgrading the crime fighting image of the police, even though this is what some officers continue to see as 'real' police work. Secondly, there have been the managerial reforms initiated by Kenneth Newman at the Metropolitan Police. This ushered in the language of objective setting and the devolution of managerial responsibility. Thirdly, and probably most importantly, there has been government pressure. Its origins are probably to be found in the Financial Management Initiative since 1982. For the police this led to the famous circular 114/83 and the three e's: economy, efficiency and effectiveness. The stress on efficiency has been

maintained by the Audit Commission and gone along with the managerial emphasis on budgeting and performance measurement. Alongside there has been some attempt at identifying a narrower role for the police. The multi-agency approach is a direct sign of this, reducing expectations of what the police can do, as well as defining the limits of their responsibilities. Whether all of this has led to changes in the level of demands made on the police is uncertain. Police officers maintain that public demands and expectations are insatiable (cf Waddington, 1993), a feeling underlined by their status as a '24 hours last resort' emergency service.

5. Reputation can be significant because it may attract novice and other buyers into an arena where they expect drugs to be available. In one particular example - Operation Mint in Notting Hill Gate (see Dorn et al., 1992, chapter 7) - the aim of police surveillance was to observe and record, but not intervene, in a street market. Drug buyers were then followed out of the area and the arrest made later, thereby seeking to establish the view that this drug market was 'bad news'.

6. One of several reasons why I have chosen not to identify the actual city and road is a concern that it can serve to reaffirm the very reputation that ought to be being questioned (see also Murji, 1998).

7. Compare these remarks from a drugs worker talking about police raids in Wolverhampton: 'The drugs squad enjoy a bit of publicity when they make a good raid. Apart from that they like keeping the lid on things, they know what's what and where things are and they don't like people smashing it up'.

8. I do not make any great claim for my own observations since they are based upon limited field work. But for what it is worth my observations suggested that, while drugs could be bought from dealers who operated in the road, the level of dealing was unexceptional; I was told of other places where it was much easier to buy drugs. Equally the level of crack availability seemed to be greatly over-stated; ecstasy was much more widely available both here and in the city in general.

9. The scope for malicious calls should be noted here. In some cases 'neighbour disputes' lead one party to create trouble for another through allegations made anonymously to the police.

10. The question of whether the police are more or less open to public pressure remains an open one. In Empire Road it was notable that complaints about drugs registered infrequently at the local police consultative committee. One could draw different conclusions from this: either drugs are not as much of a problem as some claim; or if they are, people find other channels through which to register their views (such as the meeting between the traders and the police); or the consultative committee is something of an irrelevancy.

11. For example, domestic or neighbour disputes. These, as has often been noted, are precisely what some officers regard as not 'real' police work (Kinsey et al., 1986; Reiner, 1992).

12. Manning (1980) describes a mixture of prospective and retrospective methods employed by narcotics agents. Four in particular are: (i) buy-busts consist of the agent setting-up and making a buy and then arresting the seller; (ii) head-hunting involves cruising known drug dealing areas and using an informant to point out suspected dealers, thought to have drugs on their person and then arresting the dealer; (iii) targeting is aimed at major violators and consists of compiling information on them until a case can be established; (iv) warrants and raids are used after undercover work has produced information to enable the search and arrest of suspects.

13. The prospective strategies described by Moore (1977: 138-146) include observing sales, search warrant cases, buy-busts, undercover buys, and long term covert operations.

14. The problem of displacement between areas is sometimes taken to mean that 'nothing works'. But displacement, or 'deflection' as Barr and Pease (1992) prefer to call it, might be thought of as a means through which policing aims or helps to re-shape the form of drug markets, in line with broader policy objectives such as demand reduction or harm minimisation (Dorn and Murji, 1992a, b; Pearson, 1992; ACMD, 1994).

15. Though this should not be taken for granted. The capacity of a bungled reactive approach to generate flak for the police is considerable and even 'successful' ones can provoke criticism of 'heavy handed' policing (Waddington, 1992; Silverman, 1993, 1994).

16. It is conceivable that enforcement action might follow rather than lead the actions of other agencies.

17. This could entail a variety of method such as establishing a long term street presence, undercover and buy-bust work, long-term surveillance, or a combination of strategies (Dorn et al., 1992).

18. For example, see the newsletters of the London Association of Neighbourhood Watch schemes from the early 1990s.

19. For an example see 'Our streets, our law, our way', *The Guardian*, 7 April 1993. The case of Alan Hocking received some coverage after he kidnapped an 18-year-old drug dealer suspected of selling LSD to a friend's son. Hocking said that 'I was intending to give him the fright of his life. I called him a little scumbag and a bastard'. He also threatened that he would do the same thing again because he said that there was a big drugs problem in schools in the locality, but, he said to the media, 'the police seem more interested in protecting the dealers and victimising people like me.' ('Kidnapper 'given chance'', *The Guardian*, 14 September 1993: 6; 'Anti-drug vigilante found guilty of kidnapping pusher', *The Times*, 12 August 1993: 3).

20. Similarly, it has been reported that residents and parents in the Liverpool 8 area set up road blocks to prevent 'joy riders' driving through streets at speed.

21. For Wilson 'The problem for the administrators of investigative agencies is to control the behaviour of operators - the agents. This involves obtaining valid information about what the agents do, comparing that information to some reasonable standard and issuing instructions that alter behaviour, where necessary, in the direction of the standard' (Wilson

1978: 59).

22. This is the operation reported in chapter 6 in Dorn *et al.*, 1992.

3 Principle or Pragmatism? Debating Drug Legalisation

When drug taking is said to have become as commonplace as drinking a cup of tea, and when even police officers and judges say it is time for a re-examination of the drug laws, can there be any question about the validity of the arguments for legalisation?[1] Simon Jenkins has no doubts. In his view the case for change is obvious because it is based on 'reason and experience' and is disputed only by 'emotion and ignorance' (*The Times*, 8 June 1994). In chapter 6 I criticise some of the ways in which reason is counter-posed to emotion. Here I seek to delineate some of the key features of the debate about drug control and legalisation (see also Inciardi, 1991; Kraska, 1991; Reuter and MacCoun, 1995).

It is worth clarifying a couple of key terms. First, 'drugs' are commonly taken to mean illicit drugs. While alcohol, tobacco and caffeine are also drugs, as are tranquillisers, because all alter the body's chemistry, they are usually not referred to as such. The significance of this seemingly trivial point is that definitions have consequences for policy. The US National Drug Control Policy, as Zimring and Hawkins (1992) show in their analysis of it, never actually defines what a drug is. It is not unique in that respect. The failure to define what is and is not regarded as a drug has consequences for the ways in which the 'drug problem' and matters such as 'dependence' and 'addiction' are defined, categorised and understood (Zimring and Hawkins, 1992). Even considering only those drugs that have been classified as illegal, it could be pointed out that they include a wide variety of substances with different properties, effects and methods of usage. While it would not quite be true to say that all they have in common is their illegality, they are sometimes all lumped together and undifferentiated. The National Drug Control Policy not only fails to define a drug or drug problems, it also treats 'all levels of drug use as equally troublesome and threatening' (Zimring and Hawkins, 1992: 7). Supporters of cannabis decriminalisation often seek to distinguish it from other illegal drugs, for instance by claiming that it is a 'soft' and not a 'hard' drug. This distinction suffers from the problem of how drugs such as amphetamines and ecstasy should be classified and what makes a drug 'hard' or 'soft'. Another problem is that those who claim that cannabis should not be criminalised because it is 'different' from other drugs often reaffirm an unquestioning demonology of other drugs which that are then seen as 'really bad' (Dorn, 1980).

Secondly, *decriminalisation* means that the possession of small quantities for personal use would be ignored, but controls on drug suppliers would be maintained. *Legalisation* entails the removal of legal controls on the possession, supply and production of some or all drugs. As Reuter and MacCoun (1995) point out, legalisation is a broad term that can mean anything from a permissive regime (as with alcohol) to government controlled distribution of drugs to and for addicts. For present purposes I shall refer to those supporting legalisation and/or decriminalisation as 'legalisers' and those who oppose them as 'prohibitionists', though these broad terms do not necessarily describe the views of any given individual. While it can be the case that the positions of the two camps are mirror images of one another, these labels do gloss over differences within both the legalisation and prohibitionist lobbies. In the conclusion, I will contend that 'soft' prohibitionists and legalisers can actually converge on a pragmatic basis.

A brief history of the emergence of controls

When and why were drugs made illegal? Controls are mainly a product of the twentieth century. Beginning with the US, Zimring and Hawkins (1992) see many parallels between the prohibition of alcohol and narcotics in that country. But the convergence came about in this century. In the nineteenth century opiates were freely available and the only restrictions on their availability were connected with anti-Chinese sentiments in California and some other states which restricted smoking in opium houses and importation by the Chinese, though not by Americans (Musto, 1973; Bakalar and Grinspoon, 1984). The first prohibition was the 1914 Harrison Act which made the sale or possession of opiates illegal except through medical sources. Concerns about drug use by soldiers may have been a factor in the emergence of the Act. Another was that the US was responding to or fulfilling its obligations under the emerging 'international control system' such as the 1912 Hague Convention, which called for national legislation to control the production and distribution of opium. The prohibition of cannabis or marijuana developed in several states from the late 1920s onwards until the 1937 Marijuana Tax Act superimposed a federal prohibition over state legislation. The Federal Bureau of Narcotics played a significant campaigning role in the emergence of the 1937 Act by declaring marijuana to be a cause of violent crime (Becker, 1963; Musto, 1973).

In Britain, as in the USA, there were, throughout most of the nineteenth century, no controls on the production, sale, import and export, or possession of drugs. Misgivings about this lack of regulation came from a number of sources. Doctors and pharmacists sought to extend their professional power by seeking the authority to control the availability of drugs. Moral crusaders - such as the Society for the Suppression of the Opium Trade - saw drugs as linked to vice, while others worried about the health of workers. Another similarity with the US was the association of drugs with the small Chinese community in east London, which is ironic since Britain fought the 'Opium wars' against China because the latter wanted to stop sales of opium. The association of drugs or 'opium dens' with a minority community is one of many instances when drug scares have been linked to 'foreigners' and 'outsiders' (Musto, 1973; Helmer, 1975; Berridge and Edwards, 1981; Kohn, 1992, 1993). Restrictions emerged during the first world war. In 1914 controls were introduced on the export of various commodities, including opium. A penal response came about in 1916 when Regulation 40B of the Defence of the Realm Act made it a criminal offence, with a maximum penalty of six months imprisonment, to sell any 'intoxicants' to members of the Armed forces, apparently because of anxieties about drug use by Canadian soldiers. Further concerns about cocaine use and selling by prostitutes and the fitness of workers in factories led to the law being extended to civilians too (Bean, 1974). In addition, pressure for prohibitionist policies had been building up from a number of international conventions, beginning in Shanghai in 1909, and, over time, these led to the Dangerous Drugs Acts of 1920 and 1923 which extended controls to heroin. Cannabis was added in 1925, while controls on amphetamines and LSD came as recently as 1964 and 1966 respectively (Dorn et al., 1992).

Current legislation in Britain is framed by the Misuse of Drugs Act, 1971. The Act defines various offences of possession, supply, production and import/export of drugs. It divides drugs into three classes, A, B and C. Class A drugs, such as heroin, cocaine, ecstasy and LSD, are considered the most harmful when misused, Class C drugs, which include tranquillisers and mild opiod based medicines, are thought to have the least potential for harm from their use. Cannabis and amphetamines are in Class B. Penalties for drugs offences, which were increased sharply under The Controlled Drugs (Penalties) Act, 1985, when the Conservative government chose to 'get tough' on drug trafficking, vary according to the class of drug involved and whether the offence is one of possession - simple possession, usually of a small amount - or supply, importation or exportation, or production, when larger amounts are involved. The latter are now called 'trafficking' offences and carry heavier penalties. The maximum penalty for possession of Class A drugs is 7 years; for trafficking the penalty can be life imprisonment. Class B has lower maximum penalties of 5 years for possession and 14 years for trafficking. Class C has the lowest penalties of 2 years for possession and 5 years for trafficking. In all these cases an unlimited fine can also be applied (Dorn *et al.*, 1992). Less serious offences are usually dealt with by magistrates courts where the maximum penalty cannot exceed 6 months imprisonment and a £2,000 fine.

Turning from legislation to policy, it has often been argued that drug policy in Britain has been dominated by a medical/treatment model in which drug users or addicts are seen as sick and in need of treatment, rather than as criminals who should be punished. The division in penalties between possession and supply offences reflects this, which has been characterised as a view that while users are 'sad', suppliers/traffickers are 'bad'. The so-called 'British system' of drug maintenance by prescription has allowed some doctors to prescribe drug substitutes (such as methadone) and, sometimes, even heroin and cocaine to addicts. The view of drug addiction as an 'illness' has been used to privilege a medical model of drug use and to oppose a criminal response. However, medicine and the law are better seen as different regulatory systems, rather than opposed ones. The history of control and regulation in the twentieth century can be read as a struggle for dominance between law enforcement and medicine in terms of defining and responding to drug problems (see also Dorn and South, 1994). Arguments for more emphasis on medicine and public health policies as a counter-weight to enforcement can come from a variety of perspectives, including campaigners for legalisation.[2] However, legalisers have mainly based their case on individual rights, on the counter-productive effects of controls, and on the expected benefits of legalisation.

Individual rights

The case for legalisation can be based upon strong beliefs in obtaining maximum individual freedom and choice, and minimal interference by the state and the law in private domains. The essence of this position was succinctly expressed by Morris and Hawkins (1970): each person has the right to go to hell in their own way, provided that no one else is directly injured.[3] Legalisers argue that the criminal law should not be used as a way of compelling people to behave in particular ways. The wide range of activities subject to the law is seen as infringing the rights of individuals, particularly when it comes to matters of personal morality (Husak, 1992; Gaus, 1995). What is the scope of, and what should be the limits of the law when matters of personal morality are concerned? Is drug use a personal moral choice? The question of how much freedom individuals should have and what the dividing line should be is one that raises issues of competing basic values as well as pragmatic concerns about defining what is in or out. John Stuart Mill's 'harm principle' is an attempt to address this issue and to establish the limits of the law in interfering with the rights of individuals. Mill's principle, of which Morris and Hawkins' (1970) statement is a summation, said that behaviour should only be subject to the criminal law if it harmed others: 'the only purpose for which power can rightfully be exercised over any member of a civilised community, against his will, is to prevent harm to others'.[4] Everything else is a matter for each individual to decide, protecting people for 'their own good' was not, for Mill, a sufficient reason. Applied to drugs the principle has been used to argue that each person has a basic right to determine what happens to her or his own body. Legalisers following Mill have therefore privileged the principle of autonomy. For Husak (1992: 81) 'someone violates my autonomy by prohibiting me from doing what I have a moral right to do.' But identifying the dividing line between autonomy and constraint proved to be problematic for Mill himself. He acknowledged that children and the mentally ill had to be excepted because they were adjudged to require protection from themselves.

In contrast, prohibitionists put forward an alternative basic principle, paternalism, in which the state or the community has not only the right, but also the duty, to intervene to prevent people from harming themselves. For strong paternalism, intervention is justified even if the choice to self-harm is fully voluntary and competent; a weak paternalism would justify intervention on the basis that the choice is not a genuine one because the person is in some way acting under duress or in ignorance (Gaus, 1995). In either case, prohibitionists adopt the view that 'no person is an island'. Prohibitionists argue that the state has a paternalistic duty to protect some people from harming themselves or being harmed by others. Thus, for instance, in Britain people routinely accept restrictions such as the wearing of seat belts and crash helmets. But in other European countries such restrictions appear to be less acceptable and more commonly ignored. A similar argument can be seen in the case of gun control. Following the massacre of schoolchildren in Dunblane, restrictions on the possession of handguns were introduced. The policy was not enforced without protest, as the pro-gun lobby argued that their rights to use guns responsibly were being interfered with. In that case paternalism won over individual rights, though a very different gun culture in the US means that a similar prohibition on what is seen as a matter of individual freedom, is much more difficult to envisage. The same positions have been applied to drugs. For instance, if someone chooses to take drugs and then becomes a burden to others and creates misery for families, prohibitionists argue that account should be taken of this indirect harm. But the question of what counts as a harm to others again leads back to fundamental philosophical and policy differences. A strong rights-based autonomy position which underlies some arguments for legalisation can appear to be a version of the view that there is 'no such thing as society' and, for some, legalisation is unacceptable precisely because of its individualist assumptions. For legalisers, paternalism is a problem in itself. Szasz (1992) argues that the prohibition of drugs because of their presumed dangerousness camouflages the fact that life is dangerous. Autonomous adults learn to cope with such dangers and he sees the state's attempt to regulate behaviour as symptomatic of the over-reach of the law and its intervention in the lives of individual citizens. Moreover, the view that the state has a paternalistic duty to stop people from harming themselves by taking drugs is contradictory and incoherent, since there are other potentially harmful activities, for example, people engaging in dangerous sports, that are not treated in the same way as drug use (Szasz, 1992).

The failures of control

Legalisers believe that it is the definition of drugs as illegal which itself creates problems. Drugs should not be criminalised because users choose to indulge, therefore it is a 'victimless crime' (Schur, 1965), which is why the idea of the 'pusher' selling drugs to unwilling buyers is inappropriate. Controls produce harmful consequences in terms of crime and health. As far as crime is concerned, the argument is that the illegality of drugs makes them profitable goods to supply. Organised criminal networks such as the Mafia therefore prosper. The financial power of organised crime leads to the corruption of public officials such as the police, particularly if they feel that they are being asked to enforce laws which the public does not support anyway. The 'laundering' of the profits of organised crime threatens banking and legitimate businesses. Moreover, law enforcement is expensive as well as counter-productive. The criminal justice system consumes public resources in prosecuting offenders, but since drug use seems to continue unabated, the system is ineffective. Enforcement bears down most heavily on and stigmatises the young, the poor and on racial minorities, while middle-class users are largely un-touched. Illegality also makes drugs more expensive and leads users into committing crime to support a 'habit' (Kraska, 1991; Nadelmann, 1991). Meanwhile, the rhetoric of the 'war on drugs' undermines civil liberties as drugs are made an exception to the rights afforded under the US constitution (Wisotsky, 1986). For Bennett, however, constitutional liberties are under jeopardy not due to drug policy but from drugs 'which everyday scorch the earth of our common freedom' (Bennett, 1990: 18).[5] Turning to health aspects, legalisers see criminalisation as a problem because it leads to an unregulated market where users are at the mercy of dealers who can sell them adulterated drugs of uncertain quality and purity. Illegality means that users are socially marginalised and therefore less likely to come forward when or if they need help. It therefore carries a moral and physical cost in terms of the lack of health and treatment provision, and the loss of lives where the AIDS virus is also involved.

How valid are these claims? Alcohol prohibition in the USA in the 1920s is frequently cited as the classic example of the counter-productive effects of enforcement. But it may not have been a simple failure as is usually believed (cf Woodiwiss, 1988; Zimring and Hawkins, 1992). Heavy alcohol use did decline and the incidence of alcohol-related diseases rose again after prohibition was lifted (Shapiro, 1994). Bennett goes further in maintaining that:

> When we had laws against alcohol there was less consumption of alcohol, less alcohol-related disease, fewer drunken brawls, and a lot less public drunkenness. Furthermore, contrary to myth, there is no evidence that Prohibition caused big increases in crime (Bennett, 1990: 17-18).

Prohibitionists argue that illegality itself restricts availability as well as raising prices, and that problems with alcohol are precisely a consequence of its ready availability. Because illegality forces people to deal in illicit markets which carry social disapproval, this also acts as a disincentive (cf Kaplan, 1988). The major accomplishment of prohibition may be that it creates a ceiling under which there are only modest numbers of frequent users of the most expensive drugs (Reuter and MacCoun, 1995). Legalisation would remove these barriers as well as lowering prices, all of which would contribute to greater usage and perhaps increased drug-related problems. In turn, legalisers argue that illegality itself contributes to an interest in, and the glamorisation of, drugs. If they were not illegal there would not only not be illicit markets, but there would be no more interest in selling drugs than there is in selling cold remedies (Morris and Hawkins, 1970). Prohibitionists respond by saying that illegality would not necessarily do away with illicit markets because there would still be an incentive to undercut the legal price, hence users could be at risk from adulterated drugs.

If consumption did rise would this be an acceptable price of legalisation? Or should legal controls be maintained because they contribute to lower overall consumption? Legalisers agree that enforcement does increase the price of drugs, but they contend that price increases are counter-productive because they lead users into more drug-related crime. The idea of the drugs-crime link has seeped into common sense and is often unquestioned. But the issue of whether there is a *causal* link continues to be debated. The view that users commit crime to raise money for drugs relies on an idea of 'enslavement', that is, that drugs are so powerful, physiologically or psychologically, that they 'compel' users to turn to crime to feed a habit. The compulsion or enslavement model has been challenged by studies of the economic behaviour of drug users. In times of 'drought' when their usual drug is not available or if the price goes up sharply, even long term users may simply 'switch' to other drugs, or not use at all (Wagstaff and Maynard, 1988; George and Fraser, 1989). Demand for drugs is therefore more elastic than has usually been assumed and this has led to interest in the idea of enforcement as a 'tax' on drug suppliers (Reuter and Kleiman, 1986). In other words, policing imposes costs on suppliers because it requires them to invest in surveillance (to keep a 'look out') and to deal with known customers - because new or unknown customers might be police officers working undercover. These costs suggest that enforcement can have a considerable impact on drug markets (Moore, 1977, 1979; Dorn et al., 1992; Dorn and Murji, 1992b).

Interestingly, it has been suggested that if users think that drugs really are addictive they may be more likely to believe that they have to turn to crime to finance a drug habit (Hammersley et al., 1989). This idea is supported by social learning theory, when it has been applied to alcohol, for example. If some users believe that they are enslaved and have a habit, there may be real consequences of such beleifs. Because expectations of drugs may shape experience, social factors can be as important as pharmacology. It has also been argued that the drugs-crime relationship could be the other way round. Rather than drug use leading to crime, perhaps involvement in crime generates income which may be used to pay for a desired lifestyle, including drugs. There is also a third position in which drugs and crime go hand-in-hand and it is not possible to identify a causal or deterministic relationship either way.[6] As a general proposition, legalisers are correct to maintain that enforcement can never produce a 'drug free' society. The history of public policy contains few examples of things that we have freed ourselves from. A 'drug free' society is no more possible than a 'heart disease free' society. The rhetorical excesses of the 'war on drugs' has undeniably had much to do with politicians seeking to appear 'tough' on law and order (Wisotsky, 1986; Reinarman and Levine, 1989; Weisheit, 1991). But it would be misleading to imagine that the rhetoric does not engage or 'connect' with the experiences of people at some level. The appeal of the 'drug free' society is based on the illusion that there are neat and simple solutions to social problems. Ironically, legalisers mirror this rhetoric in presenting an equally simple solution to a complex issue.

Benefits and costs

We have already seen some of the benefits which legalisers say will flow from removing legal and criminal sanctions. These include reductions in drug-related crime, removing profits from criminals, undermining illicit markets and reduced expenditure on law enforcement. To this list can be added the proposition that legalisation would enable governments to impose taxes and therefore raise revenue. But there are a series of problems with these apparent advantages. If taxation raises prices, an illicit market may undercut the legal system and continue to be a source of supply. Unless all drugs are made legally available the illicit market would still supply the remainder. Even if all existing drugs were legalised, new synthetic drugs may be manufactured. Should everything be made legally available? Legalisation would not wipe out illicit markets if unauthorised suppliers could provide drugs of a different variety, purity or price to that which would be legally available.

Prohibitionists say that the costs of legalisation are rarely considered. One of these is a rise in health care provision arising from increased drug usage. If individuals get into trouble with drugs, the cost of care is effectively a burden on everyone else. Legalisers respond by pointing out that the health costs of alcohol and tobacco are already a burden on society. In any case, consumption would not necessarily rise because prevention programmes would be used to dissuade people from taking drugs. However the faith that this places in prevention (including education) can not be supported by the evidence from programmes to date (Dorn and Murji, 1992a). Similarly, health education campaigns on alcohol and smoking have produced mixed results. Kraska (1991) does not contest the view that decriminalisation would incur costs. The key issue, though, is whether the costs of decriminalisation exceed those of current policies. If the answer to this is no, then the benefits of legalisation and/or decriminalisation would outweigh its costs. But one problem with these sort of cost-benefit propositions is that they can easily be turned round by conservatives, employing a zero tolerance approach stressing 'user accountability' (Inciardi, 1991), to argue that, if benefits exceeds costs, then the answer is to increase the costs (or consequences) of criminal activities such as drugs possession. The former US 'drugs czar' William Bennett has expressed this position most succinctly:

> Casual use is not just a matter of personal preference. It has costs - wide, horrible social costs. The suburban man who drives his BMW downtown to buy cocaine is killing himself, of course. But he is killing the city at the same time. And his 'casual' use is best deterred not by empty threats of long, hard punishment, but by <u>certain</u> punishment. Compel him, as authorities are doing in Phoenix, to pay a steep fine and spend a weekend in jail. Seize his BMW right after he has bought

some dope, and when he is convicted, take the car away from him for good. That is what they do in Philadelphia (Bennett, 1989: 5).

Legalisers are often criticised on practical grounds, that is, the question of how a legal supply system would operate? Ethan Nadelmann has justifiably complained that prohibitionists use scare tactics in suggesting that legalisation would mean that drugs would be available 'like candy' (quoted in Leitner *et al.*, 1993).[7] A licensing system, as with alcohol, could be one method of supply. But even so, Inciardi and McBride (1991) raise a challenging set of questions for legalisers: Which drugs would be legalised? What potency levels would be permitted? Would there be age limits to restrict availability to children and young people? Should some drugs, for example heroin, only be made available to those who are already dependent on them? Where and how would drugs be made available? What restrictions would there be - would transport workers and operators of heavy machinery, for example, be banned from drug use? These issues indicate that, unless a totally free, unregulated market is being proposed, there would continue to be some restrictions and controls through the state or state regulated agencies. Hence, prohibitionists argue that there could still be an illicit market for under-age drug users. They also contend that increased availability will lead to greater use and that companies will target sales amongst lower socio-economic groups, thereby reaffirming social disadvantage (Inciardi, 1991).

The last point leads on to a further criticism of the legalisation perspective. Legalisers have been accused of employing a Euro-centric perspective in which the world's poorer countries continue to be dependent upon Western consumers. Drugs may be a source of income for farmers in some countries, but as a cash crop they hardly amount to a development policy appropriate for their home markets (Dorn, 1992). Legalisers say that farmers would be able to keep more of the profits after legalisation. But others argue that it would have counter-productive effects. It is the very illegality of drugs such as heroin and cocaine which makes the poppy and coca leaf attractive to produce because they are worth more than other plants. Legalisation would mean a drop in prices and, consequently, less money for farmers.

What about cannabis only?

Many people may oppose the legalisation or decriminalisation of most drugs, but still support the case for decriminalising cannabis only. Criminalisation has usually been justified on the threat to health which drugs are supposed to pose. Opponents say this cannot be applied to cannabis. A number of government committees have found little or no evidence that cannabis is harmful (Shapiro, 1994). Its illegality appears anomalous when alcohol and tobacco are widely available, even though there is plenty of evidence of the health problems they can lead to. Public policy therefore appears confused at least, or governments are accused of 'double standards'. A frequent claim for cannabis decriminalisation and/or legalisation is that 'it is no worse than' alcohol and tobacco, both of which are legally available and from which the state derives considerable income through taxation. Thus law and policy are seen as hypocritical and biased. But, if cannabis is no worse than alcohol and tobacco, that is not in itself an argument to change its legal status. Should people be encouraged to consume more substances which are harmful? Should there be more controls on alcohol and tobacco instead?

Prohibitionists claim that cannabis is 'a substance that impairs memory, concentration, and attention span; why...foster the use of a drug that makes you stupid?' (Bennett, 1990: 17). Some would add that cannabis is a 'gateway' drug which leads on to usage of harder drugs, though this is open to some doubt, not least because of the question of how one substance is supposed to 'open the gate' to the use of others. It has, somewhat flippantly, been argued that most alcoholics have once tried milk but that hardly makes the latter a gateway into alcohol abuse. In relation to cannabis, prohibitionists probably mean that trying one illegal drug denotes a loosening of moral bonds that makes use of other 'harder' drugs more probable. But this chain or sequence tends to be undermined by questions about causality, the much greater availability of cannabis and the relatively modest consumption of other drugs compared to cannabis. In addition, there are once again issues about whether, and how, prohibitions on under-age users should be maintained. Prohibitionists argue that decriminalising cannabis would send out the message that 'drugs are okay' and that it cannot be long before all drugs are decriminalised. For legalisers, however, this last point clinches their view that drugs laws are essentially part of a moralistic campaign, rather than justified by an objective measure of harm.

> The "Drugs are Okay" argument.....is probably one of the greatest hindrances to the decriminalization of the drug laws. Americans have become highly reliant on the law to delineate moral boundaries.....to regulat[e], organize, control and teach (Kraska, 1991: 130).

Thus, here we are once again back at first principles: should the role of the law be minimalist, or should it express condemnation of immoral behaviour(s) too? And what counts as moral or immoral?

Could legalisation and/or decriminalisation be tested empirically so that we can know what the effects would be? Reuter and MacCoun (1995) suggest three possible approaches. First, a social experiment would legalise drugs in some communities and see what the effects or outcomes are. But in an increasingly mobile and globalised world the idea that there could be 'oases' of drug legalisation which would not be 'contaminated' by outside influences is difficult to believe. The city of Amsterdam, for instance, is often regarded as a haven for casual drug use and therefore upheld as a model for a permissive regime. But often not considered are what the consequences of 'drugs tourism' may be, as well as the fact that there has been some opposition from local residents to the prevailing culture (Inciardi, 1991). Secondly, a natural experiment might ask what the differences are between any two given cities with different regimes. But this encounters the same objection as the previous case, though there are others too (see Reuter and MacCoun, 1995). Thirdly, Reuter and MacCoun (1995) suggest that a laboratory experiment could seek to model the process of individual decision making in different environments. But, they argue, this would be unpersuasive when generalised to society as a whole. Prohibitionists say that even an experiment might lead large numbers of people to try drugs and that it would be difficult to turn back the clock. A resolution to the debate seems unlikely, if only because there are practical constraints on legalisation imposed by UN international conventions which make it difficult for any country to go the whole way. That however does not stop all developments in policy. Debates about control seem to come and go, while the circumstances in which it is possible to foresee governments changing the law seem as far away as ever. The choice appears to be between two absolutes: legalisers point to the irrationality of controls and offer a series of 'what if' arguments which purport to spell out the benefits of change. Meanwhile, prohibitionists remain unconvinced and offer a set of disadvantages and, sometimes, the accomplishments of controls.

Perhaps though by focusing on policies 'on the ground' rather than principles or rhetoric, there is another way to see these issues. There are two aspects to this, one concerned with health, the other with enforcement. During the 1980s harm reduction has sometimes transcended debates which tend to stress either supply (mainly enforcement) or demand (mainly prevention) reduction. The impact of HIV/AIDS has led to the development of syringe exchange schemes and guidance on safer ways of using drugs (ACMD, 1988; Pearson, 1991, 1992). And the police - in response to the increased numbers of offenders being dealt with - have made much greater use of cautioning, which has seen a tenfold increased over the decade from 1985-95. It was applied to over half of all offenders in 1995 and to four out of five of those aged under 17. Cautioning for drug offences has risen from one per cent in 1981 to 52 per cent by 1995. It has replaced the fine as the most common method of disposal for drug offences (Home Office, 1996).[8] If enforcement is concentrated on suppliers rather than users then this can be read as *de facto* decriminalisation.[9] Such pragmatism is unlikely to satisfy ardent legalisers or prohibitionists. It is undoubtedly a messy compromise, one that could at any time be tilted in a particular direction. This 'pragmatic incoherence' (Turner, 1991) would not satisfy zealous advocates of controls or no-controls. But it does at least address mid-term harm reduction policies, away from the zero tolerance rhetoric of the 'war' on drugs. It enables advances in treatment based upon harm reduction (for examples see O'Hare *et al.*, 1992), the reduction of social and legal harm (for example through cautioning) and a degree of casual, unproblematic and unproblematised drug use. To the extent that it provides a basis on which 'soft' legalisers and prohibitionists can agree, it means that pragmatism can overtake ideology in the debate on drug control.

Notes

1. For some examples in relation to the police, see 'Drug dealing licences urged', *The Independent*, 14 May 1993, and 'Police chief want drugs 'nationalised'', *The Guardian*, 6 August 1994.

2. Prohibition makes drugs a crime problem with a modest health component, while legalisation makes drugs a public health problem with a modest crime component (Reuter and MacCoun, 1995).

3. Bennett (1990: 16) regards this as the attitude that: '"If those people want to kill themselves off with drugs, let them kill themselves off with drugs"'.

4. In *On Liberty*.

5. The image of a 'war' on drugs has been a convenient one for both ardent prohibitionists, as well as their critics who have used it as freely as their opponents. More reflective accounts have sought to question the terminology itself. For example, Weisheit (1991) asks, who is the enemy? What type of war is envisaged? What would constitute victory? Where is the 'battle front'? Nonetheless, the theme is used repeatedly. For instance, the *Evening Standard* (22 April 1994) used the headline 'Biggest ever war on drugs' to discuss the Green paper *Tackling Drugs Together*.

6. As a parallel, there is also a point about the relationship between policies and drug use. Weisheit (1991) suggests that it as likely that patterns of drug use give rise to different policy responses, as the opposite, i.e. that different policies - for example, between the USA and European countries - create different patterns of drug use. As with the drugs-crime debate, a third way would stress the interaction between these two aspects.

7. Compare these remarks: 'has anyone thought about what [a] legalized regime would look like? Would crack be legal? What about PCP? Or smokeable heroin? Would they all be stocked at the local convenience store, perhaps just a few blocks from an elementary

school?' (Bennett, 1990: 17).

8. The cautioning rate fell to 51 per cent in 1996. There are notable variations between police forces, with half the forces in England and Wales cautioning fewer than 50 per cent of drug offenders (Home Office, 1998). In a leader headed 'The cannabis casino', *The Guardian* (7 February 1998: 20) recognises that a form of decriminalisation has occurred, but regards the geographical variability as 'arbitrary justice' and calls for a national policy on soft drugs. A survey of 200 police officers on their attitudes to cannabis revealed that one in five did not take any formal action against people they found in possession of small quantities of the drug (*New Statesman and Society*, 10 March 1995).

9. Henham has written that increased cautioning for drugs possession reflects 'a trend towards general relaxation of penalties for soft drug use... It is apparent that a de facto decriminalization of soft drug use and possession has occurred in certain European countries without necessitating deliberate sentencing policy changes' (Henham, 1994: 231).

PART II

DRUG REFERRAL

4 Drug and Arrest Referral in Trafford, Merseyside and Southwark

Introduction

Referral schemes - variously called arrest, drug and, once upon a time, family referral schemes - are essentially a simple means for the police to refer people to drugs advice agencies. At their most elementary they are no more than a formalisation of an advisory and 'befriending' role that may have been practised by some police officers, in some places, some of the time. Naturally, such informalism depends a good deal on the attitude of individual officers and their awareness of the existence of drug-related problems and local drugs advice/treatment agencies. The referral schemes discussed in this and the following chapter represent a variety of attempts to formalise the referral procedure. In terms of their *type*, they may be aimed at drug offenders only, or at all people who come into police custody. In between these two poles, there can be various forms of 'targeting' in which referral is aimed at a particular 'type' of person, for example persistent property offenders suspected of activity in acquisitive crime to finance drug purchases. The *referral mechanism* is generally a card or a leaflet, either of which may be supplemented by posters on the wall. A related issue is *where and by who* the referral occurs. In most of the case studies, referral is the responsibility of the custody officer whose role it is to 'book in' and oversee individuals brought into police custody. In some other cases, the referral card and invitation to self-refer may be made by an investigating officer, such as a detective from the drugs squad, perhaps as an informal 'bargaining' counter. Another aspect of the diversity within referral schemes is about the *agencies at the receiving end* of the referral process. It could be one or several drugs agencies; it could also include alcohol advice services and, as we will see, in one case it includes a wider range of advice agencies including the Samaritans. But in all the areas where referral schemes operate a consistent series of problems recur, in particular whether the referral card or leaflet is issued by police officers in the first place and, subsequently, whether it will be accepted and/or lead to self-referral.

There are at least two main points from which the impulse to develop referral can be identified. One of these is Family Referral, an idea arising from work that examined family feelings when drug use by a young person was discovered (Dorn et al., 1987). Since this often occurred when parents were notified that a child or young person was in police custody, the rationale for Family Referral was to enable the police to have to hand a simple means of referring parents - and perhaps young people too - to advice and counselling agencies. Family Referral never really took off, mainly because the police and drugs agencies were primarily interested in drug users and, at best, saw the parents as a secondary concern (Dorn et al., 1990). Another point of origin for referral schemes began from the question of whether arrest could act as a key point of intervention for drug users to seek advice and treatment from drugs services. This was the staring point of the Southwark Arrest Referral Project, which is discussed later in this chapter. These two approaches to, or understandings of, referral suggest two initial ways of characterising referral schemes (cf Dorn, 1994). Family Referral prioritised *welfare* concerns, that is the provision of advice, counselling and reassurance services for parents. This may be combined with information and education for drugs users and their relatives, but the over-riding concern is still to provide police officers with the information to direct people to the appropriate local services. In contrast, the Southwark Arrest Referral Project envisages referral into drug treatment services as a means of intervening in offending behaviour (perhaps as a version of persuading or forcing drug users into 'taking early retirement' - Gilman and Pearson, 1991) so that, over time, rates of both drug use and drug-related property crime will decline. This *crime-control* perspective is an expression of a 'controlling user crime' policy (see Kleiman and Smith, 1990; Wilson, 1985). A secondary pay-off of referral from this perspective is that it forms part of a 'carrot and stick' approach that enables police officers in cultivating informants or garnering intelligence. The distinction between welfare and crime-control is not absolute and they are combined in police practice. Either or both can also be combined with a third way of comprehending referral schemes. From an *efficiency* perspective, which has become more central in the thinking of police and other public sector agencies in the past decade, the value of referral should be assessed in terms of its benefits and costs. If referral consumes resources and has a limited pay-off, then its value is questionable.[1]

While the third perspective is closest to what Dorn (1994) calls a 'business' outlook on referral, the welfare perspective approximates to a police *service* image, while crime-control can be equated with a police *force*. However, the distinctions between these three perspectives and, for that matter, between business, service and force, are 'blurred' in practice. These perspectives can exist together in the same area because of the different understandings and meanings that police officers and others attach to referral schemes. Nonetheless some of these distinctions are reflected in the ways in which referral schemes are set up and operated. The welfare view stresses police information provision. A crime-control oriented scheme may involve drugs workers screening in and out those suitable for treatment, thereby aiming to intervene in the careers of active offenders. This intervention may also influence bail and later prosecution decisions. While the case studies are not organised under neat headings following each of the three perspectives, it is possible to see that some referral schemes began with, or came to place greater emphasis on, one perspective or element than others.

Before proceeding there is a further issue that arises at this point. In Trafford and Merseyside - both of which pre-dated both Southwark and Family Referral - referral emerged as part of an overall policy package based upon multi-agency working. This suggests that in addition to the welfare and crime-control viewpoints, referral came about from developments in multi-agency work, and that this orientation preceded the welfare and crime-control perspectives. It also transcends the force, service and business views of referral. The multi-agency framework therefore forms an umbrella within which the case studies and the differing perspectives on referral should be read. The push from government since the early 1980s for multi-agency co-ordination between the police and other agencies has been subject to extensive debate. Sampson *et al.* (1988) suggested two ways of thinking about multi-agency work: the benevolent view is that multi-agency coordination is unproblematic because it seeks to further common interests such as crime reduction; the conspiratorial view is that multi-agency is a process for enhancing the reach of the state and its power to regulate and survey individual lives. Research on the ground has inevitably demonstrated that matters are more complicated than either of these views and that local arrangements display a variety of configurations reflecting differing circumstances, the history of cooperation or conflict between agencies, and the ways in which the role and responsibilities of agencies are defined and perceived (Sampson *et al.*, 1988; Blagg *et al.*, 1988).

In terms of social prevention (Bright, 1987, 1991) the basic rationale for multi-agency work is that addressing crime and social problems will be more effective if the actions of diverse agencies are conjoined to the same ends (Hope and Shaw, 1988). This has proved to be an attractive vision, but aims and practice have often not matched-up and research has identified persistent problems in multi-agency working between the police and other agencies. One of these is that conflicts arise from the differing cultures and practices of distinct agencies that are exhorted to work together. In referral schemes for example, while the police are a large bureaucratic organisation with well established procedures and considerable resources, the drug agencies at the other end of the referral chain can range from organisations with few staff and insecure funding, to semi-established treatment agencies, sometimes linked to a hospital or local health authority.[2] As well as these differences in size and resources, the personnel or staff may have very different backgrounds and orientations. Police officers will have undergone formal training, including the law and, increasingly, an emphasis on human relations and skills training. The training of drugs workers could cover a wide variety of possibilities that are not easy to summarise. Some may have backgrounds in social work, counselling, health or nursing. Some may be former drug users or addicts. Furthermore, there may be very different attitudes to working together. For example, one of the issues that will be evident in the case studies is that of client confidentiality. Drug agencies may place a premium on maintaining the confidentiality of every individual who seeks advice from them, while the police may sometimes believe this to be an obstacle to cooperation particularly when making a decision about whether to caution an individual or recommend prosecution.

Difficulties such as these led Bottoms (1990) to ask three questions about multi-agency working. First, do discrete agencies have different amounts of power and does it matter? Second, how much autonomy is it necessary for each agency to have and how much are they willing to lose for the common good? Third, to what extent is it necessary to recognise that different agencies (e.g. the police and drugs agencies) have different assigned functions which may necessarily limit the extent to which they can ethically co-operate? For the benevolent view, the differences that do exist are not very important since there is a shared overall goal that all public agencies are aiming for. For the conspiratorial view, differences do exist and matter a great deal, particularly if welfare agencies are to avoid being subordinated to crime-control objectives.

To return to the practical issue of referral schemes, the Advisory Council on the Misuse of Drugs (ACMD) noted that the police and drug agencies had not developed effective joint working. It argued that both needed to develop a 'shared agenda' or common purpose, despite differences of philosophy (ACMD, 1991, 1994). The Council said that while the police have moved towards drugs agencies, the latter 'have been relatively slow to broaden the client-based focus of their work to incorporate a recognition of the wider interests of the community' (ACMD, 1994: 3). This concern with the wider community is significant because it indicates that community safety considerations (for example, concerns about and fears of drug-related crime) should play a role in the thinking of drugs agencies, beyond treatment and advice for individual clients. It thus fits in with an emerging consensus that 'working together' is not just about crime prevention in a narrow sense, but the contribution of diverse agencies to feelings of safety and 'quality of life' considerations (cf Dorn and Murji, 1992b). The ACMD emphasised that a local partnership needs to represent all relevant agencies, identify strategic objectives and to monitor progress. It also stated that partnership requires investment, information sharing and the building and maintenance of local alliances, including the involvement of the local media (ACMD, 1994). The ACMD (1994) recommended that the Inspectorate of Constabulary should monitor (a) consultation structures on drugs; (b) whether a local strategy had been devised; and (c) how law enforcement takes account of harm reduction objectives.

The content of most of the discussion in these two chapters focuses on police orientations and attitudes to referral schemes.[3] There is some mention of the views and experiences of either drugs advice agencies or those people offered the referral card, but this is secondary to the spotlight on the police. This is an unavoidable consequence of the nature of the action research from which most of the material is derived. All police forces were informed about the idea of referral schemes and of places where it was already operating. Subsequently, information and advice about referral through briefing meetings (including the ways in which it was working in other areas) was combined with some observational research and interviews with custody officers and others; most of the material is derived from these sources. There was also some attempt to obtain the views of individuals who should have been offered a referral card or leaflet, as a means of evaluating whether the schemes did increase self-referral to drugs advice agencies. Because of the stress on the police side of things there is a relative neglect of the reasons why individuals may choose to take-up referral, be willing to disclose drug misuse to the police and whether this is, or should be, tied in with police decisions on cautioning and prosecution (ACMD, 1991; Dorn, 1994).

The case studies of referral schemes that follow have been organised in broad chronological order.[4] In this chapter I examine the referral schemes in Trafford, Merseyside and Southwark, the first and the third mostly on the basis of reports on those schemes. In each of these areas, referral was initiated by local players such as police officers and drugs agency staff. The latter two are among the best publicised examples of referral arrangements, though there are significant differences between them. For example, the Merseyside scheme covered the whole force area and was linked to an existing drugs advice agency, while the Southwark scheme began in a much smaller way - initially with only two police stations - before being widened to all police stations in the London Borough of Southwark. Unlike Merseyside, the latter employed a full-time dedicated drugs advice worker, initially funded by the Home Office. At the end of this chapter I present a relatively brief account from two people arrested by the police.

Trafford: Developing a relationship between treatment and enforcement agencies

In the late 1980s a two year project focusing on 'problem drug users in the criminal justice system' operated in the Trafford area of Manchester. A joint effort between various local agencies, principally the Trafford Community Drugs Team (CDT), the Lifeline Project and the Greater Manchester Police, its core was an arrest referral contact leaflet giving details of the services offered by the Trafford CDT. A short report (Kay, not dated) describes some of the lessons learnt from the project. During the two years of the project, there were a series of 'active dissemination weeks' when leaflets were issued, alternating with periods when no leaflet dissemination took place. The report describes dissemination being done by 'custody office staff'.[5] The contact leaflets were only given to those people who were being either charged or cautioned. This means that leaflets were not to be given to those who were bailed but not charged, though some of these people may have got the leaflet if, upon their return to the police station, they were charged or cautioned and it was in an active dissemination week. Nor were the leaflets given to people who were being held temporarily pending escort to another police jurisdiction, or to those released without charge. In the latter case it is stated that it would be 'undiplomatic....to suggest that they might have drug problems' (Kay, n.d: 10) by handing out the leaflet.

The complex dissemination strategy inevitably, and probably forseeably, encountered difficulties. The report mentions 'a tendency for the dissemination rate to decay over time. This was not surprising as the dissemination of our leaflets had to compete for the time and attention of charge office staff with a multitude of day to day pressures and tasks' (Kay, n.d: 10). This experience led to recommendations for simplifying the dissemination process, by giving the same information to everybody. The report claims to reliably identify an extra 3.5 referrals[6] to the Trafford CDT in the active dissemination periods during the first nine months of the project. But, in the second year, this declined and is attributed to a 'saturation effect' because most drug users either had already received the leaflet or already knew about Trafford CDT. The report concludes that the leaflet was held responsible for increased awareness and, sometimes, a more sympathetic attitude towards drug users by charge office staff. Thus the project was deemed to be successful in two respects. First, in developing a relationship between enforcement and treatment agencies; and secondly, in that 'a new layer of drug users were given information about local drug services. It seems a significant number acted upon that information [the leaflet] and made contact with services' (Kay, n.d: 19). The report recommended that: (a) in future leaflets advertising helping services should be attached to or incorporated into the Police and Criminal

Evidence Act (PACE) leaflet that is supposed to be given to all people in custody to inform them of their rights on arrest; (b) advice leaflets should be given to all those who enter custody; and (c) the areas covered by the helping agencies should be extended to include HIV/AIDS and other drugs such as tranquillisers.

The report on the Trafford scheme does not contain sufficient detail to enable an evaluation of its claims that the additional referrals to the Trafford CDT can be attributed to the existence of the contact leaflets available from the police station. As the research on which the report is based found, the complexity of the dissemination process created problems and, sensibly, it recommended that the process be simplified and that the scope of referral should be broadened. This is a lesson that can be applied to virtually all referral schemes. Two other elements of the Trafford scheme can be highlighted. One is the multi- or inter-agency element, stressing cooperation between the police and drugs advice agencies. Hence it is significant that the report notes an increased awareness about the needs of drug users by the police. Secondly, as the title of the project itself suggests, the initiative can be characterised as being largely welfare oriented in seeking to bring users into the ambit of the community drugs team. All referral schemes contain some greater or lesser emphasis on these elements. However, other schemes to be discussed below contain additional elements that lean towards the crime-control and efficiency models sketched in the introduction.

Merseyside: 'Responsible demand enforcement'

The Mersey area has become internationally renowned for its approach to drugs and drug users, involving measures taken by the police, the health authority and local drugs advice agencies (see O'Hare et al., 1992). The origins of this policy is probably to be found in the particular set of local circumstances tied to the sharp increase in heroin use by young people often through 'chasing the dragon' in the early 1980s (Pearson, 1987; Parker et al., 1988). The scale of the heroin problem or 'epidemic' led to considerable public pressure on local health and enforcement agencies to produce a meaningful response. Supply side or law enforcement measures are often to the fore in such circumstances as 'fire brigade' policing is perceived of as a stop gap. For reasons particular to the locality however, including the actions of key individuals in the area, a wider policy mix emerged. It is this which has come to be characterised as the 'Mersey approach'. The basket of policies included increased cautioning and referral of drug users by the police through to harm reduction and encouragement for more liberal prescribing by the health authority. It entailed a recognition by the police that demand side measures were just as important as supply side ones. A sense of the development of this policy is to be found in this statement by Detective Superintendent Derek O'Connell, the then head of the Merseyside Police drugs squad:[7]

> When I left the force and went over to the Caribbean we didn't have the heroin problem that we came back to, I must confess that surprised and shocked me. But prior to going away it was obvious that the drug situation was increasing and obviously mere arresting and taking them before the court was just not the answer. So we were already in the throes of trying to formulate a policy like what we've got today.

Drug referral is seen as just one element of the process, and probably not all that important a one at that: 'Our own referral got going round about '85, '86. Referral, you're talking about the leaflet, that started about 1985, '86, but we had started way back in 1980 trying to work to the system that we've got now, which I was part and parcel of, because I was the originator of the first cautioning policy which was for cannabis'. It is therefore not easy to neatly separate out the referral scheme from other elements. What follows moves between general policy measures and referral specifically. There is no doubt that developments in Merseyside have sometimes been at the forefront of advances in drug policy in Britain, although many of these measures are now to be found across the country. It is this which underlies the sense of having been the 'market leaders' that is sometimes expressed in the words of Mersey spokespeople. In the 1980s the Merseyside Police force, along with the Metropolitan Police, led the way in the use of the caution for drug possession offences. Starting with cannabis, both forces have gradually widened out the scope of their policies to include the possibility of cautioning for first possession of a Class A drug such as cocaine or heroin, and the use of the caution for minor supplying offences. The policy has not been without its critics however, as DS O'Connell explained:

> Even when we were first talking about it there were people who were cynical of the fact that you gave a caution to somebody for drugs, it was just something that was totally foreign to their way of thinking, and I think the more you explained and the more that people came to see that it was working and it was practical, then their views changed. They weren't enlightened in the initial stages, it was a case of having to be proved right. I think one of the difficulties of dealing with some of the areas of harm reduction - we call it responsible demand enforcement - is the fact that things might go slightly wrong and you're going to be seen as being a participant in that arena and therefore your whole judgement, understanding and perception of the drugs situation will come into question. Let's be honest, you can't be right all the time.

Within the police force, developments in drug policy have been allied to a training programme for police officers, both those involved in drugs work as well as other officers.

> You can't change people's attitudes and philosophies just overnight. But we also have in Merseyside police a very in-depth on-going training programme, not only for the detectives involved in the major side of drug investigation but also for the uniformed officers. We have a very involved package for our uniformed bobbies on the street, and I think that we carry out more drug training than possibly any other force in the United Kingdom.

As with many similar courses, external speakers are brought in to present their views and experiences.

> Now in-built into that drug training is what we call our Drug Appreciation Course, part and parcel of that training is that outreach workers come in, consultants come in, people from the needle and syringe [exchange] come in, and they explain to our unformed officers as well as our detectives what their role is, what they're doing, what their policy is, what they're trying to achieve so that we are educating our officers so that they are aware what the other people are trying to achieve, so that each is aware of what each other is doing and what each other's roles are, to ensure that we get or remove any preconceived notions that uniformed officers may have that these people are only do-gooders out there, they don't really understand, when in fact they do understand. So you're making sure that information and knowledge is out there and is brought in.

Increasingly the policy is presented as an integrated approach between various public agencies, though it is probably better seen as having developed into an integrated policy rather than having been created as one. Because of this emphasis on joint working, for the police referral cannot simply be a way of shunting people out of the police station into the drugs agency.

> I think that when you embark on the kind of programme that we've embarked on here in Merseyside you've got to really congratulate not only the Mersey Health Authority but all those connected with it, as well as central government because central government provided funding to enable those initiatives to be able to get off the ground. And I think when you start on these initiatives it's no good saying 'go to this place and you'll get help', you've got to make sure that the help is there, that the facilities and the right staff are there, that they have got the money and the time to be able to meet that requirement and that demand. So before you embark on it there's so much infrastructure that's got to be put into place. I smile when I go down to these conferences in London and we think we're going to learn something new and innovative. But really they're about four or five years behind us, they're talking in terms of we've got to harmonise, we've got to work together, we've got to do this that and the other. These are things that we've been doing for

five, six and seven years.

Because of the way in which the policy has developed, initiatives including, but not solely, referral, have not been seen as trial measures, but rather as part of an overall package.

> Here in Merseyside we have not just embarked upon things for a trial period or in a particular area. We've considered everything and then believed that it is to the advantage, the betterment of everybody, so that it becomes a force initiative, a force objective. Therefore when we do that, we do force orders which come out under the authority of the Chief Constable so that the whole force is informed and aware of whatever that particular agreement, that initiative or package is.

As far as referral itself is concerned, the Mersey police force has moved from informal referrals by individual police officers through to a referral leaflet given to drug offenders and, latterly, to a drugs advice leaflet which is given to everybody brought into custody.

The views of three custody officers

Three custody officers were interviewed in Merseyside about how referral worked. The officers designated as A and B were based at the same station, while officer C was based at another station in the Mersey police force area. All three officers were asked who they would give the drugs advice leaflet to. These are their answers:

> Well, we just give it to people who are arrested for a drugs related offence; now the policy is that we give it out to everyone.
>
> Q. But you [personally] don't give it out to everyone?
>
> Certainly not (Officer A).

> It's basically for people who are arrested for possession of drugs or anything that's drug related, like burglary, thefts, stealing vehicles - they might be doing it to support their habits (Officer B).

> Those people who are arrested for offences of possession primarily, or those that have been arrested for obstruction where the obstruction has been to swallow what we consider to be a controlled substance. Those are the people that those forms [leaflets] would be aimed at in the first instance. And you do get an awful lot of people in through the back door, being arrested for other matters - crime in particular - who do have a drug problem and as such you'd be aiming it at them because they usually wish to volunteer that information when they come through the door, because if there's a chance that they are going to be banged-up in the cell

for some considerable time, they would want the doctor to give them some painkillers and as such they would volunteer that information. So it's not directly related but because they bring it to our attention the form would be pushed to them as well (Officer C).

After the interviews, I asked the head of the drugs squad about the differences between these replies. The answer acknowledged both that the act of referral will not always occur, and that referral itself is seem as a relatively minor component in the overall policy package.

> I think you're always going to get that no matter who you are....if you'd have got exactly the same answer to the question, you may have turned round and said 'blimey', do you know what I mean? I think there is always going to be some discrepancy in terms of the numbers of forms there are and who you give them to. The whole objective is to ensure that our officers know that those forms are there and do give them out, or attempt to give them out. It's like when you've cautioned somebody for drugs and they say 'yes I'm going to go round [to the drug agency], I'm going to get help' and when they get outside the police station they don't bother. You can't reinforce certain thing obviously. If we considered that there was a major breakdown in our harm reduction approach we would be looking to improve it positively, so we're just as keen to listen and to see, just as much as you are, to see if there are areas that we can improve upon.

A possible reason for these differences is a change in force policy in the past year. This meant giving the leaflet to all people, as O'Connell outlines: 'We made that changeover this year. It was a result of a survey we did with Mersey Regional Health Authority when we realised then that there was people who were coming in who were arrested for non-drug offences who had drug problems, so therefore we decided we would try to reach them as well'.

The Mersey force is far from unique in facing the problem of having a paper policy and making it work in practice. Even something as simple as giving or offering a leaflet to everybody cannot be guaranteed, a finding that recurs to some extent in every force. Referral leaflets or card may be expected to be low on the list of priorities but, in several areas, custody officers admitted that the statutory PACE leaflets giving advice on rights in custody were also sometimes forgotten about. Apart from that, there is an additional problem. The leaflet is not always offered, sometimes it is simply left for individuals to take if they wish to do so:

> We tend to leave the forms there [on the counter, clearly visible] so if somebody wants one they can take it, they don't have to wait for us to say here is a form for you. We try to leave them, it's like the posters on the walls [large versions of the referral leaflet], we don't hide them. Somebody who wants to take advantage of what's up there, well that's what they're there for (Officer C).

Hence officers use their discretion in how, or even whether, the leaflet is issued. Of the three Merseyside custody officers, only one explicitly stated that he did this.

> You use your own judgement [in deciding when to hand the form out], I mean people get an awful lot of forms when they come into the police station these days, to be perfectly frank, my desk and the cells end up littered with those pieces of paper that people don't consider to be relevant. Whether they consider that [drug referral form] to be relevant is up to them. If it's given to them, I can't really do any more, I'm not going to make a nuisance of myself to make sure that somebody actually takes a piece of paper at the police station with them or chase them down the street saying, 'you forgot this'. They will either take physical possession of it [the leaflet] or they will have their attention drawn to it, what happens after that I don't know. I think it's like the big black book we have about referring prostitutes to a member of the clergy. As a young officer you might try it once and then quickly realise that it has no importance at all, when you see somebody coming in again and again, you say to yourself well, they've made their mind up which way they wish to conduct their life, so that's up to them. [And] it's not worth giving it out (Officer C).

The other two officers reported some similar experiences from people given or offered the leaflet.

> For those who have not seen it before, they'll look at it, one or two might take it away, the others won't bother. For those who've been through the mill before, usually they see what it is and throw it away. [He does not specify a number or percentage who will not accept it, other than saying 'most' of them]. Those who've had it [the leaflet] before will just brush it aside (Officer A).

> [I] basically just hand it to them and say you got a problem? Think about that. [The reaction is] very mixed. There's the general 'well I don't want to know about it' syndrome; we have a very good system for drug people so they know what's available for them and where they can get it. I'd say it was more than half [who say they don't want the leaflet]. But it's very occasional that they say anything. It's like a lot of things, we dole them out these PACE sheets with their rights and we have to read them out to them and [then] give them that [drug leaflet] as well and they're left on the desk. We can't physically force them to take it (Officer B).

While all three officers were unsurprised to hear that take-ups from the referral leaflet were very low, they all felt that there was something worthwhile about having the leaflet available and offering it to people.

> I would say that [low take-up rate] fits in with the reaction [we find] here (Officer A).

> It doesn't surprise me [that most people don't take up the referral], the help's there

if they want it, maybe they don't want it. I don't consider that what I'm doing is a waste of time, but I think there's an awful lot more influences which could be brought to bear on people other than any influence I'm able to bring to bear to point these people in the right direction. Anything I say is only going to have a minuscule effect on them (Officer C).

They're a group that are using drugs, they want to stay basically in that group, I don't think they really want to get off it. You're fighting a great problem, I don't know the answer to it, I think you have to carry on fighting, there's no way we can hoist the white flag and give up. It's like what I do here, a lot of it is drug related, but we have to just carry on. If it makes a difference, so that's a success isn't it? One person is a success (Officer B).

There are considerable difficulties with any evaluation of referral in Merseyside. On the one hand it is almost impossible to treat referral as if it is separate from the other policies that have been put into operation in the area. Referral is only one part of a process, and a relatively small one at that. But on the other hand, anecdotal evidence from drugs advice agencies indicates that very few referrals could definitely be linked to the advice leaflets issued by the police. For the length of time referral leaflets have been available (even if not always handed out) and the numbers of people who should have received one, it is almost inconceivable that they could have had no impact at all. It could be that users are already well apprised of local drug services, that agencies have not been sufficiently attuned to picking up referrals through this route, or that there are problems at the point at which leaflets are issued. All, or any, of these could be possible explanations. The information from which any meaningful conclusion could be drawn simply does not exist.

At a broader level, the set of policies in place in Merseyside have been well trumpeted and possibly quite influential. The Mersey approach is one which includes and combines diverse objectives. It has a clear welfare element, stressing harm reduction, the relatively low incidence of HIV infection and the number of drug users in treatment. It also includes a demand reduction aspect within a crime-control/efficiency model, though that is unsurprising since this account is based almost entirely on the police's version of events. But as an indication of such thinking in other quarters, it is notable that the view that prescribing drugs of choice to users will decrease their tendency to crime has been advanced by treatment agencies. Furthermore, it has been argued that all the policies in place in Merseyside have contributed to a decrease in recorded crime rates in the area. A Merseyside Assistant Chief Constable has written that the 'Merseyside area had the highest number of recorded drug addicts in country. They receive care and treatment which helps their withdrawal from the unlawful market. Our force takes a full part in these initiatives and it has a vigorous policy aimed at the dealers. Containment of the explosion in drug abuse may have contributed to the wider fight against crime'.[8] Consequently, the Merseyside scheme might be seen as combining welfare elements, in the form of a harm reduction policy, with a crime-control pay-off, since one significant justification for what has sometimes been seen as a permissive policing policy is in terms of the benefits of a lower crime rate.

Southwark: The Arrest Referral Project

Probably the best known of all the referral schemes is the Arrest Referral Project in Southwark, south London. It is certainly the scheme which has been most intensively researched and hence about which there is the greatest amount of information. As well as receiving the most attention, it also received the greatest resources, enabling it to employ a specialist worker from a grant provided by the Home Office. A report to the Home Office described the background to and the findings of the first two years of the project (Southwark Arrest Referral Pilot Project [ARPP] Monitoring Group, 1991). A separate article provides a succinct summary of the report (Barker, 1992). The project began in 1989 and in its first phase ran for over two years up to March 1991. It was initially based in the Southwark police division of the London Borough of Southwark and subsequently extended to the neighbouring Peckham and Carter Street divisions.

> Its principal aim was to determine whether arrest can be a positive and effective point of intervention (providing information, advice and referral) for people who want help in tackling their problem drug use. The project also sought to determine whether, through arrest, services could begin to reach the suspected majority of drug users who do not self-present for help and at least expose these users to the helping choices available (Barker, 1992: 15).

A referral card was designed to be given to all people brought into the police station, regardless of the suspected offence. The rationale for this was that while drug use might be a contributory factor to offending behaviour, in some or many cases, drug possession or supply might not be the actual offence for which a person had been arrested. In other referral areas, this rationale was combined with a simpler, administrative reason for giving the card to every person 'booked in' at the station. Giving the card to everybody was seen as one way of removing the need for custody officers to be reminded that 'if drugs, then hand out card'. In theory it also removes the need for officers to exercise any discretion. Nonetheless, as in Merseyside and in many other areas, the card is simply not given out or officers continue to use their discretion in dispensing the card. The Southwark card invited individuals to ask the police to make a call to the drugs advice worker on their behalf, or suggests that they might call the number themselves:

> All people arrested receive a card introducing them to the ARPP....regardless of the nature of the offence for which s/he has been arrested, thus ensuring that those whose charges do not clearly reflect drug-related offences are, nevertheless, made aware of the ARPP and can, if they choose, act on their own recognition of the relationship between their offence and their drug use. Those who then choose to take up the ARPP can - themselves or through a police officer and whilst still at the police station or following their release - contact the ARPP worker (Southwark ARPP Monitoring Group, 1991: 1).

One particularly notable feature of the Southwark card was that it contained the strongest statement on confidentiality found in any referral scheme:

> This is a special service, set up to help drug users who have been arrested, run by independent drugs workers. You can talk freely - nothing you say can be used in criminal proceedings (Southwark referral card, reproduced in Southwark ARPP Monitoring Group, 1991: 82).

Confidentiality is a persistent issue in referral schemes, as in other inter-agency ventures. Drugs advice agencies in particular have an understandable concern about how they might be seen by existing or potential clients if they are perceived to be working 'hand in hand' with the police. However, as we will see at the end of this chapter, one person who received the referral card took the view that the police and drug agencies routinely exchanged information. The dilemma for the latter is that some people would, presumably, be perturbed if they found that their relationship with the agency was not wholly confidential. In another police force area the wish by drug agencies for a similar statement on the referral card was strongly, and successfully, resisted by the police. The latter argued that it was impossible to give such a *carte blanche* undertaking. The strong statement on the Southwark card was certainly seen as being significant, since the monitoring group found that over half of those who took up the ARPP had not been arrested for drug offences. By asking the police to contact a drugs worker they therefore ran the risk of exposing their drug use: 'Presumably they were reassured by the card's assertion that any information asking about the project would not be used against them' (Barker, 1992: 16).

After an initial trial run, the Southwark project received Home Office funding to employ a specialist worker based at the Maudsley Hospital's Community Drugs Team. It was this designated worker who acted as the recipient of calls from the police or from people directly, after which the worker would arrange to see people either in the police station or elsewhere.

> The first meeting normally involved an initial assessment leading to the identification of an appropriate programme of help. It was at this stage, therefore, that one of the pilot project's principal objectives was met - exposing the arrestee to the help options available. Whether those who took this first step went on to take up and sustain the identified programme of help was entirely up to them. So too was the decision whether to cite their participation in a programme as mitigation in court or in applications for police to use their discretionary powers, such as to caution rather than to prosecute (Barker, 1992: 15).

The monitoring group's report on the operation of the ARPP relates that over 18,000 people were arrested in the three police divisions which were covered by the scheme and should therefore have received the referral card. In the twenty five month period up to the end of January 1991, 78 people were referred to the ARPP; of these 76 were drug users, and two were not. Of the 76 drug users, 75 met with the scheme's worker, completed the initial assessment and were assisted with identifying a programme of help. The people who took up referral were mostly male (78 per cent) and white (over 80 per cent). The average age was between 25 and 26 years old, the vast majority were resident in the London Borough of Southwark and unemployed (over 80 per cent in both cases). Of the 76 drug users, 23 were arrested for drugs offences, 53 for other offences, of which the greatest number were burglary offences. Over 80 per cent had been arrested before, though for nine people it was their first arrest. 40 per cent of the ARPP's clients had never sought help in connection with their drug use before, while a third had been in contact with helping agencies before, but not in contact at the time of their arrest. Around 80 per cent of the drug users in the ARPP's client groups were known to have made contact with the programme of help identified after their initial interview with the project's drugs worker (Southwark ARPP Monitoring Group, 1991; Barker, 1992).

ARPP clients were also able to call on the project for the purposes of mitigation.

> In at least ten cases, ARPP reports were submitted to the court (and in another case to the police for the purposes of an application for cautioning), citing clients' participation in the pilot project as mitigation. In all but one of the cases the client had been charged with and faced prosecution for one or more serious offences and faced a possible custodial sentence. In eight of these cases, the defendants received sentences which were alternatives to custody (Barker, 1992: 15-16).

While take-up of the ARPP was lower than anticipated, the project's monitoring group were encouraged by the take-up from people who had not sought help in the past, that most seemed to follow up the programme, and that people used the help programme as a source of mitigation in court. There were problems in inter-agency cooperation, with the level of commitment to the scheme by police officers and drugs agencies, and with the blurring of their separate roles. In its second phase the ARPP in Southwark moved more into line with all other schemes by working with drug workers at an existing agency rather than employing a specific worker.[9]

The Southwark project therefore combined welfare and crime-control elements, while the stress on take-up rates and throughput indicates an efficiency concern, that is, to show that the project was delivering referrals, a need probably sharpened by the external funding of the project. One conclusion that could be drawn from the Southwark scheme is that the take-up rate from referral schemes is low. This does not necessarily mean that arrest cannot be an effective point of intervention in a drug-using career, but it probably does mean that intervention following police action is not the most cost-effective means of targeting drug users who may want to enter into drug treatment facilities. This suggests that there are two lessons for drug referral schemes in general. One is that they are best thought of as low-cost, low-yield interventions. They may not produce any significant results, but this need not matter if they cost very little anyway. A second lesson is that referral rarely makes sense on its own: rather it may be better to see it within a range of inter-agency initiatives, as in Merseyside, or as a way of opening the door to the possibility of improved inter-agency coordination, an achievement claimed for the Trafford project.

A view from the other side

Referral schemes began as a means of offering information about drugs advice services to people who had been arrested by the police. With the assistance of the police and drugs agencies it was possible to speak to a small sample of people who had been in police custody (mostly for drug offences) and should have received a referral card/leaflet. What follows are some of the points or themes which emerge from their experience of being at the receiving end of the process. Given the small number of people interviewed, there did not appear to be any point in seeking to draw lessons about police practice, or the operation of a referral scheme, in any particular area. Accordingly the following discussion does not identify which police force is being talked about by the individuals below.

An arresting experience

Two referees described their experience of being arrested by the police.

> I had some cannabis and sulphate. It's a long time ago, it was so scary that I've kind of put it out of my head quite a lot. But it was at five o'clock in the morning, myself and my children were in the house and a friend that was staying. And I just heard a terrible noise, the police broke the door down and came running in, there was six policemen and two dogs which freaked me out because I'm allergic to dogs...they just came rushing in. First of all they gave the warrant to the guy that was staying here [the friend previously mentioned] and I said 'this is my house, this is where I live' and they gave it to me and then they said to me 'we're going to search the house'. I said 'you don't have to, I'll give you what I've got' and I showed them what I had and they searched the house anyway (Referee A, female, first arrest).

> It's not the first time I've been arrested. I'm not really like keen on the police, but when they came they came with a hammer and a big bar to break the door down.... for what they achieved, for what they got you know it was just a waste of time. Smashing innocent people's doors in for something I was doing in my own home, I wasn't like selling it or anything, I was just doing it in the confines of my own home, I thought it was all wrong. To come in, you know three of them came and when they came in searching my house, I have a young child - she was crying and she couldn't like get it sorted out or anything you know. They had a search warrant but they just put it under my nose, they wouldn't let us have a look at it until they found something and then they let us stand and read through it. I didn't get a chance to read it like before they searched me, they stuffed the paper under my nose, the warrant, pushed us against the wall, searched me and carried on. They didn't let us read it or anything (Referee B, male, several previous arrests).

It may be that people who have been subjected to particularly unpleasant experiences are more motivated to make contact with researchers to whom they can report the experience. Whether this is true or not, both people admitted that while they were in possession of drugs, they felt that the police had over-reacted in making the arrest.

In the station

Neither referee could remember what was said to them on the way to the police station. They were asked if they were given the referral card after being booked in by a custody officer. Referee A did receive the referral card, but does not recall from which officer or at what stage of the process it was. In contrast, referee B related that:

> I didn't get any cards or anything like [that]. You know the cards you sent the

questionnaire with, I didn't get one of them at all. When you sent us the letter you sent us the card with it didn't you? It had like drugs on and where to call and things like that (Referee B).[10]

Custody officers are responsible for ensuring the welfare of prisoners in the police station, but referee B reports a unsatisfactory experience with the two custody officers he encountered on this occasion:

> I smoke cigarettes as well and if you have cigarettes they say you can have one when you want one, just ring the bell. I was there an hour and a half and the desk sergeant came round three, four times checking us but he wouldn't give us a cigarette till about five minutes before they come to question us. I mean his attitude was probably worse than the officer that arrested us.
>
> Q. Was it the same custody officer all the time?
>
> No they changed over. The one that came on second was even worse than the first. Like sometimes they let you have your cell hatch open so that you can talk to the other prisoners, well when the other desk sergeant came on he slammed all the cell hatch closed, there was no communication at all, you had to talk under the doors then.[11]

Referee A did receive the referral card. She recalled it as follows: 'I felt grateful for it [the card], yes at the time I felt grateful. It felt like these people would be more on my side than the police were, that's how it felt, it felt like a little ally in my hand'.

Referee A related her experience during an interview by the police. She says that she was offered 'a deal' in exchange for information about suppliers.

> I was absolutely scared stiff and they knew I was scared, the police actually said to me they could drop the supply charge if I gave them a name and a number and I was really really scared, I was just crying and everything and I was under quite a lot of pressure and I gave them a telephone number and then when I saw my solicitor I told him that they'd said they would drop the intent to supply charge, but they didn't do it anyway.
>
> Q. Did they deny making you the offer?
>
> I didn't get a chance to speak to them after that. The solicitor spoke to them... because I did a tape in the interview and I'd actually said [on tape] that I'd given somebody some [drugs], they couldn't drop it, but at the time I believed they would drop it if I gave them this telephone number. That bit [the offer to drop the charge] wasn't on tape, he [police officer] said you know 'this is not on tape, this is just between me and you, you won't get into trouble with anybody if you give us a number', that sort of thing.

Afterwards: in court and at the drugs agency

Referee B did visit the drugs agency, but at that time (shortly after the arrest) her motives for doing so combined the need for support and advice with a view that it might help her case. So there were at least two reasons for her attendance at a local agency. First, 'I actually went along after because I was scared in case I did have a problem which turned out that I haven't which is great'. And secondly,

> At the time I was doing it because I thought it was the right thing to do. I was very scared, I'd never been in this situation before, I didn't know what the hell I was doing, I was very jumpy... But the reason I went was because I thought it was required of me by the law to go, or at least it would look good if went and when I did go it was brilliant and I went again and again without having to.
>
> Q. Was the 'requirement' idea suggested to you by any officer?
>
> No, I don't think so, I think that was in my head. At that stage...I was all over the place. I though it was part of the law [to attend at the agency].
>
> Q. Did you think the agency would report your attendance to the police?
>
> Yes.

One of this referee's main concerns was to seek to use attendance at the agency as a source of mitigation in court. She said that at the drugs agency

> I did ask, I said, when I'm in court can you make it known that I came here? Because after the first few visits we decided that I hadn't got a problem and I said I need this saying to the court, by which time I'd got a solicitor and they [the drugs agency] wrote a letter about me...for me on my request. I'm not sure if they do that all the time but I asked them to do that. She [counsellor at drug agency] said that was fine and did that straight away. It was mentioned very very quickly [in court]...just fleetingly, and it said that I don't have a problem and that it was one-off thing so that was quite good.[12]

Having not been to a drugs agency before she expected it to be 'full of junkies and, you know, drop-outs and stuff'. But she found that:

> There were all sorts of people there and I've also come across people that just go there for a chat, just a general chat. I mean the people I talked with, we realised that at the project half the time if you did pop in - there was a drop-in afternoon - a very very small percentage of the conversation is actually drug-oriented. So it felt...it was great, I really needed it at the time, I really did and a lot of other people have said to me 'yeah, I pop along quite often for a cup of tea and a chat'.

It's great, it's brilliant.

Views on referral schemes

Being interviewed some time after the events they describe, both referees were asked what they made of the referral card and what they thought the relationship between the police and the drugs agencies was. Referee A has already said that she expected the agency to tell the police that she had visited the agency, but that on her first visit she was assured that her visit was confidential. Despite this reassurance and her own positive experience of the drugs agency, she felt that there would be some scepticism towards the referral card:

> I'm not sure how credible it is [getting a referral card from the police], I mean anything that the police say once something like this has happened, I think a lot of people's attitude would be, you know, that goes straight in the bin. It feels like a word of mouth thing, I mean I told a couple of people about the drugs project and how good it was and they went along just because I was saying how good it was but....in any circumstance they'd have been given anything by the police that these particular people would have just have thrown it in the bin, that's how it seems... I'm speaking from the point of view of the people that I spoke to after.

Referee A has reported feeling grateful that she did receive the referral card. Referee B did not receive a card but felt that in principle it was a good thing for the police to be doing. However he added that there were more important things (he gave the example of sexual assault) about which the police should be making information available. He felt that, in general, police officers were unconcerned about the welfare of drug users: 'Well they've arrested us haven't they, and he [police officer] says to me 'I don't care what you do to your head', they don't care like, he wasn't bothered if I had a drug problem or anything'.

Whether the referral card existed or not, referee B's belief was that the both agencies already work closely together. 'We sort of think they tend to go hand-in-hand. Well I just think that anyway [even before or without the card]...in these agencies they're people like social workers running them and they work hand-in-hand with the police'. Referee A also started out with a belief that the police and drugs agencies work together, though she was reassured by the agency's guarantee of confidentiality. She is one of a handful of people whose contact with a drugs agency can be attributed to a referral card.[13] Her reasons for doing so varied but, despite her positive experience of the agency's service, she concluded that, 'I was grateful in the end that the police did give me the thing and I ended up there and it was fine you know, but I think if I'd have felt that it wouldn't have made any difference in court to me, I don't think I'd have gone'.

Notes

1. Dorn (1994) uses welfare, justice and business perspectives to characterise referral and defines and elaborates them in somewhat differing ways.

2. In 1989 the Home Office established the Drug Prevention Initiative. Local Drug Prevention Teams were intended to encourage and support local action against drug misuse, through drawing in all relevant organisations and individuals. See Howard *et al.* (1993) for discussion of issues on drugs multi-agency work beyond referral schemes.

3. Though because of the nature of the research it would be more accurate to see the perspectives as identifying the attitudes and concerns of individual police officers and their organisations. It is possible that the welfare, crime-control and efficiency perspectives could also be applied to the concerns of drugs agencies in referral schemes. While the account presented in these two chapters does make reference to these occasionally, it would be fair to say that these are underplayed, certainly compared with the police perspective. In terms of police orientations, these perspectives could be mapped onto Reiner's (1992) categorisation of 'cop culture'. Thus 'the bobby', the peace-keeping oriented officer, is most likely to equate with the welfare perspective. The crime fighting 'new centurion' is likely to prioritise the crime-control perspective; and the ambitious and career conscious 'professional' is likely to encapsulate welfare and crime-control within an efficiency perspective. Harder to place is Reiner's 'uniform carrier' - the cynical, disillusioned officer. Reiner (1991) does the same sort of thing for Chief Constables. Of these, the 'bureaucrat' style is closest to the professional above and the 'baron' approximates to the new centurion. Reiner's other two types do not fit into these perspectives.

4. Apparently there were early examples of arrest referral that operated in Birmingham in the 1960s and in Wandsworth, south London in 1986. But there appears to be no published information about these.

5. This is the term used in the report. It is not clear if it means the same thing as custody officers.

6. It does not say whether this was per week or per month.

7. The following quotes are taken from an interview with him in 1991.

8. From an article by R. Adams in *Police Review*, 16 November 1990.

9. An additional report provides a detailed profile of ten people referred to ARPP-2 between February and May 1992. Most were heroin users; four had never been in contact with a drugs agency before (the same percentage as in ARPP-1), while - at the time of referral - eight were not in contact any agency (Southwark Arrest Referral Pilot Project - Phase 2, 1992).

10. The questionnaire was sent out by the police, in this case with a referral card attached, and individuals returned the form directly to ISDD, with their name and telephone number, if they were willing to be interviewed.

11. Though this referee was not of the opinion that there was a particular or worse form of treatment meted out to drug users: 'They don't treat us [drug offenders] any worse then motoring offenders and things like that'.

12. She said that the outcome of the case was: 'I was actually taken to court for possession and intent to deal because I'd actually given somebody a piece of hash and I'd actually told the police this in the interview. Later on the solicitor said I shouldn't have said that, but I'd just given some away, I hadn't sold any at any point, I'd given it away, but that is supplying, so I'd actually agreed on my record [taped interview] that I'd supplied. For the possession I got a £100 fine and for the intent to deal I got £200 [fine]'.

13. She reported that she had heard of one of the drugs agencies on the card before, but had never been a client.

5 Drug Referral Schemes: Local Case Studies

The operation of referral in Trafford, Merseyside and Southwark has revealed some of the key difficulties that arise. At the most practical level, referral relies upon police officers handing out a referral card or leaflet in the first place. But this first step sometimes does not occur, or officers use their own judgement in deciding when to issue the card. Because of this, problems in referral have been most apparent at the police's end, especially when the first link in the chain breaks down. This, plus the occasional rejection of the referral card by those it is offered to, as well as the low take-up of referral, has led to questions about the level of resources that it is appropriate to devote to referral schemes. Beyond that, there are also issues and concerns about how the schemes work in practice, both in terms of multi-agency working in general and the possibility that police officers might use, or misuse, referral as a means to solicit information from arrestees. Many of these issues, as well as some additional ones, are also apparent in the case studies presented in this chapter, which aims to chart local developments in a number of areas of England and contribute to a more 'rounded' picture of referral schemes.

Wiltshire: The politics of multi-agency work, part one

The Wiltshire referral scheme is based on a card listing the names and telephone numbers of local drugs advice agencies. It is available to be given to all people who are brought into the police station, thereby avoiding confusion about when to hand it out. Nonetheless, the Wiltshire referral scheme exhibits some familiar problems. The main one is that the cards are not always handed out and that custody officers report a reluctance from people to accept the card.

In Wiltshire, a force order instructed custody officers to hand out a small yellow referral card to all people. The card was not included within the 'custody folder' handed to prisoners containing the notice of entitlement to a solicitor, etc. In other words, this requires the issuing of the referral card as a separate act, which can mean that 'sometimes he [the custody officer] forgets to give it because he's under a bit of pressure, and other times it doesn't seem appropriate so he doesn't give it. And of course [there is] the reaction that comes back from the other side of the counter....that is a problem' (Custody officer D). Similarly,

> It [the card] would be low on their [custody officers] list of priorities definitely...when they're busy, I mean the first sort of forty five minutes yesterday I booked in six prisoners, in all probability that [the card] would have been low down and possibly forgotten about, I don't know. But a lot of things get forgotten about, not just your card specifically, you know signatures on records things like that (Custody officer E).

Secondly, there is the matter of some people's reaction to being offered a 'drugs card'. Officer D described the reaction that he has encountered over the counter in the following terms:

> We give some people a yellow card with, if you want drugs assistance go to this such-and-such an address. A lot of people take it as a slight against themselves because they say 'I'm not on drugs, what do I want this for?' I give [out] the card and they say, 'I'm not on drugs', and they give it back, and we put it on the pile again (Custody officer D).

Interviewed separately, officer E related a similar set of experiences and views. 'People were sort of taking offence at it [the referral card], so it was only people that you identified as being in for drug related matters, or that might be of that fraternity that you would hand one of those to. A guy in for drink-driving might take offence [at the card]' (Custody officer E). This view is confirmed by a senior detective from the force drugs squad.

> I haven't spoken to many sergeants but I had three or four of them come down to my office to talk generally about drugs and they have found that people as soon as they saw the big bold 'drugs' on there [the card] they didn't want it, didn't want to know, they didn't consider themselves to be drug addicts and they just didn't want to accept the card. [It's] just a personal feeling, perhaps at some stage we could remove the word 'drugs' from front of the card and say 'can we help'....so at least they'll take it and won't reject it just because it says drugs on it.

So from its earliest stages, the operation of the scheme encountered resistance from people offered the card, and from custody officers asked to issue it. Hence, thirdly, an unofficial though *de facto* policy change occurred in which custody officers used their discretion to give the card to drugs offenders only and 'those that are of that ilk', as one officer put it. The drugs squad officer recognised that this had occurred and that there were variations in practice between custody officers:

> Being realistic about it, I suppose as in any other walk of life you get good, bad and indifferent policemen, custody sergeants or whatever. You'll get some that'll stick rigidly to the rules and make sure that it's given out a hundred per cent, you'll get some who won't bother and it wouldn't matter to them if you offered them ten pence a card [to hand it out], and you get a grey area in between where some do and some don't. Certainly the cards are in the custody suite, they know about it and it's very much down to the individual (Drugs squad detective).

Supervision of the operation of the referral scheme is left in the hands of individual police station managers, with the drugs squad taking a hands-off approach:

> I personally haven't done any checks. I've spoken to the Chief Inspector here [a central police station] and he knows about the cards and that they should be handed out. They're in the custody suites and one can only assume that they are given out. The only thing that does bother me is that if the custody sergeants continually try to hand them out and they are continually rejected, you may get to a stage then when they think to themselves that 'I'm not going to offer it because they're going to turn it down anyway'. It may be that we'll put out a reminder that despite the fact that people are not taking them, that they should still be handed out (Drugs squad detective).

The referral scheme therefore seems to occupy a low priority in the work of the police and it could be argued that this is more or less as it should be, given the low yield from the scheme.

Two reasons were advanced for entering into the scheme in the first place. One is the 'it might just help someone' justification that we also saw used by custody officers in Merseyside.

> It must help some. You've got drug organisations and needle exchanges, if it saves one person's life because he can use a clean needle rather than a dirty needle it's got to be worthwhile because it's going to save the health service vast numbers of pounds in treatment for someone with HIV or Hepatitis B. So it's got to be a good thing....if you haven't got anything there they can't take advantage of it. For the effort of handing a card out, which is nothing, and for the cost of a card, which is negligible, I think it's got to be worth it (Drugs squad detective).

One custody officer expressed a similar view, allied to the recognition that the card can not be more than a source of information about drug services.

> There's nothing that you do or say, unless they want to that, in my opinion and, I might be totally wide of the mark, that [the card] is not going to prompt them into going on the straight and narrow, they have got to do it because they want to. I think the majority of them do it because they like doing it and when they need help they'll go for it, that's it they'll go to Release or whatever have you. It [the card]

will be worthwhile if one in a hundred that you hand out turns them round, but I just think they take drugs because they want to take drugs....I think it needs something to spark them into....[seeking help] (Custody officer E).

A second justification for the referral scheme in this area is that it represents a form of multi-agency liaison between the police and drugs advice agencies. A cynical view might be that whether it works or not seems to be less important than being able to say that there is multi-agency liaison going on. The view from the police is that there has been a slow but significant attitude change about the limits of enforcement.

> I think everybody accepts now that we cannot beat drugs by enforcement alone. We have got to have liaison with the people, if you like, that the druggies are going to trust. They don't trust us. [As a result] liaison with other agencies has gone on in leaps and bounds over the last two years. There are people I talk to now, discuss drugs matters with, that I probably wouldn't have been allowed to four years ago...
>
> Q. Allowed by who?
>
> By the police service.
>
> Q. Because it was feared that confidential information was being exchanged?
>
> That's right, or that we were compromising ourselves, [it was a] lack of trust. So we have to have liaison. My opinion is that certainly in the short-term the outside agencies get more out of it than we do. It may be that if it works in the long-term that we may get more out of it... I suppose it would be nice if the [local drug agency] said this is our list of druggies for this month! But obviously we're not going to get that (Drugs squad detective).

Thus, for the police, the referral scheme is guided by welfare principles. But allied to that is a wish to develop multi-agency relations with drugs agencies, in itself part of a climate where the force has to be 'seen to be doing so'.

Avon and Somerset: The politics of multi-agency work, part two

The case of the referral scheme in Avon and Somerset demonstrates a different kind of problem arising in and from multi- or inter-agency relations. The fact that there should have been a problem at all is perhaps surprising given that the force regards itself as a leader in multi-agency policy and practice. The drugs squad said that they took the lead in initiating their own multi-agency contacts rather than seeing it as a matter to be led by the force's community involvement branch, as a detective from the drugs squad told me:

'Because we've got the liaison we've introduced community involvement to the people we know [in drugs agencies] and not the other way round. Anything to do with drugs is dealt with by the drug squad'. Asked about the state of inter-agency relations in the force area, this officer replied that:

> They are excellent. They're not just good, they're excellent and no, they haven't always been in the past... In the last eighteen months we've made gigantic strides forward and its become very apparent to everybody that we've got an exceptionally good relationship with the other agencies.
>
> Q. How has this come about?
>
> We've done it in the main through personal contacts with them [drugs agencies], obviously it's probably more difficult for them than it is for us because we don't really expect anything of them. We can tell them things but they can't necessarily tell us things.... But current trends, problem areas, that sort of thing we discuss openly, not the people but the areas which are a problem and the drugs which are problems.... I wouldn't say there was any conflict [before]. We just never had anything to do with them full stop. We knew they existed [but] we never contacted them, they never contacted us. We didn't sit on any committees [together], there was no interchange of chat, nothing.
>
> Q. Why do you think that was?
>
> Because I think it was felt on both sides....they thought well, 'you're the police' and they didn't necessarily seen any reason why there should be contact. It was felt on both sides, well what good will it do? What do we need to talk to each other for? And if we [drug agencies] talk to the police will people [i.e. clients] be suspicious of us? (Drugs squad detective).

Unfortunately despite this positive report of the state of inter-agency relations (which was confirmed by some drugs agencies too) the referral scheme encountered a significant hitch. After the scheme had been launched, one agency reported that it had never even seen the referral card being used by the police. Staff from this agency also reported that enquiries to their local police station revealed that it did not have any referral cards and possibly that officers there did not even know about a referral scheme. Subsequent telephone calls showed that at least two other agencies had not seen the card before either.[1] At a meeting about six months after the launch of the scheme, which was in fact the first meeting at which all the parties to the scheme had been brought together, two agencies expressed other concerns. One reported that two individuals arrested in their town had not been given the referral card. Another agency said that their agreement extended only to having their name and telephone number placed on card and they had heard nothing about being involved in a 'referral scheme'.

These difficulties appear to have arisen from the way in which the scheme had been established. A precise history cannot be reconstructed, but a general lesson can be drawn from this experience. In most, and probably all, other areas the setting up of a referral scheme was preceded by a joint meeting between the police and the drug agencies. In Avon and Somerset there was no such meeting for reasons that have not been stated. What appears to have happened is that the agencies to be named on the card were telephoned by a police officer who sought their agreement to the card/scheme. Somehow, during this process, it became simultaneously possible for some drugs agencies to feel they were not consulted - whether adequately or at all is not clear - while the police, and NACRO's Drug Misuse Unit based in Bristol who played a hand in setting up the scheme, were adamant that all the agencies did give their agreement. If nothing else, this establishes a basic lesson that face-to-face meetings are preferable for establishing agreement and the details of arrangements. Even if the meeting simply 'rubber stamps' what has already been agreed, it can at least give the impression of having been collectively decided or function as an arena in which players actually give their consent.

Turning to some of the detail of the scheme, within the police force the scheme was launched in this way: 'Every week we have force orders printed in which any instructions, any details of what goes on in the force. It's sort of an official document that we're all expected to read and the instructions [about the referral scheme] were put there so everybody could see it' (Drugs squad detective). It was possible to interview only one custody officer in this area. He had this to say about the referral card itself.

> [There's] a lot of these things, I mean besides that [referral card] there's the community action trust card which we hand out. But sometimes it [handing out the referral card] does get done when it's quiet and you're not under pressure, other times when you're under a lot of pressure and there's a lot of things to be done under PACE it's something that does get overlooked. It [the handing out of the card whenever a drug offender is brought in] doesn't always come into mind, no (Custody officer F).

Despite this, his view on the referral card in general is that, 'It's not a problem being asked [to hand the card out], that's not a problem at all'. The officer described the reaction of people being offered the referral card, or indeed other literature, by custody officers as follows:

> A lot of people you give it to them and they just put it down on you, leave it down, a lot of them do, I mean with a lot of the forms we're supposed to give the people, they don't accept them. Whether they realise the actual form is for them...you say, this is for you, this is for you to take, but I mean a lot of them just

leave them down.... I would say perhaps about half receive them, why that is I don't know, perhaps a lot of them think 'oh well, I'm getting out of here now, I'll take everything I'm given and go' and others say 'oh no, no', I mean those sort of words (Custody officer F).

The overall rationale for the referral scheme is not easy to distinguish. The earlier snag in the scheme made police officers sensitive about discussing the scheme and much of the emphasis was on promotion of the force image and its good relationships. Thus this case study, and to a lesser extent the one in Wiltshire, suggest that there is an additional level to the welfare, crime-control and efficiency orientations. Public relations and the image of a police force to local (through the force's Annual Report) and national constituencies - such as the Inspectorate of Constabulary and the Home Office - may also act as a spur to development of referral arrangements, even if the practice encounters broadly similar problems in all areas.

West Yorkshire: Referral and policy development

The West Yorkshire police force area includes the metropolitan centres of Leeds and Bradford. In common with almost all other police forces, most drugs squad work is occupied with cannabis and amphetamines. Other drugs, including LSD and Ecstasy, are to be found, but still make up a minor percentage of police statistics. The West Yorkshire force has a strong emphasis on prosecuting most drug offenders, with cautioning used as the minority option. As Detective Chief Inspector [DCI] Brian Taylor the then head of the force's drugs squad put it:

> We do cautions for drugs offences, but there has to be a reason for giving a caution. For example, if you've got a 13 year old boy with small, amount of cannabis then he'll get a caution. But it doesn't follow that a 23 year old fella will get one. We have a policy of prosecution and well over 90 per cent of people who are arrested are taken to court. We maintain that if we keep the lid on here then maybe we'll contain it instead of, well, condoning it.

But the same officer acknowledged that enforcement in itself can feel like a futile exercise: 'Really it's a revolving door syndrome and nothing is achieved, except keeping them off the streets and in prison for a while, but when they come out they go right back on the drugs again'. It is in this space that the room for a referral scheme opens up:

> A lot of us realise that you need to be pointing these people in the direction of the agencies. So one of the things I did was to contact the 11 drug agencies and say,

we are planning to start a drug referral scheme and do you have any objection to your name going on this leaflet?. What I did then was to write a document to my chief constable outlining the scheme and he supported it.

The document recommended the development of a referral scheme alongside an amended cautioning policy. The former meant that drug offenders would be provided with an opportunity to obtain drug information and advice. The latter would lead the force to adopt a policy of cautioning for possession of small amounts of cannabis. There is no necessary link between these two developments, though it may be that the former afforded an opportunity for a change to the force's cautioning policy. An A4 leaflet listing eleven local agencies offering advice about drugs and HIV/AIDS was produced for distribution through custody suites to drug offenders only. An official instruction stated:

> It is important that officers take every opportunity to encourage drug misusers to make contact with available drug treatment services.... All persons now dealt with for drugs offences, whether by means of criminal proceedings or caution, should be handed a Form 208 [the referral leaflet] which contains details of the drug treatment agencies in the Force area.

As in all other areas, a persistent problem is translating such instructions into practice. DCI Taylor listed five measures taken by the West Yorkshire police to ensure that the message about the leaflets would get through to officers on the ground: (i) an article was placed in the weekly bulletin circulated to every department; (ii) information about the scheme was circulated to every sub-divisional officer; (iii) sub-divisional officers were asked to inform shift inspectors and custody officers; (iv) later, some information about referral was added on to the end of a drugs up-date video; and (v) reminders were issued to drug squad officers to inform/remind uniformed officers when they were working together. In spite of all these measures. Taylor acknowledged that making the referral scheme work at the police end would inevitably take time: 'It takes a while to get the message across. It will probably take a year or two before it's properly running to everyone's satisfaction'. There was an equal sense of realism about the possible impact of the scheme.

> Even if we just get one referral, then we've achieved something. No, I'm not really disappointed, because having dealt with them [drug users] for a few years you realise that there's quite a bit of resistance to going to the counselling agencies. You can't always convince them what's good for them, and it's their life at the end of the day. It's worthwhile for the police because if we can get just one percentage of these people to the units then there is the chance that they won't re-offend. So it will be easing our workload in the long term.

Hence the low yield from referral was held not to be a problem, as the scheme is seen as a low level intervention, provided because it a service that the police ought to offer, with the possibility that it may just help some people. This, in a nutshell, is the welfare justification for referral.

The views of three custody officers

Three custody officers in West Yorkshire were asked about their experiences of the scheme. One of them offered the following as a typical scenario for drug offenders coming to light:

> When they come in, when you're talking possession, invariably the possession has come to light because you're talking about being under the influence [of alcohol]. What lads [police officers] are doing is that they're finding someone that's staggering about or that's flopped in a doorway. They go to him, and the smell that's coming off him is either a solvents smell or no smell at all, and his eyes are gone and he can't stand up and he'll be brought in and while you search him you find something. The original basis of charge is Breach of the Peace and you find a tin of lighter fuel or a drug. And once the [drug] possession is found, the possession becomes a second offence (Custody officer G).

A second officer reported that the leaflet would be given to 'well, normally any drug offender' (Custody officer H). A third narrated the circumstances in which the leaflet would be handed out.

> The offence is on the charge sheet, that's read out to them, they're asked for a reply, they sign that [charge sheet], the bail form is made out, then I explain to them that they've been bailed to a court and it's up to them to be there otherwise they get nicked again. And then I point out that when I give them one of those forms, the drugs thing, saying you know we have a form here that we give basically to anybody who is caught with drugs.... (Custody officer J).

Officer J estimated that perhaps three or four out of ten young first-time cannabis offenders would take the card. But his view was that since they are just young people and, presumably, novice rather than serious drug users, the card is an irrelevance:

> As I say, its cannabis or whatever in the majority [of cases] and its the first time and there's no [drug] problem. They either take it [the card] for the sake of taking it or they don't want it. The majority, basically, they've been arrested for possession, they've lost the money, they haven't even had time to try the drugs before it's taken off them by us (Custody officer J).

Officers G and H shared something of the same kind of view, recalling that the leaflet is generally rejected by people. For them this called into question its usefulness in the first place.

> Well, speaking on practical terms, when you give them that [the referral leaflet] they say 'I don't want that' and just throw it back in your face. I would say that more than half the time [they refuse to accept the leaflet] - they don't see themselves as having a problem - that's cannabis users, yes. I can't say that in the case of ...the heroin users they say something like well 'I know about that' [but] they're all loath to accept advice. I would say that the majority of people are loath to accept this particular orange form [referral leaflet]. Even some heroin users say 'I haven't got a problem, I can handle this' (Custody officer H).

Officer G saw a visit to an advice agency occurring only if the card had been accepted and subsequent reflection suggested that it might be helpful to the offender's case: 'If they've been charged, then you give them a day when they're going to court, they take the bit of paper [referral card] and I think that the solicitor has more influence than us because the solicitor can say 'well I should get yourself round there'.

Given a situation where these officers relate that the leaflet is not welcomed and their impression that users are uninterested in help from the advice agencies, did they consider it worth doing at all?

> I will give this out [because] a lot of them may not be aware of the agencies that can help them. It's part of my instructions in fact to hand this out and say, well listen these are the people who can help you with your problem - if you want to take it, read it. Most people as I said just throw it back in your face; in relation to why they do it, really I can't answer that. I would say that the majority of people that come into our custody are anti-police, they look upon us really as the enemy and the enemy is supplying them with information that may well do them some good. What the reasoning behind that is I don't know (Custody officer H).

> I'm sure my view differs from the Force view. The official view is that we should give them every opportunity. I tend to think that we are wasting our time (Custody officer G).

However, officer H also argued that the referral leaflet fits in with the police's general responsibilities and can also serve a public relations purpose:

> One of the jobs of the police is the prevention and detection of crime. Possessing drugs is a crime, supplying drugs is a crime, so we must be seen to be doing something about preventing and detecting that. Now if we didn't give them that advice to prevent them from committing further offences then we're not undertaking our duties properly.... We are a caring agency - a lot of people who come into our custody are unemployed people who commit offences for various reasons whether

it's need, greed or [to get] a kick out of drugs.

Echoing the sentiments of the head of the drugs squad, Officer H concluded that, 'I think nothing's a waste of time. If you achieve a small percentage of results then it's not a waste of time is it. If you can wean a small proportion of prisoners off drugs to lead a normal life then of course you've served your purpose'.

The West Yorkshire referral scheme was designed to be targeted at drug offenders only. This raised two familiar problems. One, that custody officers sometimes forgot to hand the leaflet out to drug users. Two, that some officers believed the exercise to be futile anyway. Despite both these factors, leaflets did appear to be being handed out, from the interviews above and from information from some referees. Although the start-up effort may have consumed some resources, it seems probable that, as the scheme comes to be part of a routine, it would settle down as a low cost, low yield venture. It does not create any pressure on workloads for the drugs agencies, but it does offer an opportunity to a few people who may wish to consider taking up the services available. Both the police and the drugs agencies in West Yorkshire reported that existing inter-agency liaison is well established, so referral in itself does not open the door to further collaboration, though it may be seen as a useful complement or adjunct to what is already going on.

The West Yorkshire scheme is one that provided an unusual combination of circumstances. In many ways the scheme operated on a welfare model, principally concerned with diverting some users into treatment and advice agencies. There is little emphasis from the police on crime-control or efficiency concerns, though it is notable that some custody officers express more concern about efficiency and economy than the head of the drugs squad, who sees the value of referral primarily in public relations and multi-agency terms. At the same time, though perhaps not quite going hand-in-hand, a force that has traditionally emphasised enforcement through prosecution of drug offenders undergoes a partial liberalisation in its cautioning policy. It cannot be claimed that the latter development was precipitated by the referral scheme, though the coincidence is worth noting, as is the operation of welfare within an enforcement policy.

Views from the other side

It was possible to obtain the views of ten people who had been in the custody of West Yorkshire police.[2] All were drug users, seven were male, aged 17-24, the other three were female, aged over 25. Of the ten, eight reported receiving the leaflet, while two had not received it. All bar one thought that, in principle, it was a good idea for the police to issue such leaflets, though seven out of the ten already knew of at least one of the agencies named on the leaflet. The other three had never heard of any of the advice agencies. Only one person reported visiting an agency subsequently, while one other person was already in contact with a drugs agency. The other eight did not contact any agency. Three of the eight said they did not do so because they did not consider themselves to have a drug problem, one because s/he was too upset after being arrested and one because s/he knew nothing about drugs agencies. While these are small numbers of people and there can not be any claim to representativeness, these findings do serve some indicative purpose and confirm that the take-up of the advice services offered is low.

Norfolk: An attempt at following the Southwark model

The referral scheme in Norfolk drew heavily on the Southwark scheme for its design. Its principal notable feature for current purposes is the effort put into launching the scheme. Before describing that I briefly mention some other features of the scheme. The initial proposal for an Arrest Referral Scheme in Norfolk was explicitly linked to two of the key elements of the Southwark ARPP. One, arrest as a point of intervention for people who have not previously sought help for their drug use; and two, the availability of drugs workers to meet with people held at the police station. The scheme operated by using a local agency, the Matthew Project - Drug Aid, as the first port of call. After an initial assessment, Drug Aid would refer people on, if appropriate, to one of the specialist drug services in the county. The rationale for this approach is stated in the project proposal.

> We feel it is important that the offenders are not just given a list of sources of help and are then left to decide on the most appropriate agency for themselves. Our reason for this are that they would probably not be in a state to make these decisions at the best of times, let alone at what may be an extremely traumatic time.

Thus Norfolk, following Southwark, envisages active intervention by drugs workers seeking to identify those who may be suitable for treatment. If, in welfare-based schemes, it is police officers who play an advisory role, in crime-control schemes it is drugs workers who play that role, when they are called into the police station.

In Norfolk a referral card was designed to be given to every arrested person brought into police stations. The card would be handed out by custody officers and backed up with large posters in the custody suite. Some 30,000 cards were produced for use in the first year of the scheme. Drawing on the experiences of other schemes, especially the problem of ensuring that the card is actually handed out by custody officers, a local inter-agency group decided that the scheme would best be launched by a series of local meetings throughout the county. It was felt that at these meetings police officers could meet drugs agency workers, thereby giving both sides an opportunity to meet in person, making the scheme rather less abstract than it might otherwise seem. Five presentations, each following the same format, were organised for a mixed audience of custody officers, drugs agency workers, social services and Crown Prosecution Service employees. I observed one of these, which took the following form: A slide show with commentary explains the idea of referral schemes, with pictures of the referral card and poster. The role of the custody officer is explained, including the different forms s/he has to hand out. The referral card is shown as an additional piece of literature to be handed out. The commentary states that acceptance of the card is voluntary, while giving it to everyone avoids the problem of deciding who should or should not receive it. A custody officer is shown explaining the various leaflets handed out - one on rights in custody, another on entitlement to legal advice - before handing over the card with the words '....this card tells you how you can get advice for drug related problems'. Further slides show the drugs services which users might be referred on to, while the commentary states that advice on HIV/AIDS is also available from these agencies. The role of probation and social services is then outlined and it is stated that the referral scheme could help to identify those who might benefit from alternatives to custody. Drugs workers who can visit people at the police station are issued with a card by the police, on which are written the words 'Independent drugs worker'. Finally, it is stated that the success of the scheme depends on (i) its credibility to clients as an independent service; and (ii) on the police seeing it as a means of helping people, but in a way that does not hamper investigations. The slide show is followed by a question and answer session, with a panel made up of representatives of various organisations involved in the referral scheme.

It was possible to speak informally with a custody officer and to observe officers at work on one occasion. This officer said that cards were not being handed to everybody because 'there are some people whom it's not appropriate for'. This officer also said that at busy periods in the custody suite it was much less likely that the card would be handed out at all. The officer was then observed 'booking in' a prisoner. After telling the prisoner his rights, the officer placed a referral card on the counter and said: 'You might have seen this while you've been here', pointing to a large poster of the card on the wall, while passing the card across the counter. The man being brought into custody looked briefly at the card and left it on the counter saying 'I don't need it'. There is no way of generalising from this encounter to make any claims about custody officers or about people being offered the referral card. All that can be said is that, as we have seen, there is corroborating evidence from many other areas which shows that referral cards are not always handed out, either because custody officers regard them as a low priority, or they forget, or they use their discretion. The drugs agency reported receiving 15 telephone calls in connection with the referral scheme in the first three months of its operation, a significantly higher take-up rate than achieved anywhere else.[3]

The Norfolk scheme, drawing on experience elsewhere, pursued a conscious strategy of 'selling' the referral scheme to some of the key groups of people needed to make it work. There is no real evidence about how successful or not this strategy was, but it is noteworthy as an attempt at addressing a problem that can arise in inter-agency endeavours.

Leicestershire: Generic referral

The Leicestershire referral scheme is one that could become the model for many other areas. Two aspects are described here. One is about how the scheme came into being. The second is about how the scheme operated. From its earliest stages the scheme developed as one jointly involving both the local drugs and alcohol agencies. A historically close relationship between these two agencies served the additional purpose of easing the drug agency's worries about how it might be perceived by its clients if it was linked to the police thorough the use of a referral card. This was a concern that the police understood. An agreement that there would be a referral scheme with a card advertising both agencies appeared to have been reached. But, subsequently, none of the parties could explain why nothing more happened.

Misunderstandings?

Sometime after the scheme seemed to have been agreed, with only the details to be dealt with, there was an apparent breakdown of proceedings. A police officer reported that the scheme appeared to have become 'stalled' and asked what could be done to get things going again. No clear reason underlying this breakdown has emerged, but these are the accounts offered later by the drugs agency and the police.

> I honestly do not know what happened. A myth was generated somehow that everybody had pulled out of the scheme because it was unworkable. I don't know where that myth came from. I knew about the original meetings and they were fine, my assumption was that it was all going along. When you rang me that day it

jolted me and I checked around a few people and everyone thought it was the other person who had pulled out! So we contacted each other and met [and agreed the final leaflet]. It was absurd, it was a myth. Nobody had any coherent reason why, they just didn't know [why the scheme seemed to have stopped] (Drugs agency manager).

To go back to the difficulty we encountered at the very beginning of this project when there was a breakdown of communication between their [the agency's] workers and their management....because there was certainly, I detected, a concern with their credibility with their clients and the close association with the police, and I can accept that because obviously there has to be a degree of credibility between the worker and the client and we respect that by not going down there [to the agency's offices] in uniform. There must be difficulties on their behalf of being seen to be hand-in-glove with the police, albeit the management don't seem to have the same difficulty (Police officer).

But by this time, and independently of the difficulties reported above, another broader conception of referral had emerged.

The generic help card

Uniquely in Leicestershire the local agencies came up with a proposal for a generic advice services leaflet. This, it was felt, would avoid the problem reported in other areas where a leaflet or card about drugs met with a hostile or indifferent response from some people that it was offered to. In contrast, the Leicestershire leaflet advertised a range of local services. As well as the local drugs and alcohol services, it also listed agencies offering advice with relationship and money problems, and the Samaritans. The telephone numbers of each of these agencies was listed inside a folded A4 leaflet, with a cover that asked 'Can we help...?' This was designed to be given to each person coming into custody and to not be seen as a 'drugs leaflet', or one which required custody officers to make a decision about whether to issue it or not. Some 25,000 leaflets were produced for the first year of the scheme.

The following measures were taken to make the scheme known to all officers and to wider audiences.

Obviously one of the big problems we have with any big organisation, certainly a large organisation like this, is disseminating information from the nucleus down out to the troops on the ground. How did we go about it? First, there was an order from the Chief Superintendent here [force headquarters] to all sub-divisions to tell them what we were doing and what we expected custody officers to do. That was followed by copies of the leaflet for them to have available. So that was a direct instruction, a force order that came out through this department that we would be doing this through custody suites and if it wasn't done that would be a breach of an order. But what we also asked in that order is that, through their sub-divisional information arrangements, the existence of this scheme was also relayed through to the ground. We also included it in our weekly orders which go out from here [headquarters], signed by the Chief Constable. We also included it in the force magazine, on the front page, which goes out to libraries and other outlets in the county to let people know what we're doing (Police officer).

Custody officer interview

It was possible to interview only one custody officer in Leicestershire and there is of course no way of telling how representative the experience reported here is. Unfortunately, despite all the good intentions behind the scheme, it highlighted much the same problems that have been seen in all other referral schemes. Despite the generic advice services on offer, this custody officer appeared to see the leaflet as a drugs/alcohol advice service only:

> A number of times....more often than not I've given this leaflet out I've given this information out after they've been in for some time. They've sat down they've thought about it, usually it's alcohol, I would say three-quarters of it is alcohol....they find out they're over the limit and suddenly it hits them they're going to lose their licence for 12 months, 18 months and they think 'well, okay, maybe I shouldn't have done it, maybe I do need help'. There's not all that many [like that] to be honest of the ones that I've had dealings with.... When you've got time, when you're able to have a little chat with them - which is not always possible, because you've not really got that time - I've often said to them, look you've got a problem, perhaps you ought to be thinking about whether you can get some sort of help and they say 'well I don't know where to go' and invariably that's when I give them that [the leaflet]. It's usually alcohol, very occasionally it's drugs because if I have somebody in here who's on drugs, it takes several hours for them to come down (Custody officer L).

This officer reported that the leaflet is liable to be rejected by drug users: 'If somebody comes in arrested for drugs [and] I give them that, they screw it up and throw it on the floor, they will do'. But it is not clear whether this is based on personal experience or on a pre-conceived idea of the characteristics of drug users, or a mixture of the two. The officer continues:

> Some of them aren't interested, they won't accept it [the leaflet], they don't want advice - you've got to catch them at a certain stage. They don't consider they've got a problem, they don't consider it's wrong.... We don't get a lot of cannabis users here, well it varies from three, five, six a month and a lot of them don't really think they've got a problem, they're not interested. We can't always say to them, look, you know it's not going to do you any good, we are not necessarily the right agency to be saying those things, depending on the circumstances some will respond to it, some won't, most won't, they don't really want to know (Custody officer L).

Despite this, the officer concluded that the leaflet did serve a useful function. 'There are times when people have asked for advice [and] we have not had this leaflet. All we can do really is leave it with them...[saying] look at that, go home and it's up to you to decide whether you want to get some help. My own personal opinion is that it is a pretty good eye-opener'. But even in a generic referral scheme, it seems to be impossible to ensure that officers are aware of the existence of an advice leaflet, or that they will be not be too busy to remember about it, or they will not use discretion in deciding when and to whom to issue the leaflet.

> My main concern [as a custody officer] is making sure that they've have got the documents which they have by law got to have, okay. It's up to the officers in some respects that are dealing with people to also consider whether this [the leaflet] ought to go with it. It doesn't get given out by everyone. We often have custody officers who come in here occasionally who don't know about it, who don't know where to look for it, wouldn't even know where to find it.
>
> Q. Are these *regular* custody officers?
>
> No, not regular custody officers... I think most of them are aware of it, I know where it is and I know what it says and in what circumstances to use it. It's [the leaflet] not as much of a priority as for example making sure that they've got their rights, they've had their rights read to them. Some will say to you, 'not another form', quite a few will say 'oh no, not another form'. It depends how seriously we take this job doesn't it? I'm not a social worker primarily, I'm a policeman and I've got to try and make sure that the law is upheld first, the rules...I've got to make sure that that's done first as custody officer. I'm not saying that it isn't [a good idea]... I mean if you'd been here this morning you would very well understand how busy we were. There are so many different people that as custody officer I'm responsible for and I've got to deal with. As a matter of priority this [the leaflet] is not going to be my priority. I've had arguments with solicitors, I've had discussions with inspectors, I've had phone call from solicitors, phone calls from all sorts of people. I've got to make sure that everything runs smoothly according to the list, according to PACE.
>
> Q. But the leaflet is not just for drugs and alcohol, it includes other services, so shouldn't it be given to everyone?
>
> A lot of people we give to it just chuck it straight back at us, they don't even want to look at it. I've found that as far as drugs goes we get a particular [kind of] person (Custody officer L).[4]

The referral leaflet in Leicestershire attracted a good deal of attention and could be a model for others. It is designed to be handed to everybody, to advertise a range of helping services (thereby avoiding the possible stigma of a 'drugs leaflet'), and it need cost no more than a drugs referral card alone. There is no reason to believe that the take-up on the drugs or alcohol side will be notably higher than anywhere else. There is no information about the take-up of the other services offered on the leaflet. In its underlying aims, the Leicestershire approach combines welfare and multi-agency priorities. While cost and resource implications were sometimes raised, and there is no way of knowing whether and how the leaflet could be used in interview situations, the efficiency and crime-control perspectives appear to be in the background at best.

Nonetheless, the Leicestershire scheme suffered from the same kinds of problems that effect all the schemes we have seen. At the police end there is the difficulty of publicising the existence of the leaflets and their purpose within a large organisation. More problematically, there is some evidence of the persistent difficulty in ensuring that custody officers do actually hand the leaflet out, or of overcoming their use of discretion in deciding when and who to give the leaflet to. These problems are not ones to which there are any glib or 'quick fix' solutions. Among the remedies that have been proposed are that the advice leaflets or cards should be attached to, or even integrated into, the statutory rights leaflets issued by custody officers. Another is that if more junior officers had the scheme explained to them they might perceive it less as 'another directive to be obeyed'. A further possibility, following the Norfolk scheme, is to arrange for police officers to meet with staff from agencies named on the card so that the scheme has a more obviously human dimension. More simply, it has been suggested that the leaflets should be left on the counter to be picked up by anyone interested in them, accompanied with large posters in custody suites to act as a prompt to custody officers to offer them, or so that people can note their availability. This is what occurred in Merseyside though it does not in itself appear to increase take-up of the leaflet or of referral opportunities.

Problems in practice

Drug or arrest referral schemes could be evaluated at three levels: One, does the existence of referral cards enable or encourage drugs users to self-refer? Two, does the treatment/advice agency help to reduce levels of drug misuse? Three, does reduced use lead to reduced criminal activity?[5] This research on referral schemes was originally intended to address mainly the first of these questions, though the Southwark project did aim to examine the subsequent ones as well. However, before the first question can be answered, the research uncovered a basic problem, that of making the schemes work at the most practical level. This and some other practical difficulties in referral are considered here.

Issuing the card

The single most common problem encountered in the operation of referral schemes has been to check whether the card or leaflet is actually handed out by officers. We have seen many times that custody officers freely admit that, particularly at busy times, the card can simply be forgotten about. There are understandable reasons why that happens, though various ways around that, such as leaving the card on the desk, or attaching or incorporating it within the statutory literature, have been suggested. No alternative point of dissemination makes sense other than through custody officers.[6]

A more difficult matter is the use of discretion by officers. Some of the officers interviewed seem to have decided to issue the card on the basis of who is seen as respectable or unrespectable. In practice this operates in contradictory ways. In one area (see the Wiltshire case study) the respectable are those who are offended to be offered a 'drugs card', apparently resenting the implied suggestion that they might be drug users. But in another area (see the Leicestershire case study) it is those who are receptive to the advice leaflet who are regarded as respectable. However, some police officers seem to regard all drug users as unrespectable, because either they are unconcerned that their drug use constitutes any kind of a 'problem', or they are uninterested in any possibility of help.

> There are some people who by their demeanour and attitude you would not want to offer anything (Inspector in a drugs squad).

Police stereotypes of drug users as particular kinds of people never seem very far below the surface, though the extent to which they actually influence willingness to issue the referral card is difficult to determine.

Even the generic help card which, in theory, ought to overcome some of these difficulties, encountered comparable problems, though this finding is based on an interview with one officer only. In principle a generic referral leaflet appears to be the most straightforward form, even if the specificity of multi-agency liaison around drugs is submerged or lost. One of the officers from Wiltshire arrived at this conclusion independently:

> You're talking about a particular thing [a drugs card]. That's very narrow. And when you push it to them and say this is for you and they look at it and say, 'I'm not on drugs, what do I want that for?'.... They've got problems across the spectrum, the whole blooming gambit, the whole thing - housing, money problems, driving while they're not allowed to, unemployed people, just to name a few. And invariably, most who come through that door are unemployed. Most of them do

> feel the pinch, that's why most of them have some form of crime [record]. Because circumstances have pushed them in that direction. For women, shoplifting - financially-related again - you can see it in their faces that look of hopelessness that they've been caught and there is nothing they can do about it (Custody officer).

Thus there is a view that a general help card instinctively and logically makes more sense to custody officers. As such, it may help to increase motivation and willingness to dispense the card.

Low yields

The second main issue has been that even when the card/leaflet is issued, virtually all evidence suggests very limited take-ups through self referral. Should the low take-up rate be considered a problem or not? For the efficiency perspective it is, because cost and other resource considerations make it questionable whether the effort involved is worthwhile. The account presented in the case studies has stressed that low yields need not matter since running costs are low. Curiously though, energy expended in making officers aware of referral schemes, as in Norfolk, could then be regarded as a time-consuming and inefficient use of scarce resources. Whether the effort involved in seeking to increase take-up in areas such as Southwark and Norfolk has been worthwhile or not is open to question (cf ACMD, 1991). The crime-control pay-off that forms a part of the rationale for referral in both areas illustrates the further criteria by which these schemes could be evaluated. Schemes with such an orientation may reinforce the idea of a strong link between drug use and acquisitive crime, and perhaps make it more likely that people suspected of burglary and theft will be offered a card.

Generally though, most of the officers interviewed seem to follow the view that 'something is better than nothing', an acknowledgment that welfare considerations, even if they have limited impact, are still significant:

> It was only a dozen or so that we knew about who had referred themselves because of our cards to these agencies and when you consider there was probably two or three hundred cards sent out, is that percentage worthwhile? Some people would say it's a waste of time for the number of people that take-up the referral is so small... Is it worthwhile? Is it cost-effective? It probably isn't, but on the plus side if a dozen people have taken notice and sought referral that is a bonus and that's twelve more than we would have got (Drugs squad officer).

Similarly, in most of the case study areas, custody officers informed about the low take-up rate continued to believe that referral is worthwhile. One custody officer seemed to make a representative statement on behalf of many others:

It's a sensible thing to be doing, we should be doing our best to stop it but I don't think there's many people who will stop it by receiving the card. It is worthwhile, even if you're stopping one or two, you are stopping some.

Of course the numbers of people who take-up the scheme need not be the only objective or the only measure of whether referral schemes 'work'. The welfare and efficiency criteria are only some of the relevant factors in play. There are also other aspects of the crime-control and multi-agency perspectives to consider.

Cultivating informants

As well as the drugs-crime link, the crime-control element is evident in the capacity to 'turn' a suspects into informants. Officers may seek to cultivate informants, perhaps as some kind of 'carrot and stick' strategy, where cooperation in naming a supplier is exchanged for some favour in kind. Is there any evidence that referral schemes have been drawn into this process? We saw in the previous chapter that one referee claimed to have been offered a deal in exchange for naming a supplier. Turning to the police view, two possibilities that referral could be used as a lever, or as part of bargaining process, were mentioned by officers. One drugs squad officer explained that:

> Most drug offenders, certainly those that are nor charged on the day, are bailed under section 47/3, Bail Act to appear at a police station on a Monday afternoon to enable drugs officers to go and talk to them, to get to know them and various other reasons.
>
> Q. Is the card useful in those situations?
>
> Yes, it all comes into it. It all comes into the conversation.

This does not reveal much more than the fact that a referral card can be introduced in a situation where an officer may seek to 'get to know' someone to elicit information about suppliers. How the card may be used in such situations can only be guessed at.

In another area, two other police officers based in a community liaison section were asked about whether the issuing of a police caution could be linked to attendance at a drugs agency.

> It's offering them a carrot, it's an inducement to plead guilty [on the understanding that doing so will mean a caution] for something they might not have done, we get criticised for this with juveniles where they admit to the offence and are cautioned (Officer P).

[But] it's what we're doing now really (Officer Q).

These examples suggest that referral schemes can not and will not remain unsullied by the informalities of police practice. Indeed it would be naive to expect otherwise given the considerable literature on police discretion and police culture (Reiner, 1992). What happens in practice though and how useful, if at all, the availability of referral is in the process of garnering information remains an empirical question, requiring more detailed investigation. What is clear is that an element of crime-control can easily co-exist with both the welfare and efficiency perspectives.

Multi-agency policing?

The domination of multi-agency forums by the police and their priorities is usually taken to indicate the shortcomings of the multi-agency approach. Though this is a real concern, the research uncovered some ironies of multi-agency drugs liaison. For example, in one area a police officer commented that:

> Across the whole spectrum of the [local drug liaison] committee - probation, local and county authority, health coordinators and all the workers, they all thought it [referral] was a good idea, a positive move by the police. It was very very favourably accepted, they were all for it. But we were doing all the work, giving someone a card and telling them where to go, but tangibly we were getting no benefit from it. That doesn't matter, my point was that we were shown to be a caring agency, as well as locking them up, trying to help them as well (Drugs squad officer).[7]

Thus some officers can feel that they end up 'doing all the work' from which the benefits are at best limited.

A related matter that was frequently raised was the issue of confidentiality. In particular, there was concern from some drugs advice agencies that, in participating in referral, they might be seen by clients as 'working with the police'. As we saw in chapter 4, this perception can exist with or without a referral scheme. But for the same officer cited immediately above, the pay-off from multi-agency contact is negligible:

> None of the agencies had a clear picture of what was going on in their particular town, none of them. All they would come across would be say half-a-dozen people who might mention a few other people who were involved with amphetamines or heroin or whatever. At every meeting I was asked what the current drug situation was; they would ask for statistics, going back over a number of years, the overall county picture, age groups, sexes. It meant a reasonable amount of extra-work for myself to do that, but that was passed on to them. Now at the end of the day the

only thing I would get from them is that if I mention crack [the agencies would say] 'oh someone told us there's some crack in [names two towns]'. But if you asked who they were [the agencies would say] 'well it's confidential and I couldn't let that client be done'. So the actual intelligence information from these caring agencies was about nil (Drugs squad officer).

If the expectation of a *quid pro quo* in multi-agency liaison encounters disappointment, that does not mean that there is no low level intelligence being traded between the police and drugs agencies. Indeed at some briefing meetings informal conversations were observable. A typification of these exchanges is that they took the form of something along the lines of 'how you think things are looking at the moment?' (mostly but not always police initiated). While the interchange of any confidential information or the naming of individual people was, unsurprisingly, never witnessed, this sort of conversation opened the way to a two-way exchange of information about trends and changes in the availability of drugs in particular parts of a town or city. Whatever the frequency and status of such observations, it is clear that there can be some conflict between the attitudes of police force and drugs agency personnel. The individual client orientation of the latter makes them concerned about maintaining trust and confidentiality, while the police tend to valorise confidentiality around operational matters. Both instances reveal a 'ring fence' around what each see as their core remit and typical way of working.

Conclusion

Modest gains

Referral schemes have spread across the country with considerable rapidity. In its survey of the 43 police forces in England and Wales, the ACMD (1994) found that only seven (17 per cent) did not operate or plan to operate some referral service.[8] It also found that 26 out of 42 forces (62 per cent) had a policy of cautioning for drug offences and that in no force did the decision to caution depend on taking-up the referral. The ACMD survey, as well as interest in referral schemes from a variety of sources could be taken to mean that this is an idea whose time has come. Even if this was the case, even the most fervent proponents of referral would find it hard to make any great claims for the idea of such schemes. The ACMD itself recognised that take-up of referral via the police is low, but so are the demands that it makes upon the police. It concluded that 'referral schemes may....have a useful if limited role to play in encouraging drug misusers to make contact with services'

(ACMD, 1991: 13). This final section aims to identify a modest space that referral schemes could occupy in inter-agency relations between the police and drugs advice agencies.

At the very least there can be little doubt that referral has entailed a good deal of inter-agency communication and liaison across the country. The ACMD said that 'an incidental benefit flowing from the creation of such schemes [is] the development of closer links between the police and drugs services' (ACMD, 1991: 13). This is unfortunate, since it is clear that the benefit was not 'incidental' but intentional, even though policy and practice across the country has developed unevenly and not without impediment. Many people coming into contact with the police have been offered information about local drugs advice services and the opportunity to self-refer to an agency. But beyond these gains, it is difficult to make any claims for referral schemes in general, even though more may have been achieved in some areas. This is not intended as a dismissive conclusion, rather it is meant to be in keeping with what seems to be the appropriate scope for referral schemes within an inter-agency framework and the criminal justice system. Referral need not signal a major shift in the policy and practice of either the police or drugs agencies. Rather, it ought to represent a small contribution to inter-agency relations that either supplements existing work or, where there had been little liaison before, acts as a base or a catalyst from which other work could develop.

Points of intervention and effectiveness

For how many people are referral schemes really appropriate? Evidence from the probation and prison services leaves no doubt that there are a number of problematic drug users within the criminal justice system. But these people, including both drugs and non-drugs offenders, represent only a small proportion of the population who come into contact with the police. If their usage is sufficiently problematic it may be that users will be self-motivated, or motivated by significant others, to seek help and advice. Alternatively it may be that police referral, perhaps combined with some informal legal 'carrot and stick', opens a window of opportunity for some drug users (cf ACMD, 1991; Dorn, 1994). But all the evidence so far shows that this applies to only very small numbers of people across the country.

Within the criminal justice system it may simply be the case that a seemingly obvious point of intervention (i.e. from the police) is not the most effective one, on whatever measure of effectiveness is used - welfare, crime-control, or efficiency. It is those people who continue to be processed within the system and become liable to court orders and probation supervision who may be most amenable to advice/compulsion. At that stage of the legal process a clear risk/reward matrix can be utilised. For example, users might agree to undertake some form of treatment or counselling in connection with their drug use, linked to some system of sanctions. This is clearly a path laid out in the 1991 Criminal Justice Act, which has links to the 'justice model' of punishment.[9] But as with the underlying philosophy of that model, it is a picture that is anathema to many. Particularly with drug use, many maintain that the view of rational action implied in the model is simply not tenable or realistic for addicted or problematic drug users. Still, drugs agencies have been encouraged to play a more active role in the criminal justice system, especially by the ACMD (1991, 1994). This is certainly the state of play that now faces health professionals concerned with the welfare of drug users. There are frequent calls for more emphasis on treatment and prevention services, but even if there is a process of realignment within policy, drug users will continue to come into contact with, and be dealt with through, the criminal justice system. Apart from diversion through increased cautioning, criminal justice policy is not targeted at the police's end. So referral can make a contribution, but only a small one within the overall scheme of things. More effective criminal justice interventions may occur 'deeper' in the system.

Policing drug users

But of course the majority of drugs and other offenders who the police encounter are not problematic drugs users. Most are minor possession offences, mostly for cannabis. As one police officer stated:

> I don't find that [refusal to accept referral card] surprising at all, for a number of reasons. Most people when they go to a police station are a little bit defensive...so it's not unusual that people refuse to take away some paper. Coupled with that is the fact that the majority of people are arrested for a bit of cannabis and they don't think they have a problem (Drugs squad officer).

At this level referral can achieve little beyond the provision of information about advice services, so that individuals or those connected with them, like parents, partners and friends, may wish to seek advice or information about drugs. This after all was the starting point for Family Referral. But that was found to be useful for only a few people. In the space between non-problematic drug use and worried parents, there may be some drug users for whom, at some time, referral may be appropriate. This group cannot be taken as a basis for far reaching claims about the possible impact of referral schemes.

Local diversity

This need not mean that there is no point to referral schemes. They can, as we have seen, be widened out to include alcohol and HIV/AIDS advice services. Or, at their broadest they can be in the form of generic help cards, advertising a range of local services. From both efficiency and welfare perspectives this latter form seems to represent the most economical method, but it does not have be seen as the only way to do referral. Local circumstances, rather than a fixed blueprint, ought to dictate the nature of referral schemes. Hence there is, or could be, a place for referral even if it is for drugs alone, if that is what is deemed appropriate. Ultimately, it can reasonably be argued that referral cards or leaflets represent a low-level intervention. They might help some people at some time. Even if they do not produce any significant numbers of referrals they are an information and advice aid that is cheap and which could help the police to look more like the service that some senior mangers aspire to. It may lead to improved inter-agency coordination, or perhaps open the door to other joint ventures. It may enable both the police and drugs agencies to develop a more professional relationship where both can see what they have to gain by cooperation as well as define the limits to joint working. It is not possible to be prescriptive about the form and development of referral schemes for all situations and circumstances. Both the police and drugs agencies, as well as other local players, should be guided by local circumstances and priorities, in which case a diverse range of approaches should emerge.

Notes

1. A total of eight drugs advice agencies were listed on the card.

2. Some of this data was collected by Saeed Butt, then based at the Bridge project in Bradford.

3. Though Dorn (1994) reports a subsequent decline in the take-up of referral.

4. After prompting, and the officer saying that 'it's difficult', he estimated that about half the people he encountered fell into the category of not wanting to look at the leaflet.

5. This is drawn from Chatterton et al., 1995. Research by them in Manchester found increasing matches between a regional drugs database and police arrest records. This indicated that more individuals referred themselves after a referral scheme was set up. But the authors found no evidence that people attending drugs services had received a referral card, or whether the card, if received, motivated individuals to refer themselves.

6. Though Dorn (1994) discusses card dissemination through interviewing officers, probably detectives.

7. Compare the views of these officers:

> Q. Are there internal differences as to how the scheme is seen?

> We hold it in much higher regard than those on the ground floor [i.e. uniformed officers]. We see it as very important because we're dealing with people who administer it and people like you who report on it...they [uniformed officers] don't see that, the role of constables and sergeants is so diverse that they just see it as a card to be handed out (Officer R).

> Q. Are there any pluses in it for you?

> I can't see any great pluses for us at all, hopefully there's something for the people who've taken it up and I've met parents who've been glad that there's someone there to help them and we've been able to give them a card, but they're thanking the agency, not us (Officer R).

> Q. What about changing perception of police as not just law enforcers?

> We're still enforcing the law because the person's been arrested. They didn't get the card as an alternative to going to court, it was just an 'on-top of' this scheme, wasn't it (Officer S).

> Only about 30 per cent of the population come into contact with us because of crime, the other 70 per cent see us recovering lost dogs and have a generally favourable view. When people are arrested they try to ingratiate themselves, but you've only got listen to people talking in pubs to see that they think they've been hard done by [the police] because they were stopped for doing 40 [mph] or they were only just over the breath limit (Officer R).

8. The Council's survey did not cover Scotland, though it is known that at least two Scottish police forces operated referral schemes.

9. See Nee and Sibbitt (1993) for a study of the implementation of the 1991 Criminal Justice Act by probation services.

PART III

OFFICIAL AND MEDIA REACTIONS

6 Agony and Ecstasy: Drugs, Media and Moral Panic

> Human life is bounded by two chasms: fanaticism on one side, absolute scepticism on the other.
>
> Milan Kundera

This chapter is concerned with drugs and the media. Two broad approaches can be distinguished at the outset. The dominant conventional approach has seen the media as a key force in the demonisation and marginalisation of drug users, as presenting lurid, hysterical images, and as a provider of an uncritical platform from which politicians and other moral entrepreneurs are able to launch and wage drug 'wars'.[1] The media is thus seen to comprehensively *mis*-represent drugs, their effects, typical users and sellers and, for some, the whole nature of the drug market and law enforcement. In many ways the media may even define what we 'see' as drugs because it concentrates on solvents, heroin, crack, ecstasy, etc. In contrast, alcohol and tobacco are rarely spoken of as drugs, thereby conditioning public attitudes about the 'drug problem' and what the response to it should be. Furthermore, media coverage is not just misleading, it can also actually be harmful because it is implicated in the triggering of drug scares and moral panics which lead to 'knee-jerk' drug crackdowns and punitive responses.

Followers of this line of argument see their task as being to 'debunk' media misrepresentations, sometimes by recourse to the proposition that media reaction constitutes a moral panic, and to insert in their place a 'true' picture of drugs. This type of approach has been commonly employed in various critical approaches to deviance and the mass media. In media studies terms it fits within the continuum of 'effects' models (related terms are the 'mass market' or hypodermic models). Generally, these concentrate on the power of producers and either it is assumed that these have real consequences or effects, or the play of dominant ideology in media messages is decoded. Because of its 'media-centricity', the role of the audience is often left unexamined. In contrast, alternative approaches have stressed the ability of audiences to filter, interpret, deconstruct and even reconstruct media messages into something that can be very different from any intention that the producers may have had (Morley, 1995). This 'active audience' perspective (earlier versions were called the 'laissez faire' or commercial model), stresses the role of audiences and, in doing so, asks whether media messages work at all. Versions of this have been apparent in studies of drug prevention (for a review see Dorn and Murji, 1992a) which suggest that prevention messages and campaigns are resisted by the audience, or may even increase audience interest in experimenting with the very drugs that they are being warned about and against. Both models are problematic in various ways, not least in over-stating the power of either the media or of individual consumers.

My primary aim in this chapter is to take issue with the conventional and familiar debunking approach. I do not seek to simply adopt an empiricist view that media 'effects' are difficult to demonstrate, though this is a criticism that such approaches can be weak at dealing with. Rather, I will argue that the debunking method is itself problematic and that the argument about moral panics in particular has become virtually discredited. While I criticise the debunking perspective I should state that, in broad terms, I do not demur from the view that media representations are problematic and that they may be implicated in 'panicky' responses from officialdom. For example Reinarman and Levine (1989), Bean (1993) and Reeves and Campbell (1994) have all deconstructed the media scare or panic about crack in recent years. I instinctively share much of the distaste for the exaggerated form and context-less content of some media coverage of drugs, though I do not want to simply engage in another 'rubbishing' of media reaction. Instead, I aim to question and take issue with the counter-reaction to media reaction in an attempt at the 'disruptive evaluation' (Giddens, 1987) of the familiar. My argument is mostly based around examples of reaction and counter-reaction in the media to the case of Leah Betts, a teenager whose death in November 1995 was commonly linked to an ecstasy tablet that she had taken. I will go on to discuss a series of problems with the ways in which the term moral panic has come to be used. Before that I will argue that one of the problems with counter-reaction is the way that it mirrors certain features of the very view that it opposes.

Sorted and distorted?

In December 1995 a number of large advertising billboards were filled with a photograph of a young woman against a black background. A single word: 'SORTED' appeared in large letters next to the photograph; below it were the words: 'Just one ecstasy tablet took Leah Betts.' The death of Leah Betts received prolonged media coverage, from the time it occurred, through to her burial and when an inquest returned a verdict of accidental death. During the most intense phase of media attention *The Sun* gave over its front page to the story. Underneath a bold headline: 'Leah took ecstasy on her 18th Birthday' was an almost full page photograph of her lying on a hospital bed with a respirator on her face. Below it was an earlier, smaller picture of her smiling, next to which were the words: 'Don't become another Leah'. In the following two months a couple of other cases kept the subject of young people and ecstasy in the headlines. In January 1996 Helen Cousins fell into a coma after taking ecstasy and water to combat the effects of dehydration. After recovering she appealed to other young people not to take the drug which she likened to a 'dance with death' (*The Independent*, 13 January 1996: 3). A few days later another teenager, Andreas Bouzis, died in a club in south London after the ecstasy tablet that he had taken was thought to have exacerbated a congenital heart defect (*The Independent*, 15 January 1996).

In the aftermath of two deaths and one temporary coma all linked to ecstasy it is hardly surprising that there was a strong emotional response from the parents of the young people concerned. The parents of Leah Betts appeared regularly in the media to warn of the dangers of ecstasy. Following her daughter's recovery Mrs Cousins said: 'I'm pleading to all young people, don't chance your life, it can happen to you. If you take ecstasy it can take your life. Nothing is worth that. Don't weaken, be strong and say 'no" (*The Independent*, 13 January 1996: 3). After the death of her son Mrs Bouzis said: 'Yesterday our son had a future, he had a life... Today he is dead. Families and their love are very precious. Ecstasy tablets destroy families' (*The Independent*, 15 January 1996: 3). Elements of the media treated the death of Leah Betts and the other cases as symptoms of a general social malaise. For instance the *Daily Express* declared that the death of Leah - a teenager from a respectable home, whose father was an ex-police officer and whose mother had worked as a drugs counsellor - revealed that drugs were present as a 'rotten core at the heart of middle England'. Other dramatic images were invoked by tabloid newspapers. *The Sun* wrote of how 'evil ecstasy pushers [are] cashing in on Leah's death' to promote sales of ecstasy, while the *Daily Star* reported its horror that 'ecstasy club kids [are] still dicing with death' by continuing to take the drug despite the recent cases. Accompanying such stories were exposé style articles castigating magazines that detailed the content and likely effects of different 'brands' of ecstasy. Also, and probably inevitably, the *Daily Mirror* urged an 'even tougher crackdown on pushers'.

Reaction and counter-reaction

The intense media reaction about ecstasy at this time - with its elements of dramatisation, exaggeration and a general sense of excitability - provoked a counter-reaction from some who sought to present an alternative view of the drug in the media. I take two articles, one in a left wing magazine, the other in a liberal/left broadsheet newspaper to illustrate my argument about problems with counter-reaction. In the former Steve Platt, then the editor of the *New Statesman*, declared that media reaction to the case of Leah Betts signalled that 'we are in the midst of a moral panic' (Platt, 1995). In the latter, Alix Sharkey in *The Guardian* examined distorted media coverage of ecstasy following the death of Leah Betts. These articles have been selected for the purposes of elaborating the argument that follows not because they are regarded as 'representative' of media coverage at this time. While there is overlap between them in the ways that both unpack and seek to debunk media coverage, I want to deal with them separately for current purposes. My aim is not simply to try to 'debunk the debunkers', though in criticising them there inevitably are some elements of this. Rather, I argue that both contain a series of problems, some or many of which could also be found within more academic/social scientific texts. First I outline the case presented by Sharkey (1996). I will then look at the ways in which this mirrors aspects of media reaction. Sharkey's main points (from which all the quotations below are taken) were that:

- Media 'horror stories' about ecstasy pre-dated the death of Leah Betts. Her case merely provided a hook or peg on which to hang those stories.
- The picture being painted by the media was one of ecstasy as a 'child-killing drug, available on every street corner'.
- 'There exists a largely manufactured consensus that drugs are "evil", those who sell them are "monsters", those who take them are "victims"'.
- The death of Leah Betts generated 'an avalanche of emotive but essentially uninformative copy'. But, 'nobody asked whether the death would have received such widespread attention had it not involved a pretty, white, teenage girl'.
- The corrosive effect of this type of media coverage is such that 'even factual TV programmes now take their editorial lead from such reporting'.
- The death of Leah Betts 'was not due to the effects of Ecstasy but to water intoxication'. However, if this was the case her parents seemed unwilling to make it public, instead they championed the view that ecstasy itself led to their daughter's death.
- The risk of death from ecstasy has been greatly exaggerated. Official figures of some 60 deaths since 1987 placed against estimated consumption of a

million doses a week puts the risk of death at one in 6.8 million. The statistically greater risk of death from aspirin, let alone amphetamines, has been largely ignored. Even a Swiss skiing holiday carries a higher risk of death than ecstasy use.[2]
• Similarly, the emphasis on ecstasy as a threat to young people's lives obscures the fact that car accidents are the major cause of death for 14-24 year olds; and that the majority of drug related deaths are due to smoking and alcohol. Even when considering illicit drugs only, deaths linked to ecstasy make up only a tiny fraction.

This strikes me as a good example of the debunking of the media and the attempt to re-contextualise the issue or problem as one of media reaction (see also Saunders, 1995). It accuses the media of selective perception (why Leah Betts, when other cases did not receive similar coverage?), the promotion of folk devil images of drugs and drug sellers ('evil pushers' and innocent victims/users), misleading, simplistic and hysterical coverage (ecstasy 'caused' the death of Leah Betts, it is 'a child killing drug') and of ignoring rational evidence (the greater risk of death from other activities).

What is wrong with this? While Sharkey does not personally say so, the debunking approach can sometimes include a complaint about 'the media' itself, which is presented as undergoing periodic, inevitable and predictable phases of reaction in which crude stereotypes will be perpetuated. But the reaction that is being objected to obviously represents only some parts and sections of the media. It is certainly trite to observe that counter-reaction also takes place in and makes use of the media, which therefore can not be spoken of as an ideologically homogenous or undifferentiated whole, but while it remains unacknowledged, the criticism will still need to be made. This is but one difficulty with counter-reaction. It can contain an exaggerated tendency to see media coverage as hysterical and promoting an anti-drugs 'consensus' even when the existence of counter-reaction must signal, at the very least, a crack in any widespread consensus. Nonetheless, the media's basic message, we are told, simply apes the government's already discredited and fatuous 'just say no' policy. The likelihood that the nature of media coverage means that it can be seen as exciting interest in drug use even while it appears to be forbidding it, or that government policy, for all its simplifications, does amount to more than 'just say no' (see HM Government, 1995; Pearson, 1991) are both inconveniences best left to one side. Consequently, reaction and counter-reaction can often appear to be merely different sides of the same coin, or to mirror one another. Elements that are problematic in media reaction are no less problematic when they occur in counter-reaction. The mirroring of apparently opposite points of view has been observed before.[3] Dorn (1980) demonstrated that both supporters and opponents of cannabis decriminalisation subscribed to a common 'demonic' image of other drugs such as heroin. Similarly, in a review of Clutterbuck's *Terrorism, Drugs and Crime in Europe after 1992*,[4] Dorn and Murji pointed out that drug 'warriors' and 'legalisers' display an equal passion in hyping up the nature, or 'horribleness', of drug markets. Once things can be seen to have got 'so bad' it enables both sides to make their case that either even more and tougher enforcement is required, or that legalisation is the only option left.

Mirroring

The first way in which reaction and counter-reaction mirror one another is in their view of social consensus. Media reaction assumes that there is a moral or social consensus which is under threat or breaking down.[5] Increased drug use by young people is presented as a symptom of this decline, or as a contributory or principal cause of social decay. For the counter-reactors there is a consensus but it has been manufactured by the media and moral entrepreneurs. The image presented is one of a monolithic control culture which sees the world in terms of a binary opposition of good versus evil. In this sense counter-reaction subscribes to a simple and comforting dualistic conception of power - a world divided into 'them' and 'us'. The object of critical analysis should then be to uncover this false consensus. What remains unquestioned is the nature and even existence of any consensus. It is simply assumed to exist, either as something to be defended or uncovered. The contradictory and fragmented patterns of real life are a nuisance that both approaches prefer not to deal with. The 'one dimensional' picture presented in media reaction that Cohen (1972) drew attention to, is replaced by an alternative, but equally one dimensional view in counter-reaction.

Similarly, in its concern to denounce media hype, counter-reaction can also end up effectively substituting one over simple message for another. Either, as the advert would have it 'Just one ecstasy tablet took Leah Betts', or it was not ecstasy at all but death was actually caused by water intoxication, due to an excessive intake of water to combat the effects of dehydration. As the headline in *The Guardian* (1 February 1996) stated following the inquest verdict: 'Leah's ecstasy death caused by water'. Thus media misconceptions can find their mirror image in the counter-reaction to (which is also in) the media. It can hardly be a coincidence that both perspectives are promoted in newspapers and other media, since they make equal use of simplification and lay claim to certainty. They exemplify the 'sound bite culture' (Schlesinger and Tumber, 1994) in which complexity has little place. In this black and white world the possibility that it was *both* ecstasy and water that contributed to the death of Leah Betts fails to suit the preferred framework of either side. As Dr John Henry of the National Poisons Unit indicated: 'If she had just taken the drug alone she might have survived. If she had drunk the amount of water alone she would have survived' (in *The Guardian*, 1 February 1996: 2; see also *Druglink*, 1996). Both perspectives also contain a broadly similar, strong view of media 'effects'. Either popular culture mediated through music, magazines, television, etc., is seen as promoting drug use and activities associated with it. Or, on the other hand, over the top media coverage is seen as promoting a false social consensus which alienates those with experience of drugs and marginalises users. From both viewpoints the media is constructed as a powerful social force with determinate and undesirable effects.

There are a number of other similarities. Both perspectives can see drug users as 'victims' at the mercy of drug sellers. For one side young people are seemingly seduced by 'evil pushers'; alternatively, young people are seen as prey to being 'ripped off' by unscrupulous dealers selling them something that is not really ecstasy. Another similarity is that both can treat the parents of the young people in the cases discussed at the outset as ciphers. Either the parents grief can be vicariously used to promote a particular message about drugs, or the parents are virtually 'dupes' who are being used by the media to promote an ideologically loaded message. A third similarity can be seen in the view that both perspectives have about the extent of drug use. While media reaction might see increased use in terms of an 'epidemic', the counter-reaction concurs with the view that usage has increased dramatically; Sharkey for example refers to 'a million doses a week'. It is notable that there is no disputing (or debunking) of the claim itself, nor even much attempt to put drug use in perspective by suggesting that, as all evidence shows, cannabis is the most widely used illegal drug. Thus there is agreement that drug use is on the increase, only the language and style of media reaction is at issue. The ways in which drugs are discussed and depicted can be serious issues, though I question whether counter-reaction helps to make them so.

Both perspectives can also be seen to have an implicit conception of the 'audience' that is being addressed, constructed and reconstructed in media discourse. Eco (1979; see also Sparks, 1992) saw 'closed texts' as ones that envisage an average addressee and aim to arouse a particular response. This is more likely to be successful if the text can appeal to an existing 'common frame' of which the audience has already been 'made fond'. In the mass market place of media consumption it could be argued that both media reaction, favouring the individualising 'human interest' approach to private troubles, and counter-reaction, with its use of exposé style journalism, are forms of closed texts accustomed to constituting audiences in a particular frame of reference. But the common problem with effects models is revealed in the need to make allowance for the probability that audiences, because they remain regular readers and viewers, may also have got used to 'seeing' and constructing themselves within such a framework. Thus there is a dynamic and reflexive relationship or inter-play between media and audience.

A moral panic?

The second strand of counter-reaction that I want to examine bases itself upon the view that the media's response can be classified as a moral panic. Platt's (1995) argument that media reaction to the death of Leah Betts was a moral panic is substantiated by the use of Goode and Ben-Yehuda's (1994) five criteria of a moral panic: a heightened level of concern, increased hostility towards those associated with the activity, a high level of consensus that the activity is a real and serious threat, exaggeration of the nature of threat, and volatility. From this perspective the media and self-selected moral entrepreneurs, in cahoots with the government, are seen as conveying a simplistic anti-drugs message which ignores the fact that more and more young people are trying drugs. Hence the reality of drugs and their effects are swept under the carpet by the dominant prohibitionist mentality. Because Platt and Sharkey make similar points about media coverage I am not going to spell out the former's case. Rather I want to examine Platt's use of the moral panics model since its appearance in counter-reaction acts as a pillar for the debunking of the media that probably all users of the term aim to accomplish.

Since Cohen (1972) the term moral panic has been widely used and abused, achieving the status of a sociological concept that has passed into everyday language. A moral panic has been held to be occurring in media and official reaction to street crime (Hall *et al.*, 1978), juvenile crime (Pearson, 1983; Hay, 1995), child abuse (Jenkins, 1992), as well as alcohol, solvents and all or particular drugs (Dorn, 1983; Ives, 1986; Young, 1971; Pearson *et al.*, 1986; Kohn, 1987; Reinarman and Levine, 1989; Parker *et al.*, 1988; Ben-Yehuda, 1990; Coffield and Gofton, 1994; Gould, 1994). Sparks points out that Cohen's use of the term was 'a modest and descriptive one'. But, while the original formulation

> usefully [drew] attention to the recurrence of themes of social anxiety and their association with rhetorics of crisis, it elides all such 'panics' under a single heading, representing them as a consequence of some (hypothetically universal, endlessly cyclical) feature of social life, namely panickyness (Sparks, 1992: 65).

Cohen (1972) and Hall *et al.* (1978) did seek to carefully contextualise and theorise the model of moral panic. But this has not always been evident in the manifold uses of the term since then. As a result, moral panic has become a throwaway phrase, a 'catch all term for anything that we don't like'

(Thompson, quoted in Jenkins, 1992), and 'a value laden terminology' (Waddington, 1986) revealing as much about the view of the user as the phenomenon itself. Whenever something is described as a moral panic the intention is always pejorative, there are no instances that I know of where the user does not seem to use it dismissively against the phenomenon depicted.

It is true that one can easily find newspapers and other media that present ecstasy and other drugs in apocalyptic terms and make use of individual and unrepresentative cases to address or represent the 'state of the nation', just as it is true that there are commentators and moral entrepreneurs who 'man the barricades' and call for more law, more punishment, etc. But this ease indicates that moral panics have become commonplace and everyday, rather than exceptional (McRobbie, 1994):

> moral panics have become the way in which daily events are brought to the attention of the public. They are a standard response, a familiar sometimes weary, even ridiculous rhetoric rather than an exceptional emergency intervention (McRobbie and Thornton, 1995: 560).

There was, for instance, a fuss in the media about the film *Trainspotting*, which was criticised for virtually inciting people to try heroin and an insufficiently censorious view of drug-taking. A similar controversy surrounded the depiction of drug taking in the film *Pulp Fiction* for allegedly 'celebrating' drug use. Does the reaction to either, or both, constitute a moral panic? The problem, it seems to me, is that to say it is (or that any one of a host of other issues are) makes little allowance for the possibility that audiences may well recognise there is more than an element of commercial hype in much of this type of coverage. The moral panic has become a 'routine means of making youth-orientated cultural products more alluring' (McRobbie and Thornton, 1995: 559). It has become part of a 'promotional logic' which business practice can play upon, as Cohen (1972) recognised in his discussion of the 'exploitative culture'.

The media may be able to generate such moral panics and a panoply of new folk devils almost to order, for example, new age travellers, anti-road building protestors, campaigners against live animal exports, etc. But simply identifying their presence in the media is hardly the same thing as saying that whatever 'views' are presented about such groups are widely shared. After all, in the case of all of the 'new' folk devils just mentioned, there has been at least sufficient public support for them to make any claims about consensus, concern, hostility and the reality of the threat questionable at the very least.[6] Not each and every instance of exaggeration of the 'threat' posed by some group or activity can be regarded as a moral panic, unless the term is now being used so loosely as to refer to all and every social anxiety, however localised, and whether it is widely shared or not.

The uncovering of media over-reaction has been a key element of the moral panics framework. But the empirical basis on which this can be asserted is far from being as straight-forward as it may appear. Even one of the most sophisticated elaborations of a moral panic has been found wanting. Sumner and Sandberg (1990) have shown that, contrary to Hall *et al.*'s (1978) argument, 'mugging' was not the dominant issue in the news in 1973. Their re-analysis of newspapers found that the prime news story concerned industrial relations and trade unions. Yet no one has argued that there was a moral panic about strikes. A similar argument could be applied to more recent events. Around the same time as the death of Leah Betts, there was abundant media coverage of knives following the fatal stabbing of the head teacher Philip Lawrence outside a school in London. Despite the extensive reporting of this incident and calls for increased police powers of stop and search, there has been no case presented that this was a moral panic about knives and young people.

Claims about media over-reaction run into further problems. To return to the example of 'mugging' again, it has been argued that the scale of the reaction to it was not, as Hall *et al.*, (1978) argued, disproportionate to its actual occurrence (Waddington, 1986). Crucially, Waddington argues that there is no basis for identifying what the empirical criteria for a 'proportionate' response are (see also Reiner, 1988). Critics and counter-reactors asserting that the media over-reacts imply that news coverage is, or should be, governed by some actuarial rules. An argument could certainly be made that media coverage of heroin, crack and ecstasy in recent years has been 'out of keeping' with the actual usage of these drugs. But what is the 'right' or appropriate level of reaction? To illustrate the problem of establishing an answer to this question I will take a different example. Media coverage of HIV/AIDS in the late 1980s had many features of a moral panic (though see Watney, 1987 for a critique) when, for example, it was depicted as a 'gay plague' or as of concern to injecting drug users only. Were those who called for more resources and attention to be given to harm reduction and prevention messages, and in the process warned about a potential 'epidemic' of HIV infection, irrespective of the actual prevalence of HIV, also engaging in a moral panic? After all, 'rational statistics' could be used to say that there are far more deaths from prostate cancer. Hence both approaches can be accused of 'sensationalism' and 'over reaction' in hyping up the problem in order to attract attention. Health educators and others involved in prevention could argue that a 'disproportional' reaction can be justified by an appeal to the 'hidden' scale of a problem or its potential as a 'future threat'. However such appeals are equally open to those who issued apocalyptic warnings about the addictive power of crack (Bean, 1993). A more credible case could be made out for differences in the *style* and *content* of different warning messages, which would indicate that there are important political and qualitative differences between those who use terms such as 'gay plague' or a 'child killing drug' and others who want to promote harm reduction and safer sex and drug use messages. But, in formal terms the 'warnings' can appear similar enough to worry anyone who chooses to say that only one of these is disproportionate and an over-reaction and hence part of a moral panic.

There is a view that a moral panic is not about the 'objective' phenomenon but rather the ways in which 'social problems' are constructed (Jenkins, 1992). But some social constructionist have still felt the need to contrast problem construction with some evidence about its extent (e.g. see Reinarman and Levine, 1989). Thus, as Watney (1987: 41) has stated:

> Moral panic theory is always obliged in the final instance to refer and contrast 'representation' to the arbitration of 'the real', and is hence unable to develop a full theory concerning the operations of ideology within all representational systems.

A further problem with users of the moral panic argument is a tendency to see panics as actively promoted by a particular group, or at least as being a peg around which powerful interest groups can hang their pre-set agenda. But in this instrumentalist conception there is rarely any acknowledgment that such groups may have something to lose from moral panics too.[7] For example, following their role in the spectacular representation of drugs as a problem and continuing evidence that usage has not declined, the police are faced with two possibilities: either to 'give up' and join the drug legalisation lobby, or to campaign for even more powers and resources, etc. Both options position them in a posture of defeat: the 'problem' is either insoluble, or so overwhelming that only further special powers, the limits to which can never be specified, will do (Dorn *et al.*, 1991).[8]

Another example reveals a different problem with both the instrumentalist and disproportionality aspects of the moral panics argument. In the early 1980s there was a campaign by parents in Merseyside for more attention to be paid to the increase in heroin use by young people. Their complaint was that there was insufficient reaction by the media and the authorities. This local campaign for more action may have touched off the wider campaign that spread publicity about heroin nationally and, perhaps, stimulated the interest of others (Pearson, 1991). But the parents may have felt that their (over?) reaction was necessary in order to get the authorities to respond. Hence the media and the powerful may sometimes be forced to follow rather than lead public opinion. And, as all the examples used suggest, exaggeration can routinely be used as a means of getting the media, politicians and the public to react in cases where they otherwise seem to show little interest.

Finally there is a problem with the periodisation of moral panics. If there was a moral panic about ecstasy in 1995, when did it begin and end? Clearly for Platt (1995) and Sharkey (1996) the death of Leah Betts acted as the touchstone for the onset of a moral panic. But how would this view deal with the fact that the cultural industries associated with 'acid house' and 'rave' culture were predicting that there would be a moral panic as long ago as 1988? Or that the music press were running exposés about ecstasy at that time and asking why the tabloids were ignoring the issue? There was eventually much press attention paid to the 'rave' scene in the summer of 1988 and throughout the early 1990s (see McRobbie and Thornton, 1995) just as, well before the death of Leah Betts, there was considerable news coverage of ecstasy-linked deaths of young people. As the headlines 'Alarm grows over rising death toll' and 'Ravers play 'Russian roulette' with ecstasy' (*The Independent*, 28 December 1991: 5) indicate, the themes of 1995 were, in many ways, a replay of a well established story. How does the advocate of the moral panic explain this? Goode and Ben-Yehuda (1994) have the catch-all answer since volatility is one of their criteria of a moral panic. But, as a 'totalizing' or holistic conception of society, the media and social regulation has 'fissured' (McRobbie and Thornton, 1995), accounting for the persistence, residues and decline of moral panics requires a good deal more explanation than this (see also Watney, 1987). For all these reasons it seems to me that to say that the media promotes moral panics about drugs in general, or ecstasy in particular, raises a number of difficulties that are rooted in the way that moral panics and the role of the media have been theorised. These difficulties can not simply be dismissed in the way that Goode and Ben-Yehuda (1994) do in response to Waddington (1986) when they argue that the popularity of the term moral panics in journalism and social science establishes its verisimilitude and utility.

Reason and emotion

The implicit or explicit use of reason as a key motif of counter-reaction raises a final set of problems. The play upon and with rationality takes two main forms. It is most evident in the appeal to rational statistics, as well as the writing style and tone that is adopted. The statistics of death - the much smaller probability of death linked to ecstasy against the known higher rates of deaths due to less publicised activities - are used to highlight the media's emphasis on the former at the expense of the latter to reinforce the view that media coverage is ideologically loaded. The argument that the media constructs particular cases and deaths as exceptional and newsworthy while ignoring many others is plausible. It is certainly possible to find other cases that have not received as much coverage as that of Leah Betts. But, the appeal to rational statistics contains an implication that a moral calculus governs news coverage, or should do so. Yet the extent or amount of media reaction to deaths probably rarely corresponds simply to the numbers involved. As Kettle indicates, in Britain news coverage of a disaster is likely to emphasise 'six Brits' over '60 Frogs, and 600 more remote aliens' (cited in Walter *et al.*, 1995: 587). Pointing out the far greater number of deaths due to tobacco, alcohol, car accidents, etc., achieves the rhetorical effect of exposing media partiality. But it also glosses over the unexamined assumption that the commonplace could be the stuff of daily news. While the question of how 'the news' is constructed is an important one, it is still the case that:

> The deaths boldly headlined and portrayed by the news media are extraordinary deaths. That is why they are so eminently story-worthy as news. They are also types of deaths which, unlike the majority of deaths, occur in a public place (Walter *et al.*, 1995: 595).

Hence it is at least understandable why there was a lot of coverage given to the death of Leah Betts, though that did not occur in a public place. The revelation that other deaths did not generate as much coverage does not go beyond what is already known: that news values shape and construct what becomes the news. It does not amount to a case against the media, particularly since counter-reaction is also part of the media circle. To put the case another way, I am arguing that it is not sufficient to uncover that the media is partial, since it is difficult to know what an 'impartial' media would look like.

A second aspect of the use of reason is evident in the style adopted by the counter-reactors. Michael Keith (1992) has written about the ways in which academic writing masks its own rhetoric chiefly through the use of a dispassionate tone and style. These conventions, Keith argues, account for why writings that convey anger and emotion can be dismissed as not serious and hence are disqualified from consideration. Though the writings I have been considering are journalistic it seems to me that they employ the same strategy, and I would contend that same conventions are commonly in play. Hysteria and emotion are taken as the hall marks of that which is to be debunked and this is best done with a 'cool', dispassionate and logical tone. Reason is, self-evidently, rational while emotion is irrational and therefore not to be trusted. Hence reasonableness marks another boundary between 'us' and the 'others'. But as Sparks pointed out, reason is not the opposite of emotion: 'Rather the opposites of emotion are the 'detachment and equanimity' of a spurious objectivism and the 'sentimentality' of inauthentic responses' (Sparks, 1992: 75).

Rationality performs a key rhetorical role in counter-reaction because it makes it possible to depict media reaction as moralistically pushing a particular agenda using emotional, even hysterical, language and images. It enables the creation of a dichotomy in which only one side is seen as engaged in rhetoric, as Sharkey (1996: 2) demonstrates: 'When drugs cannot be considered outside this simplistic rhetorical context, meaningful debate is impossible'.[9] Reasonableness thus creates a space for counter-reaction to 'cloak' or suppress its own moral enterprise and rhetoric.[10] But opposing views about drugs can not be seen in terms of morality versus non-morality. Paradigms of morality imbue debates about drugs, whether those views come from the most ardent 'warriors' or the strongest libertarians (see Rouse and Johnson, 1991; Husak, 1992; Gaus, 1995). Both perspectives contain moral positions in the struggle over definitions, lifestyles, etc., rather than morality being the preserve of one side only. This criticism of counter-reaction for its use of rationality is not intended to be read as a collapse into the postmodernist rejection of reason. Rather I am arguing that we need to pay more attention, as Garland (1990) has observed about punishment, to the 'sentiments and passions' that the subject of drugs can and does arouse. The use of reason, I have sought to argue, seeks to artificially disqualify emotion, even though there clearly are sentiments and passions that underlie counter-reaction too.

Conclusion

I have argued against the conventional debunking approach to some sections of the media's coverage of drugs. The counter-reaction contains ideas or themes that are just as problematic as the views to which it is opposed. Furthermore it can be seen as relying upon a rather out-dated vocabulary about moral panics and accused of deceitfully covering up its own moral enterprise. In taking issue with the conventional reaction to media coverage I have spent more time criticising the critics than the originators. This is not intended as a defence of any of the media's reporting of drugs. It is meant to indicate that theorising about drugs and the media requires more rigour than the examples of counter-reaction that I have used here. While the sociology of the media, youth cultures and deviance has moved on (Schlesinger and Tumber, 1994; Morley, 1995; McRobbie and Thornton, 1995) the terminology of moral panics remains stuck in a time-warp that requires a model of social consensus, a monolithic media and control culture, and a seemingly gullible, or at least highly suggestive, public to work.

There are however a number of unresolved problems that can be mentioned. In drawing attention to equivalences between apparently contrasting perspectives, the differences between them have been underplayed. I have mainly focused on the form and content of reaction and counter-reaction. But it is also worth asking *where* the different views are usually to be found. At some risk of overstating the case, it is probably true that drug scares and the most extreme forms of coverage are likely to be found in the mass market tabloid newspapers while the more 'reasoned' counter-reactions are to be found in broad sheet quality newspapers.[11] If these are taken as broad indicators of the sites of reaction and counter-reaction then the ways in which separate sections of the media address and 'visualise' the audience is one difference that could be worthy of further exploration. A second difference is the possible presence in counter-reaction of multiple viewpoints of an issue, suggesting complexity and a degree of openness and debate, against the singular perspective or grand narrative adopted in reaction. A third issue is the question of weight and influence. The forces of reaction do not stand in an equal relationship to forces of counter-reaction. There are inequalities of access as well as resources (Schlesinger and Tumber, 1994). Moreover, the prevalence of political conservatism apparently makes it more acceptable to talk 'tough' about drugs (and crime and punishment) than to appear 'soft'. In the mid-1990s extensive coverage was given to a Labour party shadow minister who called for a fresh look at the laws on cannabis. The response to even this modest proposal was a howl of protest by the media which eventually led the politician to apologise and retract. Hence it is arguable that 'alternative' views get much less time and space in the media than 'mainstream' ones, although both alternative and mainstream are far from homogenous perspectives. In seeing similarities between reaction and counter-reaction we should be aware of de Certau's distinction between the strategies of the powerful and the tactics of the weak (see Morley, 1995).

There can of course be times when apparent media hysteria 'drowns out' any opposition to the orthodoxy, and the media literally circumscribe the limits of what it is possible to say in public. There is also a problem that many of the questions that journalists seek answers to are not answerable in the simple terms that are expected. Hence, there is every reason to question media representations about drugs, to ask what evidence the images presented are based upon and to challenge apparently dominant ideas. However, the simple replacement of these with equally one-dimensional views is not likely to achieve much beyond a sense of satisfaction that the 'control culture' has once again been exposed. Both reaction and counter-reaction need to be open to critical scrutiny. Ultimately, the problem with both is that they construct a terrain in which each reader and viewer is invited to position her/himself as for one side and against the other. Thus there are apparently only two absolutist positions to select from, fanaticism on one side, scepticism on the other. But as I have tried to argue, there is more than a bit of fanaticism and scepticism on both sides.

Notes

1. The last point is well demonstrated by Reinarman and Levine (1989). They show how drugs came to be seen as the number one social problem in the USA, particularly in the years where politicians standing for election tried to outbid each other in how 'tough' they were going to be on drug sellers and users (see also Chambliss, 1994).

2. Similarly, in a letter to *The Times* (27 January 1997: 23) Danny Kushlick argued that 'Ecstasy has a mortality rate of about 0.0002 per cent, whereas alcohol is about 0.5 per cent'.

3. Another aspect of mirroring has been observed in the rationale for changing the structure of law enforcement in relation to drug trafficking. The Broome report for the Association of Chief Police Officers (extracts from which are reproduced as the Appendix in Dorn *et al.*, 1992) successfully argued for enforcement to be organised on a three tier model on the basis that it should mirror the organisation of drug trafficking itself. For a critique see Dorn *et al.*, 1991.

4. The review appeared in the *International Journal on Drug Policy* in 1992.

5. In another context, the Standards Commission has referred to a culture of 'moral vagueness' in seeking to account for rule-breaking by Members of Parliament.

6. A significant change since the 1960s is that 'folk devils' and the pressure groups that represent them now produce their own newspapers and magazines, and provide spokespeople who are well versed in the ways that the media works (McRobbie 1994; McRobbie and Thornton 1995).

7. McRobbie and Thornton (1995) make a similar point by using the example of the Conservative government's ill-fated 'back to basics' campaign.

8. There is a third option in which senior police officers seek to redefine the issue as a social problem linked to or caused by structural features such as poverty, unemployment, etc.

9. In April 1996 comments by Mary Hartnoll, Glasgow's Director of Social Work, received widespread attention. In a memo, she wrote that 'The irony is that ecstasy, for example, is a relatively safe drug - risk of death has been calculated as one in 6.8 million - (the risk of dying from an ordinary dose of aspirin is very much greater) and young people tend to know this' ('Ecstasy is 'as safe as taking aspirin", *The Guardian*, 11 April 1996: 7). Sections of the media branded these comments as 'irresponsible' and Ms Hartnoll as 'a silly woman'. In one example of counter-reaction to this incident Sara Maitland made two points. One, the media quoted with approval the critical views of Leah Betts' father, while

dismissing the views of a highly-paid expert [i.e. Hartnoll]. Second, she asked, 'why do some subjects fall outside the realm of reasoned debate' (in *The Guardian*, 13 April 1996: 26). Variants of the same themes recurred at least twice. First, when a singer from the pop group East 17 said that ecstasy was a safe drug and that he had taken as many as 12 in one night (see 'Pop star trips up after singing praises of ecstasy', *The Guardian*, 17 January 1997: 1; and 'Rave on, Brian 'E' Harvey', *The Guardian*, 20 January 1997: 12). Secondly, when in the same month, Noel Gallagher of Oasis said that drug taking was as commonplace as drinking tea (for reaction see *The Guardian*, 31 January 1997 and 3 February 1997).

10. Becker (1963) saw moral enterprise as 'the creation of a new fragment of the moral constitution of society'.

11. My reservations about this are partly due to the fact that one of the most prolific proponents of drug legalisation, Dr Vernon Coleman, has written regularly for *The Sun*.

7 High Anxiety: Crack and Social Reaction

> We fear that unless *immediate* and effective action is taken Britain and Europe stand to inherit the American drug problem in less than five years. We see this as the most serious peacetime threat to our national well-being (Home Affairs Committee, 1985: iii).

If a criterion by which a moral panic can be recognised is a closure of the space between official discourse and sensational newspaper headlines, anyone seeking to argue that there has been a panic about drugs would have few problems. The past decade alone has seen alarms about ecstasy, crack cocaine, solvents and heroin. Both media coverage and official reports have utilised a narrative combining a hitherto unknown and unprecedented threat, with dreadful consequences if no action is taken. In 1985 members of the Home Affairs Committee aptly displayed their ability to feed, and simultaneously position themselves as calling for measures to quench, a panic about drugs, in seeing them as 'the most serious peacetime threat to our national well-being'. Lord Macaulay is reputed to have said that there is nothing so ridiculous as the British public undergoing one of its periodic bouts of morality, though he probably had not imagined the depths that could be plumbed by the media and politicians.[1]

In a period where there were claims that Colombian 'drug barons' were targeting Europe and Britain as new outlets for cocaine because the north American market was 'saturated' (Hargreaves, 1992; Silverman, 1994) widespread publicity about crack cocaine followed a speech by Robert Stutman, a DEA (Drug Enforcement Administration) special agent. He told a conference of the Association of Chief Police Officers (ACPO) in April 1989 that: 'We are so saturated with cocaine in the United States, there aren't enough noses left to use the cocaine that's coming in. It's got to go somewhere and where it's coming is right here' (Stutman, 1989: 7). His talk also included images of the effects of crack use, such as 'crack babies' being born to addicted women, and its causal role in parental violence towards children. He warned that crack was such a powerful drug that 75 per cent of people who tried it three times would become addicted to it. He also said that 'we have screwed up enough to write 10,000 books' and that, unless immediate action was taken, 'I will personally guarantee you that in two years from now, you will have a serious crack problem...three years from today...you will be looking back on the good old days of 1989, and that won't be pleasant' (Stutman, 1989: 8).

Stutman's claims and the research that he referred to were subjected to searching and sceptical review. For instance, Bean questions whether north America really was 'saturated' and says that Stutman's 'information was largely incorrect, his evidence uncorroborated, and his views simpleminded' (Bean, 1993: 62).[2] But ACPO members did not seem to be among the doubters (Dorn et al., 1991; Silverman, 1994), though they were hardly alone in that. Considered contemporaneous assessments (Shapiro, 1989; File on Four, 1990) were trampled in a headlong rush to relate the dangers of crack. In its 1989 report, the Home Affairs Committee repeated Stutman's figures without any qualifications. In words that could have come straight out of Stutman's speech, the Committee said:

> Crack is the most potent and toxic form of cocaine available and is five to ten times as addictive as cocaine. Indeed it can be almost instantly addictive. We were told that three doses of crack were sufficient to produce addiction. It can take over a person's life in a week (Home Affairs Committee, 1989: vii).

Other picturesque claims about crack included the then Home Secretary likening its potential effects to a 'medieval plague' across Europe. Media coverage combined such portents of dread with reports of what made crack so appealing and powerful: an 'intense high', 'better than sex'. In a piece headed 'Crack crazy' *The Sun* (25 May 1989) said that ruthless drug dealers were sending their best workers 'to peddle crack on Britain's inner-city estates'. More sensational coverage centred on the effects of crack use as *The Sun* added that '75% of crack users become hopelessly addicted from inhaling crack just three times'. Similarly, the *Daily Star* (16 June 1989) reported that 'Yardie drug fiend sat on a mum-to-be', in which 'an evil drug-crazed gang leader', is quoted as saying that 'I ate and slept crack....it became my God'. Lending further credence to the transformative powers of the drug we learn that: 'An ex-girlfriend described the former altar boy as being "like a gentleman on occasions but able to pass for the Devil himself when under the influence"'. And the *News of the World* (30 July 1989) ventured 'Inside the crack castles' to feature pictures of black men smoking crack with accounts of the drug's terrible effects, mirroring Stutman's claim that 'it is drug that produces violence....it gives you a feeling of omnipotence' (Stutman, 1989: 8-9). Just in case people were insufficiently attracted by such publicity, Clutterbuck related that 'pushers are now secreting quantities of crack in cannabis so that victims smoking cannabis become addicted to crack without realizing it' (Clutterbuck, 1990: 112).

The media and political over-reaction to crack, as well as the lurid language and images used, could be grounds for developing the idea that this was a moral panic (Reinarman and Levine, 1989; Bean, 1993; Reeves and Campbell, 1994). I have criticised such approaches in chapter 6. Here I want to begin by briefly mentioning three antecedents of Cohen's (1972) use of the term to characterise social reaction. First, Gusfield's (1963) 'symbolic crusade' described the alcohol temperance movement, which he regarded as a struggle for hegemony by the protestant middle class in nineteenth century America. Secondly, Becker (1963) characterised moral entrepreneurs as either rule creators and/or rule enforcers who campaigned for controls on drugs and alcohol. He used the term 'moral enterprise' to characterise 'the creation of a new fragment of the moral constitution of society'. Thirdly, in its most functionalist formulation, social reaction was seen as an inevitable and recurring feature of a society's need to reaffirm or redefine its moral boundaries (Erikson, 1966). All of these ideas could be applied to the social reaction to crack. However in doing so, albeit to a limited extent, I want to draw attention to discontinuities and inconsistencies in social reaction. The uneven character of social reaction is, it seems to me, glossed over in the use of the term moral panic as a shorthand way of dismissing reaction to a particular issue as 'merely' a panic. Criticising uses of the term moral panic is not the same thing as denying that there are far-reaching consequences which result from social reaction.

Symbolic crusade

Dorn et al. (1992) argue that in the 1980s the category of the drug *trafficker* came to replace the drug dealer, or pusher, of earlier decades. While users were 'sad', traffickers were 'bad' and 'evil'. In the 1980s the Prime Minster Mrs Thatcher issued a warning to criminals and drug traffickers: 'we will get you'. One reason behind this punitive turn may have been President Reagan's new 'war on drugs' in the US. Another could be Mrs Thatcher's search for new enemies to mobilise popular consent against, after having vanquished the 'enemy without' in the Falklands war and the 'enemy within' in the miners strike. Hence declaring war on drug traffickers could be seen as a symbolic crusade, identifying and targeting a new 'enemy'. In the late 1980s, the emphasis on demand reduction and user accountability (Inciardi, 1991) could be seen as part of a conservative backlash against deviant lifestyles and an attempt to restate 'traditional' moral boundaries.[3]

Legislatively, two main illustrations of this reaction appeared. First, penalties for drugs offences were revised upwards in the Controlled Drugs

(Penalties) Act, 1985, with the maximum term for trafficking of Class A drugs raised to life imprisonment. Secondly, the Drug Trafficking Offences Act, 1986 permitted the investigation of the financial affairs of convicted drug traffickers and the seizure of their assets (which could be more than just the 'profits of crime' - see Dorn et al., 1992). Passed with all-party support and little detailed consideration, the Act heralded a far-reaching change to British law, enabling the courts to freeze the assets of suspects before any charges had been made, and reversing the burden of proof by placing the onus on a convicted person to prove that assets were not illegally obtained (Dorn and South, 1991). The extensive powers of the Act have been described as 'draconian' and it represents one of the clearest examples of the way in which drug trafficking has been the key force driving legislation and enforcement responses (Dorn et al., 1991, 1992). As Goodsir records, 'the apparent emergency presented by drug trafficking, and particularly fear of cocaine trafficking, has enabled politicians to introduce quite intrusive measures ....with relatively little debate or opposition' (Goodsir, 1993: 131).

As the 'law and order state' developed, civil liberties declined both here - for example, the requirement on banks to disclose financial details has been regarded as the 'death of customer confidentiality' - and in the US. Under Presidents Reagan and Bush there appears to have been a particularly febrile 'zero tolerance' atmosphere in which the drugs 'war' has been used to justify 'drug exceptions' to the Bill of Rights, vastly increase spending on enforcement, extend penalties and drug testing, and fill up prisons with drug convicts, impacting disproportionately on black males (Wisotsky, 1986; Szasz, 1992; Currie, 1993; Tonry, 1994; Chambliss, 1994; Miller, 1996). The apparently popular mood was amusingly lampooned in Tim Robbins' 1992 film of a singer turned politician, *Bob Roberts*. At one point Bob sings a duet which includes the lines:

> Drugs stink, they make me sick,
> those who sell 'em and those who use 'em.
> String them up, from the highest tree,
> without a trace of sympathy.
> Be a clean living man with a rope in your hand,
> hang them high for a clean living land.

Unfortunately, in drugs as in many other fields, reality was already surpassing the reach of satire. During this time some of the most colourful utterances came from US 'drugs czar' William Bennett, the head of the Office of National Drug Control Policy under Bush. According to Bennett the beheading of convicted drug dealers or tearing them limb from limb would be 'morally plausible' punishment (in *The Independent*, 17 June 1989). He also said that drug traffickers must suffer the consequences of their actions.[4]

> Consequences come in many forms. In terms of law enforcement, they include penalties such as seizure of assets, stiffer prison sentences, revocation of bail rights, and the death penalty for drug kingpins (Bennett, 1989: 4).

Developments in criminal law accompanied by such statements seem to typify the over-reaction to drugs. It suggests that exceptional measures taken against the threat of drugs can be combined with the interests of particular individuals and groups (Goode and Ben-Yehuda, 1994). However, one problem with seeing all of this simply as a conservative backlash is that it ignores the extent of fissures within the new right. The latter includes both conservatives who want to 'get tough' on crime and drugs, and libertarians who favour legalisation and oppose the over-reach of the state, as well as 'new realists' who argue for focused 'what works' measures, not just a crackdown.

Crack and moral enterprise

Much has been written about the police as moral entrepreneurs, responsible for re-working and generally extending definitions of criminal deviancy and, through their relationship with the mass media, their role in the popularisation of particular images of crime. To a limited extent the police reaction to definitions of 1980s drug problems, and particularly to crack, can be thought of in a similar way.[5] For instance, Reeves and Campbell (1994) have depicted Stutman as a moral entrepreneur who 'exemplified the enterprising drug crusaders who profit personally and professionally from media exposure' (cited in *Druglink*, November/December 1994: 5). A few months after Stutman's speech ACPO decided that crack posed a sufficiently serious threat to warrant a two day special seminar in August 1989. A resulting press release from ACPO called for a meeting with the Home Secretary to 'prevent the escalation of the lethal drug'. As an illustration of the vacuousness of rhetoric and reaction this has few equals. Exactly why ACPO felt this urgent need to alert the then Home Secretary Douglas Hurd, is somewhat unclear since he had already likened the threat of crack to a medieval plague and in calling it a 'spectre hanging over Europe', urged greater coordination between EU countries, at a time when there had been quite unparalleled levels of anxiety over cocaine trafficking and crack (Home Affairs Committee, 1985, 1989; *Police Review*, 4 August 1989).[6]

There is however another way of making sense of ACPO's response, which would suggest that crack cannot be seen as a slow motion replay of the 'mugging' crisis of the 1970s. In that case the police had played a major role in setting the agenda (Hall *et al.*, 1978). But in the summer of 1989, as some politicians and the media made the running about crack, the police found themselves confronted by expectations that they should play a starring role in an anti-drugs war that was not of their making, and the definition of which had spun from their grasp. The process of 'talking up' the problem, and anticipating its imminent transmutation into yet more terrifying forms, had advanced to include fears of instant addiction, inner-city gang wars and sexual abandon. Hence the police, far from feeling in command of the debate as in the 1970s, often found themselves caught in the awkward position of being required to respond to a problem which the press and politicians said did exist, but which had yet to appear in any substance. ACPO's call for action by the Home Secretary contains a wish to be seen as resolute and active, while seeking to avoid expectations that they could produce the answers too, a version of what Becker (1963) regarded as the 'double problem' of enforcement. Police clamour for more resources and powers is not an unfamiliar response. However, for some other officers drugs had spun so far out of enforcement control that the only response is to 'give up' and campaign for legalisation.

Searching for crack in the wake of Stutman's speech included a few high profile 'crack raids'. One on a public house on the Heath Town estate in Wolverhampton in May 1989 yielded a few small rocks of crack (*Police Review*, 26 May 1989 and 2 June 1989). Interviewed a couple of months later, the head of a local drugs advice agency said that: 'They [the police] say they were called in because it [crack] was there; all those resources and all those men, they'd have looked a right bunch of wallies if they'd found nothing'. But, subsequently, none of the 25 people charged were linked to crack, as the police said that the crack that was found was on the floor, not in someone's possession. A local Community Relations Council spokesman said that, 'We don't believe there was any crack' (in *The Voice*, 31 October 1989: 1). The experience of the local drug agency was that:

> There's a fair number [of clients] who will use everything and anything that comes their way....[but we] haven't seen a single client with crack, some wouldn't even know what it was. We know that some of our white users use Heath Town to score some draw; if there was crack around I think we'd have heard from them.

Nonetheless, hailed by an expectant press with large photographs of small quantities, such raids further escalated the pressure for the police to 'do something' about crack. The spectacular representation of a crack/crime control problem completely out of control did mark a break with mugging in the 1970s, when the police portrayed themselves as having problems but, conveniently, none that more resources and more public support could not resolve. Under pressure to 'nip in the bud' crack before drug sellers had seemingly even got around to providing it, police actions attracted undue attention. Finds of small amounts then increased rather than reduced demands that the police should seek out more of the same.[7] Thus ACPO's call can be seen as an attempt to appear in control, but its high profile seminar and press release may have added to the very excitability and pressure for action that the police wanted to avoid.

One feature of the reaction to crack was a disaster mentality of a problem just waiting to happen and the search for solutions. The crack threat necessitated visits to the US by the Home Secretary, members of the Home Affairs Committee and various police officers and journalists to see the problem at first hand. How this slice of life was meant to inform policy here was not clear but they returned uttering ghastly warnings (Home Affairs Committee, 1989). After his own observations in the US, the Lord Mayor of the City of London arranged for the City to fund a special conference on crack at the Barbican in 1990. Stutman appeared as a keynote speaker and his renown can be gauged by his opening remark when he acknowledged that, to some of the audience, he must appear to be the anti-Christ. He reiterated the earlier warnings, though the time frame had shifted and he was no longer forecasting a 'serious crack problem' within three years. Later, representatives from Boston appeared as the 'city that won' the battle against crack. In practice this was attributed to a proactive job creation scheme and other diversionary activities for young people during the summer (cf Dorn and Murji, 1992a on prevention programmes). Thus, these two contributions exemplified a recurrent theme in British life, in which the USA is cast as both dystopia and utopia, a source of all problems, as well as solutions. In a microcosm the conference summed up the disaster mentality surrounding crack, though disappointingly for the organisers, the audience of drugs workers and researchers were un-moved. Most of them argued that the focus on crack was too narrow and called for a broad strategy on all drugs.

Policing crack

To further chart unevenness in social reaction I now turn to look at the police response to crack from the late 1980s. One effect of Stutman's speech was to send some chief constables 'running around like headless chickens', as one sceptical police officer said to me. Chief constables apparently started asking what their drug squads were doing about crack. As a consequence, the same officer reported that his force, which had never had a single seizure of cocaine, now had a team looking for crack.

In 1988 the Metropolitan Police set up Operation Lucy to gather intelligence about organised black crime in Britain.[8] During that year the number of officers employed to track around 200 Jamaican suspects was nearly doubled (see also Platt, 1988). From around the same time an undated report from the National Drugs Intelligence Unit (NDIU)[9] refers to yardies as part of a 'rapidly growing problem' of black organised crime. But Detective Chief Superintendent Ramm, the head of Operation Lucy, reported that there was not a 'black mafia' but a 'complex matrix of much flatter pyramids than a traditional Mafia organisation' (quoted in Campbell, 1990: 6; see also Metropolitan Police, 1989).[10] Similarly Keith (1993; see also Pearson, et al., 1993; Small, 1995) observed that some officers were trying to play down the idea of a 'black mafia'. Operation Lucy was scaled down, possibly because it had indicated that yardies were not as much of a threat as had been thought.[11] In spite of what is claimed to be an 'impressive strike record [which] through hi-tech surveillance and the use of informants...managed to arrest several hundred suspects' (Small, 1995: 394; see also Davison, 1997) it was merged into the Metropolitan Police Crack Intelligence Coordinating Unit (CICU) which, under the name Operation Dalehouse, gathered all information about crack and targeted drug-related violence. That was wound up at the end of 1992 (see *Druglink*, January/February 1993). Again, we are told that 'Dalehouse was nothing if not successful...[it was] a model of its kind' and that it was disbanded because it was 'a victim of its own success' (Small, 1995: 427). Davison (1997: 146) says that Dalehouse did achieve results in terms of arrests and seizure of guns and drugs, but its 'conviction rate was disappointing...because of continuing problems of witness intimidation'. At that time there undoubtedly were officers disgruntled with the decision to end Operation Dalehouse and some signs of this were visible in the press at the time. One manifestation of the internal struggle within the police followed the shooting of a beat/patrol officer in south London in October 1993, which was widely reported as linked to yardies and/or a crack or drugs deal that he had interrupted, though both links have since been questioned (see Small, 1995). This incident led some officers to complain that the Metropolitan Police had closed its crack intelligence unit too soon. Alternatively, other officers said that anti-drugs operations had actually increased, even if the specialist response to crack had been scaled down, though in practice what seems to have occurred is not a closure of police operations but, rather, a move from a central squad to more local campaigns (see Small, 1995). The latter group of officers argued that levels of drug-related violence were low, especially compared to the US (see *The Guardian*, 23 October 1993). Nevertheless, they maintained that crack and/or yardies should be targeted because, even if neither had yet reached the scale that some had predicted, there was clear evidence of a nascent threat for either or both to become so.

For Davison however, the operations were closed down because senior police managers underestimated the potential for yardies to develop into a more organised network, played down the occasional shootings that occurred, and perhaps most importantly, were under pressure from black politicians who felt that the police operation was racist in conception and action. This version of events suggests that it was Stutman's speech to ACPO in April 1989 that re-awakened police interest and led to the formation of a specialist squad. The most insidious point is that the operation was scaled-down or closed because senior police officers were under pressure from black MPs and concerned about allegations of racism. Small (1995) says that the operation was deemed to be inappropriate, but the extent to which this was due to 'the politically sensitive nature' of the operation is not clear. Davison is less circumspect and, like Clutterbuck (1995), clearly believes that politicians successfully pressed senior officers into delimiting the operation because of its racial character. For instance, he cites Diane Abbott MP saying to *The Voice* in September 1988 that: 'I am very concerned about the way the whole Yardie myth is being promoted by the Metropolitan Police and the way the press is colluding with it. The black community both here and in Jamaica is concerned that this is going to damage community relations' (quoted in Davison, 1997: 46). Yet in Parliament the same politician said that:

> We have had much sensational coverage in the newspapers during the past couple of years of yardies, the so-called black mafia who control the drug trade in Britain. There is no doubt that there are people of Jamaican origin who are involved, just as there are people of all other communities who are involved in the trade. I speak on behalf of the whole Jamaican community here and abroad when I say that we resent strongly the sensationalist and exaggerated reports which imply that there is a Jamaican mafia which provided the key actors in the drug trade. That is a slur on millions of law-abiding Jamaicans here and abroad. Most are law abiding and want to be involved in the fight against drugs. We resent the smears against our community. In the debate on drug misuse, there is often a suggestion or inference that the problem is to do with race and involves black communities. Crack knows no colour. It and other drugs are equal opportunities scourges. They hit high and low, regardless of colour, gender or class. My community wants an effective war on drugs (in *Hansard*, 8 December 1989, col. 640).

This lengthy extract is significant because it indicates the double-edged and contradictory nature of social reaction. Speaking on behalf of the community, Abbott complains of 'sensationalist and exaggerated reports' but she also calls for 'an effective war on drugs'.

Evidence of things not seen

> In every headline you could replace 'crack' with 'nigger' and it would mean exactly the same thing (Remark by Metropolitan Police drugs squad officer, 1990).

The inconsistency in rhetoric is exemplified in another theme of Abbott's speech. One notable and recurring feature of discourses on crack is the reference to an 'equal opportunities scourge'. The origins of this attribute comes directly from Stutman's (1989) speech in which he referred to crack as an 'equal opportunity drug', apparently hitting high and low identically. But no matter how often the term was repeated and however much lip service was paid to it, it is clear that crack was regarded as anything but an equitable drug. Rather the invocation of the phrase 'equal opportunity drug' seems to act as a release mechanism that enables the speaker to simultaneously deny and reaffirm the essentially racial character of crack supply and use. For one observer, 'whereas most of the heroin users in British prisons were white, the vast majority of those for whom cocaine or crack was the primary drug of dependence were black. Although use of crack and cocaine may not be any higher than in other communities, there are growing fears that, as in America, the drug is beginning to have a disproportionate impact upon black communities'. (McDermott, 1992: 21). The examples from the popular press of the late 1980s mentioned earlier were obsessed with yardies as the chief suppliers of crack, as well as its use by them and the terrible effects that were said to result. The following exchange in Parliament is in the same vein.

> Mr. Mellor: Sad evidence is emerging that members of the Afro-Caribbean community, who have not previously been involved with hard drugs, are now becoming involved with cocaine.
> Mr. Vaz: The Minister referred to the Afro-Caribbean community and the use of crack. The evidence that members of the [Home Affairs] Select Committee.....when they visited America was that crack knew no boundaries of race and gender. Does he agree with me on that?
> Mr. Mellor: Oh yes. I hope that is not the impression that I gave. I was paying a compliment to the Afro-Caribbean community by saying that it previously had not been much involved with hard drugs....cocaine knows no racial boundaries, and it is sad that it seems to me to have started to affect the Afro-Caribbean community as well as the rest of us. I am not saying that it is a particular problem in that community because it is certainly not (in *Hansard*, Drugs Misuse debate, 8 December 1989, col. 597).

Another example also reaffirms the general point, when Clutterbuck warns that, 'throughout Western Europe, addiction is fast creating a new underclass, drawing social security and financing their addiction by crime or, more often, by recruiting new addicts. This underclass contains a disproportionate number of immigrants, whose unrewarding lives make them prey to the drug pushers' (Clutterbuck, 1990: 184).

Probably the most distinctive feature of the reaction to crack is the yoking of race and drugs, especially when the link is simultaneously made and repudiated. Such linkages were not confined to politicians, police officers and commentators, but also came from perhaps unexpected sources. One particularly active player, who could be labelled a moral entrepreneur, was Viv Reid, the coordinator of the Newham Drugs Advice Project (NDAP) in east London. In the early 1990s *The Voice*, the main black newspaper in Britain, ran a high profile campaign to warn of the crack threat. Small claims that it 'produced a welter of drugs workers, black community leaders and police officers, all of whom strongly asserted that crack was making serious inroads into the black communities' (Small, 1995: 398). This over-states the case and glosses over the fact that Reid felt that he had to risk some of the opprobrium that he encountered in encouraging *The Voice* to go public on the dangers that crack posed to the black community. But having stepped out into public, the scene was set for much more of the same. Thus in Hargreaves' book, Reid says about the crack epidemic that Stutman warned of that, 'the baby needs time to grow. But in some areas, like parts of south and west London, the epidemic is already here' (quoted in Hargreaves, 1992: 13).[12] In the same year, an article in *The Guardian* relates that,

> Viv Reid of the Newham Drugs Project, is one of the few drug workers in the UK with a sizable caseload of crack users. He says black communities are being unfairly labelled over this issue and that crack and cocaine are creating serious problems in all communities - though other agencies take a different view of the relative importance of crack. According to Reid, none of London's existing drugs agencies sees significant numbers of people whose primary problem is crack or cocaine (McDermott, 1992: 21).

In Small's (1995) book, Reid says that 'the situation is deteriorating rapidly' and that drug workers were 'starting to see the effects' of crack taking a hold in Britain (quoted in Small, 1995: 398). Thus social reaction is being led and problems defined by hitherto unusual sources. And while crack may not have lived up to Stutman's or the Home Affairs Committee's (1989) prophecies, a recurring theme is that it is just about to happen, according to Hargreaves (1992), Small (1995) and Davison (1997).

Mean streets

The focus on the yardies as a 'black mafia' is one of the key features of the racialisation of crack, making the 'black drug trafficker' the latest in a gallery of racialised characters linking race to disorderliness, mugging and vice (Hall et al., 1978; Gilroy 1987a; Solomos, 1988; Keith, 1993). I examine the construction of the yardies in chapter 8. Here I want to discuss another aspect of racialisation, the dramatisation of particular locales as a 'dreadful zone' or contaminated space (cf Goldberg, 1993; Keith and Cross, 1993). The association of specific areas, such as Notting Hill and Brixton in London, and Moss Side in Manchester with race and drugs - for example through the shorthand term 'front lines' - has been common place.[13] In the sense that certain place names can be made to stand in for a range of meanings (of which drugs are only a part) processes of symbolisation have occurred, which are furthered by the classification of some places as 'symbolic locations', especially when these places are then the focus for high profile raids (Keith, 1993; Dorn et al., 1992; Silverman, 1993, 1994; on racial aspects of drug crackdowns in the US, see Davis, 1990; Zatz, 1987). The impact that the unenviable label 'Crack City', applied to an estate in south London, after a raid by over 120 officers in February 1990, on those who routinely live there can only be guessed at (Mirza et al., 1991; Pearson et al., 1993; Silverman, 1994).

These representations are deeply problematic not just because they generate invidious images which may impact on the life chances of people who live in them. A further problem is that the depiction of Moss Side as an area where drugs are commonly available and 'turf wars' are fought out, suppresses most or any of the local histories which structure particular conflicts. Moss Side is only one among a number of locations that has come to bear the burden of representation as a dangerous place where drugs, race, guns and violence are said to co-exist in an unstable mix (Taylor et al., 1996; Fraser, 1996). It has been described as England's 'Bronx' by Silverman (cf The Guardian, 13 January 1996) who, in furthering the theme of a place/a race apart, adds that it 'stands on its own [as] the only place where drug dealing has followed the American model' (Silverman, 1994: 232). Paddy Ashdown, the leader of the Liberal Democratic party has observed that: 'I used to find the arguments about the legalisation of cannabis quite powerful until I went to see Moss Side. Now, I'd been a soldier on the streets of Belfast, but I'd never been so frightened in all my life' (interviewed in The Big Issue, 3-9 February 1997: 13). The shooting in January 1992 of a 14-year-old boy Benji Stanley, apparently caught up in a case of mistaken identity focused widespread media and public attention on Moss Side as the arena where violent 'turf wars' between gangs were being played out. Enhancing the image of territorial conflict - and, in consequence, an explicit comparison with the street gangs of south-central Los Angeles - the 'Goochies and the 'Doddies' were said to take their name from streets on a local housing estate (*The Guardian*, 24 December 1993 and 14 January 1994; Taylor *et al.*, 1996) Because of this, by the early 1990s a picture of Moss Side as a criminal area had become powerfully established as a place where 'drug gangs fight for power' (*The Independent*, 18 April 1991: 5) or 'gun gangs rule the rat-runs' (*The Times*, 29 June 1993: 7). The apparently unique dangerousness of Moss Side, and the fear that its problems or 'disease' might infect the rest of the city is summed up in the view that it was seen as:

> inescapably exerting its irresistible criminal influence on what local common sense wants to see as a relatively non-criminal city. The presence of Moss Side was symbolic in a very contemporary sense; that is, in symbolising the presence not just of a racial Other....but also of a specific kind of violent criminality, signified in particular by discussion of the 'Yardie', implicitly linked into the 'international drugs and firearms trade' (Taylor *et al.*, 1996: 206).[14]

Thus Thompson can glibly state that 'In some areas, notably Manchester's Moss Side, the Yardie-led gun culture has spread through an entire generation' (Thompson, 1995: 59).

Moss Side seems to typify Lash and Urry's (1994) idea of the 'wild zone' as an arena defined by disorder and danger (see also Stanley, 1996). Race and place become intertwined as features that demarcate the boundaries of civility, distinguishing the respectable from the disreputable. The 'stain' of infamy became even more apparent when it was reported that the author Joanna Trollope retracted a 'slur' on the Gloucestershire village of Aston Magna after complaints about her comparison of it to Moss Side. Unsurprisingly, race can be read as a key element because she saw the village as having 'a population.... significantly immigrant. It's a place where all the goings-on you are accustomed to associate with a place like Moss Side are common place' (in *The Guardian*, 20 January 1996: 2). It hardly needs to be added that there was no apology to the residents of Moss Side (Murji, 1998).

In drawing attention to unevenness and discontinuities within social reaction I have sought to suggest that such aspects are underplayed in the use of descriptions such as moral panic and symbolic crusade. Before expanding on that, continuities and closure in social reaction should be noted. One of these is the theme of the crack epidemic that is just round the corner, as we saw particularly in the comments attributed to Reid over several years. That account has been challenged (Shapiro, 1994) but there seems to be less openness and debate around 'dangerous places' such as Moss Side, and yardies, who, as I argue in chapter 8, seem to be explained in remarkably similar ways. To return to the discontinuities, it can be noted that it is possible to see the police as both promoting the idea of yardies as a black mafia and seeking to play it down. Black politicians have simultaneously complained about stereotypes and called for a war on drugs in the name of the black community. Drugs researchers and agencies have both criticised the pre-occupation with crack (or any other drug on its own) while some have discovered crack and perhaps used that as the basis for their continued funding (cf *Druglink*, January/February 1993). Hence I think that we have moved some way from the view of Stutman as a self-serving moral entrepreneur (Reeves and Campbell, 1994) and of a moral panic driven by the interests of the government and the police (to the extent that it fitted with campaigns for a national intelligence and detective agency, and for some officers, greater or even routine arming of the police - Dorn *et al.*, 1991; 1992; Small, 1995). Perhaps, in an entrepreneurial age, it makes more sense to see moral entrepreneurs as coming from all directions, probably with all sort of motives. Thus, as the police officially scaled down the search for crack, it was instead being discovered by drugs agencies:

> there are growing signs that Stutman's predictions are beginning to prove correct. In March this year, Customs arrested several Liverpool men in connection with the import of 900 kilos of cocaine, the largest British seizure of the drug to date. Outreach workers across the region report that the drug is increasingly available, street prices having dropped to £40 a gram, from a peak of £80-100 in the early eighties, lending support to claims that the Colombian cartels, having saturated the US market, have begun to target Europe. Not surprisingly, there are also indications of a concomitant increase in cocaine and crack-related problems (McDermott, 1992: 21).

On the basis of a detailed history of policy responses to AIDS, Berridge (1996) is able to chart and date three periods or stages of reaction: First, AIDS as an unexpected 'shock of the new', which officials and politicians were not sure how to react to. Secondly, the 'wartime emergency response' to AIDS as a national crisis. And thirdly, a process of normalisation and professionalisation, as the key groups developed a more coherent response. Bean (1993) delineates three phases of reaction to crack. The first from mid-1987 to mid-1989 was when the scare (or panic) about crack was created.[15] The second phase lasted about 12 months, during which scepticism about earlier claims, and doubts about a crack epidemic, surfaced. Finally in the third phase, media interest subsided and there was an impression that the problem of crack no longer existed. This may be accurate, though my account suggests that responses to crack have been more uneven and may evade classification into neat temporal categories. In applying Berridge's phases to crack it is arguable that stages one and two overlapped, and that stage three never quite happened as drugs agencies competed to discover the spread of crack. It is also arguable that the lack of a separation between crack as the shock of the new and the national emergency response may be due to the perhaps accidental way in which Stutman's talk came to be regarded as so significant. We have seen that members of ACPO appeared to be unprepared for its nature and content. Bean (1993: 62) states that Stutman's style was 'meat and drink to the British media, as most surely it was intended to be'. But it is worth recording that the public impact of Stutman's speech was not instantaneous. There was a period of at least a few weeks in which there were rumours about his talk to ACPO in April 1989, as a tape recording of it was circulated and 'transcripts of the tape circulated like wildfire round police forces and to Westminster' (Clutterbuck, 1995: 73). Media coverage took off in May 1989 and this time lag is rarely accounted for in reports of the social reaction to crack.

Problematisations

I want to suggest that instead of seeing social reaction in terms of moral panics and symbolic crusades, it may be preferable to use the looser term problematisations. Foucault used the term 'moral problematisations' to refer to 'not behaviours or ideas, nor societies and their ideologies' but the relationship between thoughts and practices.[16] Revisiting some of the themes of this chapter, my argument is that it is sufficient to problematise social reaction, perhaps by treating it as a form of social censure (Sumner and Sandberg, 1990), without making any prior judgement about whose interests it serves, and whether it is accurate, proportionate and rational, or not.

First, media coverage of drugs could be seen as fuelling scares, misinformation, stereotypes, invidious generalisations, and so on. But it is not necessary to assert that the media plays a determinate role in creating, shaping or furthering particular images. Nor for that matter, is it necessary to argue that the media creates 'moral communities' through its coverage of particular issues (cf Tester, 1994). A weaker suggestion is that the media may at least contribute to some of the problems that it describes, and that it 'excites' while it appears to forbid. This may sometimes maximise rather than minimise harm. A possible problem could be that media coverage increases interest in drugs through 'advertising'. Media coverage of particular drugs may actually increase demand for them, just as it has been found that some information based prevention campaigns can actually make young people more interested in drugs (Dorn and Murji, 1992a). Indeed media workers are hardly unaware of their double-edged role in simultaneously censoring while aiding the 'manufacture of desire' for consumption. Following the death of Leah Betts, one media complaint was that dealers were 'cashing in' on the increased interest in ecstasy that was itself enhanced by media reporting. Media scares about particular drugs can therefore be seen as a form of 'positive-negative' advertising and as assisting the creation of particular market 'niches'. To take another example, the widespread publicity about crack may have encouraged dealers to manufacture it and users to seek it out. As Dorn has pointed out, during the late 1980s and early 1990s, any dealer with a microwave was virtually given the recipe to make cocaine into crack.[17]

> the publicity [about crack] sparks in every bored and impressionable drug user the idea of using and dealing in these stimulating commodities. Dealers are told that they can make a fortune, and that crack is the world's greatest hit. More people seek out cocaine, pop it in the microwave with a few easily obtained chemicals, and hey presto, there is an enlarged pool for the police to fish in.

Much media coverage often uncritically replayed the words of Stutman without all that much judgement or consideration. Claims about the powerful addictive qualities of crack ('ten times stronger than heroin', 'three hits and you're hooked') were reported in ways that seemingly led any number of people, anecdotally at least, to believe that such claims were credible. For Campbell, much information on crime 'is one-dimensional, portrayed in black and white, learned from the screen or the headline and with little relationship to reality. A classic example is the scare over crack....dire warnings were issued by politicians, press and some police officers of an impending epidemic.... In reality crack turned out to be a small problem, compared with heroin or amphetamines' (Campbell, 1991: 11; cf Shapiro, 1994).

Secondly, the ways in which particular substances are depicted may have an influence on images of drugs. For instance, young people who took heroin by 'chasing the dragon' in the 1980s apparently saw themselves as quite different from the 'dirty' heroin users who injected the drug (Pearson, 1987). Similarly, it has been reported that young people involved in 'rave culture' have seen themselves as distinct from the apparently detestable hippies who also made use of psychedelic drugs. It is clearer in the latter example that users are unlikely to have direct experience of the groups they see themselves as different to, which is the gap in which media and other representations may have a part to play. Characterisations and demonisation of particular drugs, especially heroin, has been strong enough for even those who support some form of legalisation or decriminalisation of cannabis to draw the line at heroin (Dorn, 1980).

I have emphasised the racialising character of diverse reactions to crack, particularly in the shape of the yardies. Hall *et al.* (1978) showed how the word 'mugger' in the 1970s connoted a young black male. The continuing resonance of this word was clear in the furore in 1995 following a letter from the Commissioner of the Metropolitan Police in which he said that most muggings were committed by young black males. For drugs there is an established literature which shows the ways in which they have been associated with various minority groups. Indeed at various times, especially in the US, it is this very linkage which has driven the movement for control (including alcohol: see Gusfield, 1963; Woodiwiss, 1988; Goode and Ben-Yehuda, 1994). Like alcohol the dangers of, and need for controls on, illegal drugs have been associated with racial minorities, fears of sexual mixing, vice and violence. For example, in 1870s California a ban on opium smoking was tied in with a campaign against Chinese opium smoking, including some claims that 'yellow fiends' were using it to drug white women into slavery. Anti-alcohol prohibitions were sometimes based on the idea that controls were necessary to protect white women from black men. Cocaine was said to induce black men to rape white women. The 'cocaine-crazed negro' was though to acquire extra strength, which apparently led some Southern US police forces to change from .32 to .38 calibre bullets. And at the time of the 1937 Marihuana Tax Act the 'killer weed' was said to make Mexicans especially violent (Becker, 1963; Duster, 1970; Musto, 1973; Helmer, 1975; Goode, 1989; Reinarman and Levine, 1989). Britain too shares a history of associating particular drugs, especially opium, with the 'foreign', the 'exotic' and 'the other' (Kohn, 1987, 1992). The Chinese 'opium dens' of the East End were linked to concerns about sexual morality and calls for control in the nineteenth century. The focus on a small community had more than a hint of double standards, as Pearson indicates: 'the fear of 'stimulant' opium use by the working classes in nineteenth century England [occurred] at a time when middle class opium use for 'medicinal' purposes was openly condoned' (Pearson, 1990: 144; see also Bean, 1974; Berridge and Edwards, 1981; Berridge, 1984; Kohn, 1992, 1993). Hence, as Musto has concluded:

> The most passionate support for legal prohibition of narcotics has been associated with fear of a given drug's effect on a specific minority. Certain drugs were dreaded because they seemed to undermine essential social restrictions which kept these groups under control. Cocaine was supposed to enable blacks to withstand bullets which would kill normal persons and to stimulate sexual assault. Fear that smoking opium facilitated sexual contact between Chinese and white Americans was also a factor in its total prohibition. Chicanos in the South-west were believed to be incited to violence by smoking marijuana. Heroin was linked in the 1920s with a turbulent age-group: adolescents in reckless and promiscuous urban gangs. Alcohol was associated with immigrants crowding into large and corrupt cities. In each instance, use of a particular drug was attributed to an identifiable and threatening minority group (Musto, 1973: 244-45).

What is significant is the ways in which such links are recreated in different historical and social contexts. Thus, calls for greater co-operation and integration in European Union law enforcement often base themselves on the need to fight the threat of drugs, terrorism and illegal immigration (Clutterbuck, 1990). Britain's reluctance to abolish internal barriers to movement has frequently been based on this linkage.

Drugs have had other racial associations too, for example linkage between cannabis and black communities has existed since at least the 1950s, which seems to have made black males 'unusually eligible' (Miller, 1996) for the diagnosis of cannabis psychosis (Ranger, 1989). Drugs have also played some role in the conflict between the police and black communities in a number of ways during the 1980s: There have been reports of the over-policing of cannabis; the establishment of so-called 'front line areas' where drugs are said to be openly available, but which are apparently 'no go' areas for the police; and the contention of the chief constable of the West Midlands Police that the 1985 Handsworth riot was promoted by drug dealers either to provide a 'cover' for their activities or because they had 'incited' others against the police who were responding to local calls for a crackdown on drug dealers.[18] All of this is meant to suggest that the connection between crack and Jamaican yardies does not occur in a vacuum. It is not necessary to imply that history plays some sort of determining role by which all that follows has to be judged; merely that the words, images and style of coverage of crack cocaine is problematic, especially when it seems to be easy to write about particular groups in ways that, rightly, would seem bizarre if applied to majority or 'mainstream' communities.

Finally, I have also questioned the claims of some people working with drug users or young people. Part of my objection to the term moral panic is the fact that the reaction to many topics, including racial attacks as Waddington (1986) shows, could also be classified as a panic. I have also expressed reservations about the use of the terms symbolic crusade and moral entrepreneur. But if we are to use the latter then there is no reason why it could or should not be applied equally to people working with drug users, or who proclaim their sympathy with the 'victims'. The words of any individual(s) who has a stake in the subject matter (which is probably all of us) ought to be treated with some scepticism, at the very least, rather than privileged because of their location or some other characteristic.[19] For example, in the early 1990s a number of drugs agencies publicly discovered crack users and attracted attention for precisely that reason. And in a context where competition for funding and resources is intense, publicity may well be useful, as *Druglink* the leading magazine on drugs issues in Britain commented:

> The issue of crack use itself is high profile, and particularly so when mixed with race and violence. Careers can be made from media-friendly pronouncements and from claiming expertise in this area that are simply not to be had from more

mundane day to day drugs work. Crack supplies the 'fast track' to publicity that solvents and heroin failed to provide. Resources too are on the line and funders faced with the threat of streets ricocheting with bullets of well-heeled crack dealers may be prepared to prioritise services that promise to respond to this threat (*Druglink*, January/February 1993: 5).[20]

Notes

1. It is a form that lends itself to parody, as Pearson (1983) has most notably demonstrated. He takes seemingly contemporary headlines only to reveal that actually they came from twenty or more years ago, and shows that this is a recurring cycle.

2. See Kohn (1987) for an earlier discussion of the market saturation thesis, at that time applied to heroin.

3. However in these terms, as well as in its form and extent, the reaction to HIV/AIDS fits the idea of a symbolic crusade more closely (Watney, 1987; Berridge, 1996).

4. Though the strategy also focused on drug buyers and the 'casual user' (see Dorn and Murji, 1992a, b).

5. The article 'Drugs: Why black people suspect the police' in *Searchlight*, no. 184 (October 1990) combines elements of both symbolic crusade and moral enterprise by the police in its report of the reaction to crack.

6. In 1990 London hosted the World Ministerial Summit to Reduce Demand for Cocaine and other drugs, convened by the Prime Minister. The event marked the salience of cocaine, as well as the emphasis on demand reduction and the increasing prominence of drugs as the focus for international coordination.

7. For instance see, 'Between a rock and a hard place' in *The Guardian*, 22 May 1993. See also, 'The street where I live', *The Independent*, 2 November 1993.

8. Small (1995) reports some agitation by lower ranking officers for a special squad before Operation Lucy was established.

9. The NDIU was merged into the National Criminal Intelligence Service (NCIS) in 1992 (see Dorn *et al.*, 1991, 1992).

10. Similarly in another book, Ramm is quoted as saying that yardies are a 'loose association of violent criminals bent on making profits from drugs' (in Davison, 1997: 44).

11. Bean (1993) refers to a National Task Force made up of police and Customs officers being wound up in August 1990.

12. But as Shapiro (1994) soberly warned: 'The crack scene in the UK is currently in a volatile situation. After an initial burst of enthusiasm and activity, most drugs find a level within the drug scene, so that what is first dubbed an 'epidemic' becomes just another part

of drug culture. When eventually there is nothing left to say, crack will fade from our front pages as heroin did in the late 1980s. But for those inner-city services trying to cope with the fallout, the resource implications could be substantial' (Shapiro, 1994: 15).

13. For instance, in a 1985 Metropolitan police divisional report for Brixton it is stated that 'Railton Road has always been regarded locally as a location synonymous with the use and supply of drugs'.

14. There seems to be something contagious about this style of reportage though. Writing about Toxteth in Liverpool, McDermott (1992: 21) reports that, 'on Granby Street, in the heart of Toxteth... At 11am on a Thursday morning, ganga and crack dealers ply their trade in the rain.... Just opposite, graffiti painted on the side of a row of terraces alerts the community to the discovery of police cameras in the house'.

15. There had been some press stories about crack in 1986 and a Gallup poll found that 60 per cent of people, claimed to have heard of the drug at that time (Gallup, 1989).

16. In *The Use of Pleasure*.

17. In *The Times*, 26 June 1989. Stutman also recognised this point when he said that it did not require 'genius to realise, "I don't have to import crack from the United States". I can go out and buy a baby bottle [and] I can make my crack right here in Great Britain, and I can increase my profit....by something like 300%' (quoted in Davison, 1997: 49).

18. A Wolverhampton drugs agency worker said to me that: 'Some have said that the crack issue is a Geoffrey Dear campaign, because he's had a couple of knockbacks - he didn't get the job in Northern Ireland and the more men he wanted - so cynically perhaps this is a campaign for more men, so whether it's there or not doesn't matter, they were going to find it anyway'.

19. Including the police. See the conclusion to Dorn *et al.*, 1992.

20. To return to an article on Toxteth, it is notable that McDermott (1992) acknowledges, albeit in parentheses, that '(There is rivalry between different agencies combating drugs, each of which tends to have a different perspective on the problem.)'.

8 In Living Colour? Representations of Yardies

This chapter is concerned with representations and constructions of 'black criminality', specifically the 'yardie', in Britain. It draws upon a body of work, often considered to be, at best, at the margins of criminology, that seeks to understand processes of racialisation, that is the attribution of significance to 'race differences'. This perspective adopts an anti-essentialist view of 'race' as a socially and culturally constructed category. It emphasises the examination of the ways in which racist discourses generate and seek to fix ideas about race differences as the principal marker of boundaries between groups of people.

Since the 1970s at least, culture has become embroiled in the politics of difference and racism. Barker (1981) delineated the emergence of a 'new racism' based on cultural rather than biological differences. Conventional notions of genetic superiority and inferiority were supplanted by ideas about the incompatibility of different cultures. Cultural difference thus became a code for race, and depictions of the 'culture' of ethnic or racial minorities became a means for simultaneously denying, while implicitly reasserting, hierarchies through which racial categories are 'smuggled' back in. A 'differential' or 'culturalised' racism emerged in the writings of conservative writers and politicians where the 'pathologies of black culture', or a view of blacks as 'barbarians within Western civilisation', marked out cultural difference as a hard and fast boundary that separates 'us' from 'them'. Critics have argued that liberal, and in some cases radical, perspectives have also offered highly problematical, often essentialised, representations of black culture, making the dividing line between reactionary and liberal approaches a sometimes very thin one. For example, some explanations of drug use draw upon 'cultural deficiency' models (Dorn and Murji, 1992a) as is evident in this passage:

> Among cultural minorities within the United States, historically there have been higher rates of unemployment and poverty level existence....characteristics and stresses of poverty, such as feelings of hopelessness, alienation, and powerlesness [are] high correlates of chemical abuse within African-American communities. Youth raised in these communities are often subjected to a culture of origin that appears to tolerate and support the trafficking and use of chemicals for non-medical

purposes... This does not imply that all members of low income communities succumb to or tolerate the abuse of chemicals. In fact, the majority of people in these communities do not. Yet, in terms of prevention or intervention program development, the visibility and accessibility of trafficking and use does impact the culture and lifestyle evolution in many of these communities. It is evident historically that the trafficking of illegal chemicals within minority communities has served to fulfil some of the economic needs of a population that was systematically and legally ostracized from the job market. Over time, the culture has adapted to a situation thrust upon them but not accepted by the majority (Griswold-Ezekoye, 1986: 209-10).

The attempt to locate drugs within social and economic pressures probably marks this out as a liberal perspective. But the view that there has been a seemingly embedded cultural adaptation that tolerates the 'trafficking and use of chemicals' employs a malignant and dangerous form of culturalism. It presents a pathological view of a permissive and casual 'black drugs culture' that, in emphasising its 'otherness', is close to, rather than critical of, new right and other forms of new racism.[1]

Indeed I will argue that all kinds of texts on the yardies, whether of liberal or illiberal intent, that seek to 'understand' yardie violence, or 'explain' their social and economic origins can also be seen to lead to much the same outcome. The differentiation of 'the other' whose activities or presence demarcate 'them' from 'us', reinforces boundaries rather than questioning their construction. Edward Said argued that over time the languages, cultures, writings and people of 'the East' have been built up into a body of knowledge that he calls Orientalism. From it, various myths of the Orient have been propagated which structured the ways in which Westerners 'saw' the Orient, its places and people. One of the effects of these myths was the difference or opposition that was set up with the West. So, for instance the 'exoticism' and 'decadence' of the Orient was contrasted with the morality of the West. These differences thus shape mutually constitutive relations between civility and the uncivilised, the clean and the dirty (Rattansi, 1994).[2] The questionability of such thinking can be seen in another example on drugs and race. The Advisory Council on the Misuse of Drugs (ACMD) has, implicitly using control theory, alluded to some sort of cultural blanket acting to prevent or contain drug problems for Asian communities. But again this establishes another contrast: Asian 'culture' is seen as strong and offering protection, while the culture of African-Caribbean groups is seen as somehow lacking, or to put it another way, 'Asians have culture, West Indians have problems' (Benson, 1996; cf Pitts, 1993).[3]

A key starting point for examining racialised constructions of 'black crime' is the work of Hall et al. (1978). Drawing upon an interactionist approach to deviance they analysed the role of the media and moral entrepreneurs in naming and framing the 'new' crime of 'mugging'. In focusing upon the operation of the control system in identifying and constructing this crime, rather than the behaviour of those labelled, they drew upon the social constructionist approach to social problems. But, in *Policing the Crisis* this is developed within a Marxist framework where the period of mugging is related to a mobilisation for law and order and the construction of an authoritarian state. Crucially, for present purposes, Hall *et al.*, argued that the association of mugging as a street crime mostly, or perhaps uniquely, committed by young black men became a means for emphasising the otherness of both this crime and of blacks, at a time when 'popular racism' was on the increase and politicians sought to mobilise a consensus for more law and order. Gilroy's (1987a) analysis of explanations of black crime shows how these have utilised ideas about the 'weakness' of black culture, for example the lack of a father or authority figure within the 'matriarchal' West Indian family, or simply a lack of respect for the law and English traditions of civility. These 'characteristics' serve to define blacks as 'lesser breeds without the law', who stand outside of what it means to be English or British. This discussion suggests that there are several over-lapping layers of otherness in play. Race or blackness acts as an other that gives rise to fears about particular people and places. Race has also been a medium through which fears and anxieties about crime are focused and given a recognisable shape (Hall *et al.*, 1978; Gilroy 1987a; Solomos, 1988; Keith 1993). Furthermore, Kohn (1987, 1992) has suggested that racism and xenophobia shape complex fears about drugs. The discovery of the yardies in the 1980s meant that the 'black drug trafficker' became the latest in the gallery of racialised characters linking race to mugging, rioting and now drugs.

Using a number of sources, I will examine some aspects of the representations of yardies as a dangerous and violent group involved in drug trafficking. Taking representation to refer to 'the significance of the construction....of ethnic identities through the production of images and narratives in visual and written texts in 'popular' and 'high' culture' (Rattansi, 1994: 58), I have drawn freely from a wide variety of texts - police and law enforcement documents from Britain, Canada and the US, newspaper reports and books by journalists, as well as television and radio reports. I argue that the degree of concordance between them amounts to a form of 'closed text' (Eco, 1979) in which space for any alternative representations has been squeezed out. They form hyperreal circles of repetition, reinforcing and validating one another. Their sources are sometimes clear, for example some books acknowledge assistance received from the police, or a particular police officer. However there are also writers who seem to stand outside that circle of information, but end up re-producing much the same story. There obviously are some differences of detail and style between these texts, but there are enough similarities to suggest that the line between fact and fiction is sufficiently blurred to evade any neat divisions. These texts compete to most faithfully represent the excesses of yardies. Thus, Victor Headley's book *Yardie* (and the follow-ups *Excess* and *Yush!*) are both marketed as realistic accounts of guns, violence, drugs and sex in yardie culture. The success of *Yardie* was such that other novels use bylines such as 'here's the real Yardie!' as a selling point. Similarly Philip Baker's *Blood Posse* is also sold with the promise that 'here's the real thing, written by somebody who's really been there'. Meanwhile books by journalists are not far behind with sub-titles such as 'the global rise of the yardies' (Small, 1995) and the 'sinister spread of yardie gun culture' (Davison, 1997).

Nevertheless, it is important to avoid the simple replacement of one broad brush approach with another. While most of the police and journalistic works I make use of are indistinguishably similar, there is reason to believe that the police response should not be seen as homogenous or undifferentiated. Some officers, both in localities and centrally, were keen to play down the idea that yardies were a 'black mafia' (Keith 1993; see also Mirza *et al.*, 1991; Pearson *et al.*, 1993). Furthermore, some journalists acknowledged that the threat of yardies had been exaggerated and that the term was being applied to almost anyone who was black and involved in crime (Campbell, 1991, 1994). Campbell says 'there was a tendency in the eighties to label every major crime committed by a black person as Yardie-inspired' (Campbell, 1994: 260) and goes only as far as saying that yardies developed a reputation for 'unpredictable violence'.[4]

Before proceeding, it is worth stating that, in Britain, crack has remained largely a cottage industry and that guns and violence, whether related to drugs or not, have never figured to anything even approaching the levels found in parts of the US. Levels of crack and cocaine use have remained relatively low - lower than heroin, which is a long way behind usage of ecstasy, itself way behind the most widely used illegal substances such as amphetamines and cannabis (Pearson, 1991, 1995a; Home Office, 1996).

Drug, race and nation

Historical associations between race and drugs have been extensively explored in the US (Musto, 1973; Helmer, 1975) and to some extent in Britain (Kohn 1987, 1992). In the post-war period, it appears that African-Caribbean communities in Britain seem to have been connected with two main drugs, cannabis initially and latterly crack cocaine. It is the latter that has been seen as being almost unique to yardies. The picture of crack as a distinctively 'ethnic' drug was apparent in a speech by the DEA Special Agent Robert Stutman. In spite of comments about an 'equal opportunity drug', he told ACPO that: 'Right now crack is controlled by a fairly large number of organisations, basically of two ethnic backgrounds, Dominicans and Jamaicans....the Jamaicans have taken over control of much of the rest of the United States.... I don't have to tell any of you that you have a large number of Jamaicans in this country' (Stutman, 1989: 7). And after this speech countless links between crack and Jamaicans in particular are made, in ways that suggest the otherness of both, leading to a police description of yardies as threats to the 'very security and stability of the nation' (in *The Guardian*, 3 February 1997: 1), in addition to an earlier reference to blacks and/or yardies as posing 'the greatest threat to law and order'.

In policing terms, the connections between drugs, race and nation are not merely incidental. In the 1970s a Metropolitan Police specialist unit was set up on the basis that drugs and immigration were integrally connected:

> twenty five years ago....it [drugs] was directly relatable to illegal immigration, it was the illegal immigrants who were predominantly bringing the drugs through, hence the reason that the NDIU [National Drugs Intelligence Unit] if you look at its history was formerly known as the Central Drugs and Illegal Immigration Unit. But as that problem was dealt with so it became the CDIU [Central Drugs Intelligence Unit].[5]

Nonetheless the connection between drugs and illegal immigration has became a routine part of official discourse. Since the 1980s both have frequently been linked in the same sentence with terrorism (for instance see Clutterbuck, 1990) especially in the context of increasingly strict immigration control, racially defined, and the building of a 'Fortress Europe' policy in which European countries have to some extent pooled their attempts to control the movement of all 'undesirables' (Bunyan, 1993).

Constructing the identikit

Interest in the yardies emerged at some point in the 1980s when first the police, and later the media, began to monitor and highlight the emergence and activities of what was already being described as a 'black mafia'. The yardies were said to be migrating from Jamaica, after the political fall-out in that country in the early 1980s and now entering Britain, often illegally: the 'majority of posse members are illegal aliens', according to an intelligence report from the Royal Canadian Mounted Police (RCMP, 1988: 27). Indeed illegal immigration became one of the key motifs of the 'yardie profile': 'The

Yardie idea of status focuses on four factors: You have to have a gun; money; drugs to sell - and you must have the ability to travel freely, and that usually means false passports' (*Evening Standard*, 22 October 1993: 5). Through 'ethnic networks', or sheer force and violence, they were seen as establishing themselves as criminal kingpins in British and American cities. An internal police report described yardies as:

> Jamaican born males who, by the use of extreme violence, including murder, are dominating the drugs trafficking, prostitution, gaming clubs, both legal and illegal and possibly the black popular music industries. They inflict their violence with firearms and sharp instruments, in particular machetes and flick knives (NDIU, undated).[6]

The report rather confusingly moves between offering an identikit portrait, while seeking to deny it. On the one hand it states that: 'There is no criterion which can be used to identify a criminal of West Indian origin as being a Yardie'. But it then adds, 'from those [yardies] already identified, certain similarities have emerged':

> He would have been a born in Jamaica, probably about 1950; he would have entered the UK usually from the late 1970's direct from Jamaica or via the USA; he will be involved in black reggae-type music; he will have a violent past, not necessarily found in previous convictions; it is known for him to be polite to police officers when being arrested and during any subsequent interview; he may, when being interviewed, simulate low intellect (NDIU, undated).[7]

Again the broad brush cardboard-cutout is qualified: 'the above points are purely indications. It would be most inadvisable to use them as a 'check-list' when attempting to identify a Yardie'. Nonetheless, the identikit portrait of a new breed of organised black crime in Britain has been widely reproduced, producing a remarkable congruence between police reports (the RCMP, NDIU, as well as the US Bureau of Alcohol, Firearms and Tobacco (ATF) use virtually identical images and phrases), journalism (e.g. see Silverman 1994; Thompson 1995a; Small, 1995; Davison, 1997) and, as mentioned previously, fiction that is marketed as realistic description. Thus, a book that exists to provide factual data about race in Britain, can state, without any qualification, that: 'A Yardie is a member of an organized crime institution with it roots in Jamaican politics that has become increasingly involved in drug dealing in the 1980s-90s' (Skellington, 1996: 74).

In addition to the linkages between race, crack, violence and guns, a number of inter-related themes emerged in press accounts: aggressive masculinity, sexual promiscuity and conspicuous consumption, in the form of fast cars and flashy jewellery. As two of these terms suggest, it is significant that the yardies are not just racialised but also sexualised, in ways that reaffirm stereotypes of 'black masculinity' as potent, threatening and elemental - 'dangerous masculinities' personified. Above all, the rise to power of the yardies was linked to their domination of one main commodity, crack cocaine. The apparent characteristics of the drug - an intense rush and a general feeling of excitability - are mirrored in the erratic and unpredictable behaviour attributed to yardies, thereby establishing a homology between the drug and its main sellers/users. Hence, crack tales combined a dizzying depiction of black men with a fondness for guns and extreme violence, loose living and a fragile valuing of their own and other people's lives. Yardies are said to have an attitude that 'life is short but sweet'[8] (Thompson, 1995b: 5), or, more bluntly, 'sociopathic recklessness' (*Newsweek*, 1988: 22). This has been presented as wreaking havoc on black communities and inner-city areas, furthering a 'spiral of decline'. Discursively these themes are too intertwined to disentangle, but I will attempt to highlight some of the main features of the representation of the yardies as other.

The invasion: swamping and pollution

> In the last twenty five years I've heard the drug problem blamed on the Afganistanis, Pakistanis, Iranians....now it's Yardies. Why do we always look outside for the cause of our problems in this country? (Comment made by a senior police officer at a seminar, 1993).

The otherness of both drugs and race are combined in contemporary accounts that envisage yardies and crack cocaine as twinned threats from without that have spread within. The use of the invasion metaphor to describe drugs parallels discourses where black and Asian immigration has also been described as an 'alien invasion' that threatens to 'swamp' Britain (Gilroy, 1987a). Similarly, drugs are commonly described as 'flooding' into Britain which is at risk of being 'swamped' by, or 'awash' with, them (Kohn, 1987). For Davison (1997: 3) yardies are a 'central thread in the development...of [a] 'Gangsta' gun culture', implying that before the yardies guns were somehow unknown in Britain. The role of images of contagion and pollution within racist discourses have been examined by Goldberg (1993). These themes run right through accounts of yardies and crack, implying a racial 'stain' on a hitherto uncontaminated and unspoilt landscape. For instance, a *Newsweek* feature contained a section on 'A Jamaican invasion in West Virginia'. As with other examples of this type of reportage, there is an image of an unsullied, perhaps even idyllic, community that has been tainted by cocaine and yardies/posses:

> With its tidy clapboard houses and neat apple and peach orchards....West Virginia seems far from the mean streets normally patrolled by drug gangs. But over the last three years, an invasion of Jamaican drug dealers has turned the home of the Mountain State Apple Harvest Festival into a mecca for cocaine (*Newsweek*, 28 March 1988: 24).

The image of the external invasion operates at levels other than the despoilation of the pure. It can also be applied to 'ghetto' areas, for instance when *The Sun* (25 May 1989) reported that: 'ruthless yardie gangbosses' were sending their best recruits 'to peddle crack on Britain's inner-city estates'; or a more highbrow newspaper refers to yardies 'making their presence felt...[by] pumping crack into black housing estates' (Davies, 1997: 2).

In the case of such areas, usually in the inner-cities, that do not have so far to 'fall' the danger is that contamination may seep out and infect 'us'. The area of Moss Side in Manchester, described as England's 'Bronx' by Silverman (1994), has been extensively featured as an area where 'gun gangs rule the rat runs' (*The Times*, 29 June 1993: 7). Hence, 'The presence of Moss Side symbolis[es] the presence not just of a racial Other....but also of a specific kind of violent criminality, signified in particular by discussion of the 'Yardie', implicitly linked into the 'international drugs and firearms trade" (Taylor *et al.*, 1996: 206). Moss Side thus typifies the idea of the 'wild zone' as 'a field of disorder and ungovernability and signifies an area of the without-law(s)' (Stanley, 1996: 105; see also Lash and Urry, 1994). Race and place become intertwined as features that demarcate the boundaries of civilisation, distinguishing the respectable from the disreputable. The 'yardie gun culture' (Davison, 1997) causes Moss Side to deteriorate from bad to worse, while an 'invasion of Jamaican drug dealers (*Newsweek*, 1988) leads to the alien corruption of the hitherto untainted Mountain State. In both cases all 'indigenous' crime is neatly obscured.

Policing yardies: ethnic closure

Police discourse suggests that a major problem of policing yardies is that they are difficult to distinguish within black culture. We have already seen references to their role within the 'black popular music industries' and 'black reggae-type music'. Accounts by police officers suggest that there is a large measure of 'ethnic closure', so that officers cannot tell who is and is not a yardie, because they are so easily concealed within black communities. The, presumably mono-ethnic, police are simply unable to distinguish the law-abiding from the lawless, coming close to a view that all blacks look alike. But they do not seem alone in that as Davison (1997) describes the 'strange, alien' world of the ghetto. Having left Jamaica to 'go foreign', as one police officer puts it (Brennan, 1994) yardies are able to hide themselves with ease:

> Once in a foreign country the individual can easily be absorbed into the local community making their detection difficult. Once abroad the Jamaican criminal merely acts in an identical way as if he were on the streets of Kingston, Jamaica (Brennan, 1994: 15).[9]

Similarly, the Interpol Secretary-General (Kendall, 1990) said that criminals are able to hide within 'immigrant' communities by using 'ethnic customs, backgrounds, fears and language'. Hence the police, seemingly impervious to accusations of criminalisation, provide themselves with the legitimation for targeting entire neighbourhoods and communities, as well as black clubs because they may be used as 'cover', just in case there might be some yardies hiding amongst them. Black culture is indistinguishable from crime. After all, as Brennan (1994: 16) concludes, 'this violent group of international criminals are present and organised in our very own backyards'. These observations, including the view that everyday behaviour in black communities is indistinguishable from that in Kingston, Jamaica, reveals rather more about the mind-set and outlook of some police officers than anything they tell us about yardies.

Indeed it is not only all blacks who are now being inclusively characterised as the other, the dangers go even beyond identifiable racial minorities. The NDIU report said that: 'It is of interest to note that...tenuous links have been established between the Yardies and/or close associates with members of the Israeli criminal fraternity, the Angry Brigade and the IRA' (NDIU, undated). So the other threatens to coalesce into one all-powerful enemy. In this context it is notable that some commentators have referred to a 'clash of civilisations' in which the west as a whole stands against the rest:

> Western people have far more in common with each other than they have with Asian, Middle Eastern or African people..... Promoting the coherence of the West means both preserving Western culture within the West and defining the limits of the West. [It] requires... controlling immigration from non-Western societies...and ensuring the assimilation into Western culture of the immigrants who are admitted (Huntington, 1996: 23).

Naturally the view that the West has to spread its civilising values to the rest of the world has been contested. More noticeable for present purposes is the view that all 'non-western' others pose a threat to Western values and civilisation, and the insinuation that the west was once, and seemingly still is for Huntington, mono-cultural and undivided, before the 'outsiders' came in.

An image of inscrutable 'ethnic customs' is apparent in other aspects of drugs policing. During the 1980s the police began to 'chase the money' rather than just drugs (Dorn et al., 1992). Some police officers working on money laundering, wrote of their discovery of 'hawala' and 'chiti' banking - techniques said to be commonly employed by Indians and Asians in lieu of other form of record keeping. Hence these obscurity of ethnic customs presents a challenge to an apparently mono-ethnic, mono-cultural police. At the same time, there is also an implication that these devious methods are characteristic of the 'wily oriental', and as Gilroy (1993) has pointed out, this conception is contrasted with a 'dumb savage' image of blacks.

Another aspect of the 'impenetrability' of yardies and ethnic drug trafficking networks is apparent in the policing of yardies, particularly the use of informants. Closure of the 'yardie squad' and specialist anti-crack operations did not mean that yardies were not still being actively targeted by the police (see previous chapter). Rather the strategy had changed to focus on the recruitment of informants from within the yardies. The rationale for this can be surmised from a report which said that: 'Because of their tightly organized operations and high mobility, it is virtually impossible to utilize undercover agents' (RCMP, 1988: 29). The nature of yardie organisation is taken to mean that the use of undercover police officers, or established informants, are both ruled out. Thus there is an image of a 'tight knit' group - or 'clannish, cunning and extraordinarily violent' as *Newsweek* (1988: 21) puts it. The difficulty of penetrating the yardies is put down to their operating on a seemingly 'tribal' basis, a view reaffirmed by tracing posses back to particular neighbourhoods in Jamaica from which they take their name, which is also expressed in 'turf wars' where gangs are defined according to geography/neighbourhood. All the sources considered here do this to some extent - see *Newsweek*, 1988; RCMP, 1988; NDIU, undated; Silverman, 1994; Small, 1995; Thompson, 1995a, b; Davison, 1997). However, in at least two cases this strategy has re-bounded spectacularly on the police. In the case of Eaton Green, it seems that:

> for more than two years he had been a paid Scotland Yard informant and that his handlers had allowed him to bring known Yardies into the country.....other detectives came across evidence of the crimes Green says he committed while on Scotland Yard's payroll, but [the detectives] were blocked from investigating them by his handlers, who wanted to keep their informer on the streets. It is understood that Green has admitted that he routinely used a firearm, committed armed robberies, bought and sold large quantities of crack cocaine, and ran protection rackets.... He was never prosecuted for any of these offences, and was finally brought to book only when he committed the armed robbery in Nottingham where his handlers were unable to protect him (Davies, 1996: 7).

Such use of informants is prohibited under Home Office guidelines (see Dorn et al., 1992; Davies, 1996, 1997). So too is the unofficial policy of 'squeal deals' where people under threat of deportation from Britain had been allowed to stay in return for acting as informants for the police and/or Customs. In another case, it became apparent that the police had permitted a Delroy Denton to stay in Britain so that he could act as an informant on the yardies, despite a Home Office order that he should be deported. During this period, the man committed various crimes, including rape and murder which eventually led to his conviction (Davies, 1997). But for Davison, though 'things went dreadfully wrong with Denton, it comes down to a simple, hard fact. In order to combat the bad men the police need bad men on their side - in some respects, the badder the better' (Davison, 1997: 189).

Explaining yardies: a culture of violence

The alieness of yardies or posses is supplemented by a list of seemingly unique features. Paramount among these is the recurring theme of 'extraordinary violence' (*Newsweek*, 1988: 22); the ATF reports that posses have a 'propensity for violence' (RCMP, 1988), or more bluntly that 'these gangs are the most vicious and violent groups local law enforcement has ever encountered. They don't hesitate to kill for any reason and they don't care who gets caught in the crossfire' (*Drug Enforcement Report*, 8 March 1988: 5). Similarly, a British police officer repeats that, 'the[y] are a unique group of criminals, their illegal activities....are reinforced by ruthless violence' (Brennan, 1994: 15). A journalist adds that yardies are 'using guns and knives with terrifying spontaneity' (Davies, 1997: 2). Guns are not simply a means to an end but a status symbol and a source of pleasure. Under the headline, 'Drug gangs 'relish dice with death'', a police officer was reported to have said that: 'The gangs actually enjoy the buzz that comes from the fear of being shot at or the sense of power when carrying a gun. They revel in the 'respect' that goes with having money, access to drugs and a gun. They love to pose or posture; their sense of well-being comes from 'status'' (in *The Guardian*, 13 May 1993: 4). And the violence is random and as likely to be directed at 'their own kind' as *Newsweek* (1988: 26) reported that reggae clubs have 'a well deserved reputation for frequent homicides'.

Having been well established by enforcement officials, more or less the same refrain is repeated over and over again, as journalistic reportage or as fictional glamour. Journalists working on television and radio programmes on yardies have chosen to go to Jamaica to explain that yardies are said to have originated from a period of political conflict and patronage between two factions in Jamaican politics (Small, 1995). This is often combined with an account of the social and economic climate in Jamaica and the lack of legitimate job opportunities. This is similar to approaches that explain black involvement in drug trafficking from a political economy perspective, for example see Davis (1990). Left realism deploys some similar reasoning (see Lea and Young, 1984). McDermott (1992) provides another example: 'youths selling ganga and crack....on the street corner are excluded from mainstream economic activity and they see drug dealing as one of the few routes open to them'. But attempts to make this 'culture of violence' understandable can end up reinforcing the idea that it is somehow a cultural proclivity, or more problematically, 'in their roots': 'Yardies are simply a class apart, born as they were from an environment in which violence is the norm' (Thompson, 1995b: 5). Consequently, visiting Jamaica to look for 'root causes' of yardie violence can simply reaffirm that a 'foreign import' has been brought into Britain (or perhaps 'the west') by these 'outsiders'.

Once again there is an explicit contrast which serves to affirm the otherness of yardie/posse violence. Gangs such as those run by the Krays and the Richardsons were said to be dominant in London's East End in the 1960s. While it was a criminal culture, it was basically stable, ordered, hierarchical. But disorganised crime, accompanied by guns and violence (its randomness typified in the 'drive by shooting') depicts a culture of instability. The excitable effects of crack are mimicked in the instability of yardies. As Stanley points out:

> The 'controlled' gang violence of the 1960s and the 1970s has declined in favour of new and more arbitrary forces of violence. Where gang rule provided a veneer of respectability in the distribution of the criminal activities of protection, gambling and vice....the dominant commodities are now drugs and guns implicating embryonic Jamaican Yardie....influence (Stanley, 1996: 103).

A comparable perspective is discernible in the US when *Newsweek* (1988: 22) emphasises the exceptionality and otherness of posses in saying that 'Jamaican posses are far more violent than the Mafia'. Yardies are sufficiently other to make earlier criminal networks seem tame by comparison. For Clutterbuck the comparison between yardies and the Italian mafia is misleading because the former have no mysticism and honour, 'just the power and security derived from membership of a violent criminal community able to hold its own with guns and knives' (Clutterbuck, 1995: 72). There may indeed be quantitative as well as qualitative differences in drug-related violence, though the reasons for that are likely to be more complex than the ethnicity of the main players. It could be added that having a 'rep' (reputation - see Bourgois, 1995; Katz, 1988) for violence can serve various purposes. One of these is the reasonably obvious one of status enhancement: 'many young blacks of various ethnic origins play up their own, usually non-existent, links with the Yardies in order to reinforce their own reputations. There have even been some cases of Nigerian and Ghanian drug dealers attempting to affect Jamaican accents in order to enhance their status' (Thompson, 1995b: 5). Another is that a reputation for violence may be useful for intimidating other criminals, as Woodiwiss (1988) has shown for the prohibition period in the US. The idea of an all-powerful criminal mafia was valuable because it could be used to 'buy off' law enforcement officials and politicians Woodiwiss adds that such a reputation also served other interests: the media because it made for better stories and the police because it emphasised the size of the task they faced.

Picturing the yardie: lifestyles of the rich and infamous

Turning to another level of representation, there are clear similarities in pictorial depictions of yardies and indeed various features use very similar images of men who are said to 'love to pose or posture' (*The Guardian*, 13 May 1994: 4). The most common posture features pictures of black men, their eyes 'blacked out', displaying some gold jewellery and holding one or more handguns. Sometimes drug use is also evident. One of the first of these was in *The Observer* when its front cover featured a black man posing with two firearms and a gold chain. The text next to it read:

> He makes his money from drugs. He wears the profits in a neckchain. He loves fast cars but his women are just 'baby mothers'. Cross him and he'll blast your head away. He is one of a frightening new network in Britain.

The feature, titled 'Heirs to the Krays' (Sweeney, 1989), displayed a full-page picture of a black man toting an automatic gun in each hand. The actual article contains a slightly more measured approach, but what is striking is the headline, photographs and the 'yardie profile' set-off from the main text with its tale of large amounts of cash, a fondness for 'classy German cars', and 'many girlfriends...who are treated very badly'. The iconography is sufficiently well established so that the yardie connection does not even need to spelt out. Thus, a feature on 'The Dealers in Death' in the Metropolitan Police's newspaper, *The Job* (8 July 1994: 8-9) used pictures of gun-toting blacks, with barely a mention of crack and none at all of yardies to signify threat/menace/danger. This seems to be analogous to the ways in blackness has become the standard means for referring to the cautionary other, in ways that do not need to spelt out (Keith and Cross, 1993; Murji, 1998).

Confirming much of the composite picture of yardies, Viv Reid, coordinator of the Newham Drugs Advice Project reports that black drug dealers

> want women, fast cars [and] expensive clothes. They may carry £50,000 worth of assets on themselves, like gold chains and rings and designed clothes.... Black dealers also attract attention to by their use of mafia-style shootouts (quoted in Hargreaves, 1992: 12-13).

In the late 1980s it was rumoured that the German car company BMW had moved to control second hand car sales apparently because of a concern that their cars had acquired an image as the 'drug dealers car', a key motif of conspicuous consumption among successful dealers (see also Chambliss, 1994; Small, 1995; Miller, 1996). Given the relatively high risk of being stopped by the police for black men - especially when 'out of place' in a car like a BMW - it seems, again, that the yardie's propensity for conspicuousness implies that, while they may be violent and dangerous, they are basically stupid, or at least criminally unprofessional: the 'dumb savage'. Similarly, in another example of the invasion theme it had been reported that yardies targeted Britain because it is 'easy' (e.g. 'Yardie gangsters see London as soft touch', *Evening Standard*, 22 October 1993: 5; 'Crack trade turning to 'safe' Britain', *The Guardian*, 2 July 1994: 8), seemingly unaware that Britain has some of the toughest penalties for drug trafficking in Europe (see Dorn et al., 1992, chapter 10).

By way of contrast this account by 'James', a black man convicted for drug trafficking is noteworthy. James does not quite fit the yardie profile. He was born in the late 1950s and brought up in Britain. But because he has had some involvement with what the police would call 'reggae-type music', like Sammy Lewis (see note 4) he could be mistakenly thought of as a yardie, or at least to have some connections. Interviewed in prison, he told me about some basic measures that he took to minimise the risk of being caught by the police:

> you don't go out there totally willy nilly, I did take precautions, for instance you get yourself a decent car not something ostentatious like a BMW, but a Ford or something, you dress decently and go to places where there's no trouble. It's trying to do everything that the drug stereotype wouldn't do.

James may not be exceptional in his approach to dealing drugs, but his modus operandi does differ significantly from the image of the yardie. In place of the gang or mafia he describes himself as a 'one man operation' and a 'smuggler, period' who did not want any involvement with selling drugs at the retail level. His rationale for this was based on an awareness that risks increase with the numbers of people dealt with. Despite his personal concerns about cocaine as the drug that had become stereotypically linked to black men, his decision to deal in it was informed by a basic businesslike attitude:

> In my case it was a rational decision to smuggle cocaine. One, I knew people in America I could get it from. Two, the returns on your investment are very high. Third, the quantities you can carry in relation to how much you can get for it....so these are the things which influenced my decision.

Ironies and contradictions

The demonisation of the yardies produced some ironic consequences.[10] The folk devil image acquired a certain cachet and, in some cases, yardie status became something to aspire to rather than live down.[11] In the late 1980s T-shirts were available in street markets around London featuring the single word 'Yardie' below a picture of a muscular black man, something like the 'Mr T' character from the TV programme *The A-Team*. Another T-shirt twisted the storyline by depicting a white male police officer with boot soles prominent, apparently about to stamp on someone, with the words 'Scotland Yardies' underneath. This can be read as a barbed commentary on the police's yardie squad, or a reference to the history of police/black conflict in the area (Keith, 1993) and, perhaps, a hint to the stories about drug-related corruption among police officers from the nearby Stoke Newington police station (see Hackney Community Defence Campaign, 1992).

I have adopted a sceptical and critical stance regarding the depictions of yardies. In doing so, I do not wish to be seen as implying that there are no blacks involved in drug trafficking. Rather, following Gilroy, I believe that the representation of black people in crime (or, for current purposes, drugs) means that 'images and representations of black criminality....achieve a mythic status' (Gilroy, 1987b: 118). A seemingly casual racialisation serves to establish the boundaries that distinguish civility from dangerousness and when referred to in terms of their nationality, race or ethnicity, these groups seem to merge into an all-encompassing other 'them' who threaten 'us'. For example, an article about the decline of the mafia concluded with this warning about new threats emerging to fill the void:

> As well as the growing influence of the ruthless Russian gangs, Chinese Triads and Japanese yakusa compete for spoils. On the west coast of the United States, Korean gangs are active alongside Mexican organised crime collectives which recruit from the smaller street gangs of young disaffected Latinos (*The Guardian*, 4 January 1997: 2).

Or *Newsweek* refers to: 'black gangs, Hispanic gangs, Asian gangs and gangs drawn from specific nationality groups' (*Newsweek*, 1988: 21). When the other is characterised so all-inclusively, the 'tiny minority' approach seems rather pointless. Thompson, for instance, prefaces his account of 'gangland Britain' with these words: 'in every case, organised criminals make up only a fraction of a percentage of the population - [I] do not seek to tar every Jamaican, Colombian, Sicilian or Asian with the same brush, it [this book] merely focuses on the tiny underworld element within each group' (Thompson, 1995a: 5). But since the rest of his book concentrates on ethnic criminal enterprises and uses descriptions such as Jamaicans, Asians and so on, it is difficult to see who is being excluded from his broad brush.[12]

I have intimated that crude stereotypes of yardies are articulated from a variety of sources. These representations have a peculiar cultural character that is highly questionable at the very least, and dangerous and grossly invidious in a climate of culturalised racism that I mentioned at the outset. The representations of yardies are in many ways akin to cartoon images and lifestyles and I want to finish by highlighting some of the 'dislocations' (see Rattansi, 1994) or 'flips' in this process. Yardies, on the one hand, are seemingly driven by 'elemental needs' to be violent, powerful, sexually promiscuous and consume as much they can. This 'base' conception of them suggests a somewhat primitive, rather uncivilised set of instincts. Yardies like to wear gaudy gold jewellery, pose for photographs holding automatic weapons and drive BMWs. Yardies are therefore apparently basically stupid. They behave as if they are (still) in Kingston, Jamaica unaware that such behaviour makes them look more out of place than 'at home'. However, it seems that their stupidity can not be taken for granted as a police report states that 'it is not unknown for them to feign low intelligence' to trick police officers (NDIU, undated).

The same set of contradictions recur. On the one hand, 'the workings of the group are very simple. They are after fast money which the drug market provides. Their violence, utilisation of firearms, ease of travel to escape detection all assist in perpetuating their operation' (Brennan, 1994). Similarly, the NDIU said: 'The MO [Modus Operandi] used by the Yardies will not require a great deal of explanation, as the one crime they could never be accused of is 'subtlety'. With the aid of sound systems (discos), the Yardies infiltrate clubs [and] displace existing staff. The venue then becomes one more outlet for the sale of drugs'. But for all their simplicity, lack of sophistication and conspicuous activity, this does not seem to make them any easier to police. Rather, stories appear regularly about the police fighting considerable odds: 'Police fight to end the Yardie reign of terror' (*Sunday Times*, 1 August 1993: 5). For the RCMP: 'Jamaican posses are....a national problem. It is only through an unrelenting, unified and flexible approach by all levels of law enforcement that we can combat the threat of Jamaican posses' (RCMP, 1988: 29). For *Newsweek*: 'Outmanned, outgunned and outspent, the cops are fighting back as best they can' (*Newsweek*, 1988: 26). Hence a view that yardies are disorganised and unlike professional criminals, has to co-exist with an image of ultra-professionalism in their use of 'ruthless violence' and their ever-increasing sphere of influence. Another opposition suggests that yardies are 'unique', but they are also 'heirs' to an 'indigenous' criminal tradition. These accounts of yardies are monochrome, unidimensional characterisations that can only invite accusations of stereotyping, culturalism and racism. These portrayals contain little, if any, living colour and none of the shades that are an inevitable part of every person and every group's make-up.

In developing this argument I would contend that looking at yardies from a criminological perspective is less revealing than one that begins with their construction in racial and cultural terms (see also Ferrell and Sanders, 1995). This view implies the need to broaden the field of vision of criminology. While challenges to criminology from feminism and post-structuralism have sought to transgress its boundaries, this does not seem to have been realised in relation to race which often appears to still be caught up in, on one side, empiricist arguments about the extent of discrimination, and on the other, culturalist explanations of black crime.

Finally, I thought it best to end on this note. In 1996 a newspaper reported on an ACPO study ('Home-grown gangs 'worse than Triads", *The Independent*, 12 January 1996: 4).[13] It said that: 'Contrary to previous reports, organisations such as Triads, the Mafia, Yardies and Russian criminals, pose little national threat compared to local gangs, says the study. The report also says that the powers of foreign-influenced outfits are greatly exaggerated, particularly with Jamaican "Yardie" gangsters'.

Notes

1. In contrast, Ruggiero (1995) has argued that, to the extent that the illicit economy broadly mirrors the structure of the licit economy, we would expect blacks in the main to be at the lower end of criminal hierarchies rather than the kingpins, just as they mostly are in the legitimate world. While this approach does seek to make the visibility of black drug sellers in some streets and areas understandable, it does not do so by using a culturalist explanation.

2. In contrasting 'the West' with the Orient, Said can be accused of homogenising the former and obscuring its own fractures and fissures. For an elaboration and other criticisms see Rattansi (1994).

3. There is a broadly similar distinction made in the US where Asians (albeit from Southeast Asia rather than the Indian sub-continent, as in Britain) are seen as a 'model minority', positioning them above 'underclass' blacks and Latinos in a racial hierarchy.

4. Similarly, Thompson notes: 'today virtually every black criminal in Britain is seen as a Yardie, or at the very least suspected of having Yardie links. When black drug dealer Sammy Lewis shot and wounded a detective...the incident was immediately reported as a Yardie crime (in fact Lewis was born in Reading, his parents were from Barbados and he had never been to Jamaica in his life)' (Thompson, 1995b: 5).

5. This quote is from an interview with a senior officer from the National Drugs Intelligence Unit. The NDIU was established as a central intelligence point for information about drugs. In 1992 it was absorbed into the National Criminal Intelligence Service, which has a wider remit than just drugs (see Dorn et al., 1992).

6. A section of this unpublished internal report appears in paragraph 1.7 of the Metropolitan Police's (1989) memorandum to the Home Affairs Committee.

7. The Metropolitan Police's (1989: 47) memorandum states that '...those involved [in drugs distribution] are Jamaican illegal immigrants who have no fixed addresses but who are bound by their Jamaican origin and reggae culture and who travel from one location to another with regularity'.

8. Adding to my point about the repetitive nature of yardie discourse, consider the quote attributed to Detective Superintendent John Jones, then head of Operation Dalehouse: 'They [yardies] have a philosophy that it is a short life but a sweet one' (in Campbell, 1994: 260).

9. Small (1995: 391) describes Brennan as 'one of the world's leading authorities' on the subject of Jamaican criminals.

10. Another notable development has been the mobilisation for law and order among black communities. *Newsweek* (1988: 27) reported on Black Muslims in Brooklyn who sought to 'take back the neighbourhood' and pressed the police to take action (for other examples see Dorn and Murji, 1992a).

11. This led some police officers to express concern that the yardie label had become fashionable, and that the yardie image was creating an alternative role model: 'It has been found that many West Indian males will identify themselves as a Yardie in order to enhance their reputations among the West Indian criminal fraternity' (NDIU, undated; see also Small, 1995). And other officers expressed caution about 'seeing yardies everywhere'. A beat officer in London's Chinatown, in expressing reluctance to see all or even most criminal activity as signs of Triad activity, said that 'I was conscious of the enhancing effect that the term 'Yardie' had on the street credibility of low-level drug dealers and street thugs in north and south London council estates' (in *Police Review*, 21 June 1991: 1261).

12. Small (1995) discuses the concerns of the Jamaican embassy in London about the blanket 'catch-all' representation of yardies.

13. Campbell reports that at a 1993 Bramshill seminar on organized crime, police officers had moved on from the threat of yardies to focus on the impact of the end of the cold war and movements from eastern Europe to the west, which meant that the 'selling of arms and

the passage of drugs from the east had rocketed' (Campbell, 1994: 260).

Bibliography

ACPO (Association of Chief Police Officers) (1985) *Final Report of the Working Party on Drugs Related Crime*, unpublished; extracts in the Appendix to Dorn *et al.*, 1992.
Advisory Council on the Misuse of Drugs (ACMD) (1984) *Prevention*, London: HMSO.
Advisory Council on the Misuse of Drugs (ACMD) (1988) *Aids and Drug Misuse*, London: HMSO.
Advisory Council on the Misuse of Drugs (ACMD) (1991) *Drug Misusers and the Criminal Justice System, Part 1: Community resources and the probation service*, London: HMSO.
Advisory Council on the Misuse of Drugs (ACMD) (1994) *Drug Misusers and the Criminal Justice System, Part 2: Police, drug misusers and the community*, London: HMSO.
Audit Commission (1993) *Helping with Enquiries*, London: HMSO.
Awiah, J, Butt, S and Dorn, N (1992) *Race, Gender and Drug Services*, London: ISDD.
Bakalar, J and Grinspoon, L (1984) *Drug Control in a Free Society*, Cambridge: Cambridge University Press.
Baker, P (1994) *Blood Posse*, London: Picador.
Barker, J (1992) 'A positive bust: arrest referral in Southwark', *Druglink*, 7 (4): 15-16.
Barker, M (1981) *The New Racism*, London: Junction Books.
Barr, R and Pease, K (1992) 'The problem of displacement', in D. Evans *et al.* (eds) *Crime, Policing and Place*, London: Routledge.
Bayley, D (1994) *Police for the Future*, New York: Oxford University Press.
Bean, P (1974) *The Social Control of Drugs*, London: Martin Robertson.
Bean, P (1993) 'Cocaine and crack: The promotion of an epidemic', in P. Bean (ed) *Cocaine and Crack*, Basingstoke: Macmillan.
Becker, H (1963) *Outsiders*, New York: Free Press.
Beckett, I (1991) 'Police budget and performance', *International Criminal Police Review*, July-August.
Belenko, S (1990) 'The impact of drug offenders on the criminal justice system' in R. Weisheit (ed) *Drugs, Crime and the Criminal Justice System*, Ohio: Anderson Publishing.
Ben-Yehuda, N (1990) *The Politics and Morality of Deviance*, New York:

SUNY Press.
Bennett, W (1989) 'Restoring authority', *New Perspectives Quarterly*, 6 (2): 4-7.
Bennett, W (1990) 'Drug policy and the intellectuals', *International Journal on Drug Policy*, 1 (6): 16-18.
Benson, S (1996) 'Asians have culture, West Indians have problems', in T. Ranger et al. (eds) *Culture, Identity and Politics*, Aldershot: Avebury.
Berridge, V (1984) 'Drugs and social policy: The establishment of drug control in Britain 1900-30', *British Journal of Addiction*, 79.
Berridge, V (1996) *Aids in the UK*, Oxford: Oxford University Press.
Berridge, V and Edwards, G (1981) *Opium and the People*, London: Allen Lane.
Bertram, E, Blachman, M, Sharpe, K and Andreas, P (1996) *Drug War Politics*, Berkeley: California University Press.
Blagg, H et al. (1988) 'Inter-agency co-ordination', in T. Hope and M. Shaw (eds) *Communities and Crime Reduction*, London: HMSO.
Bottoms, A (1990) 'Crime prevention facing the 1990s', *Policing and Society*, 1: 3-22.
Bourgois, P (1995) *In Search of Respect*, Cambridge: Cambridge University Press.
Brennan, J (1994) '"The Yardies" - organised crime in our own backyards', in *Drugs and Criminality*, report of 1994 ACPO National Drugs Conference.
Bright, J (1987) 'Community safety, crime prevention and the local authority', in P. Willmott (ed) *Policing and the Community*, London: PSI.
Bright, J (1991) 'Crime prevention', in K. Stenson and D. Cowell (eds) *The Politics of Crime Control*, London: Sage.
Bunyan, T (ed) (1993) *Statewatching the New Europe,* London: Statewatch.
Campbell, D (1991) *That was Business, This is Personal*, London: Mandarin.
Campbell, D (1994) *The Underworld*, London: BBC Books.
Chambliss, W (1994) 'Policing the ghetto underclass', *Social Problems*, 41: 177-94.
Chatterton, M et al. (1995) *Performance Indicators for Local Anti-Drugs Strategies*, London: Home Office Police Research Group.
Clutterbuck, R (1990) *Terrorism, Drugs and Crime in Europe after 1992*, London: Routledge.
Clutterbuck, R (1995) *Drugs, Crime and Corruption*, Basingstoke: Macmillan.
Coffield, F and Gofton, L (1994) *Drugs and Young People*, London: IPPR.
Cohen, S (1972) *Folk Devils and Moral Panics*, London: MacGibbon & Kee.

Collison, M (1993) 'Punishing drugs', *British Journal of Criminology*, 33: 382-99.
Collison, M (1995) *Police, Drugs and Community*, London: Free Association Books.
Currie, E (1993) *Reckoning*, New York: Hill & Wang.
Daniels, T and Gerson, J (eds) (1989) *The Colour Black*, London: BFI.
Davies, N (1996) 'Yard's Yardie is too hot to handle', *The Guardian*, 1 May.
Davies, N (1997) 'Police Yardie scandal' and 'How the Yardies duped the Yard', *The Guardian*, 3 February.
Davis, M (1990) *City of Quartz*, London: Verso.
del Olmo, R (1987) 'Aerobiology and the war on drugs: A transnational crime', *Crime and Social Justice*, no. 30: 28-44.
Dorn, N (1980) 'The Conservatism of the cannabis debate', in National Deviancy Conference (ed) *Permissiveness and Control*, London: Macmillan.
Dorn, N (1983) *Alcohol, Youth and the State*, London: Croom Helm.
Dorn, N (1992) 'Clarifying policy options on drug trafficking', in P. O'Hare et al. (eds) *The Reduction of Drug-Related Harm*, London: Routledge.
Dorn, N (1994) 'Three faces of police referral', *Policing and Society*, 4: 13-34.
Dorn, N (1996) 'Drug markets and law enforcement in Europe', in P. Green (ed) *Drug Couriers*, London: Quartet.
Dorn, N, Jepsen, J and Savona, E (eds) (1996) *European Drug Policies and Enforcement*, Basingstoke: Macmillan.
Dorn, N and Murji, K (1992a) *Drug Prevention*, London: ISDD.
Dorn, N and Murji, K (1992b) 'Low level drug enforcement', *International Journal of the Sociology of Law*, 20: 159-71.
Dorn, N, Murji, K and South, N (1990) 'Drug referral schemes', *Policing*, 6: 482-92.
Dorn, N, Murji, K and South, N (1991) 'Mirroring the market', in R. Reiner and M. Cross (eds) *Beyond Law and Order*, Basingstoke: Macmillan.
Dorn, N, Murji, K and South, N (1992) *Traffickers: Drug markets and law enforcement*, London: Routledge.
Dorn, N, Ribbens, J and South, N (1987) *Coping with a nightmare*, London: ISDD.
Dorn, N and South, N (1990) 'Drug markets and law enforcement', *British Journal of Criminology*, 30: 171-88.
Dorn, N and South, N (1991) 'Profits and penalties', in D. Whynes and P. Bean (eds) *Policing and Prescribing*, Basingstoke: Macmillan.
Dorn, N and South, N (1993) 'After Mr Bennett and Mr Bush', in F. Pearce and M. Woodiwiss (eds) *Global Crime Connections*, London:

Macmillan.

Dorn, N and South, N (1994) 'The power behind practice', in J. Strang and M. Gossop (eds) *Heroin Addiction and Drug Policy*, Oxford: Oxford University Press.

Druglink (1989) Special issue on crack, September-October.

Druglink (1992) 'ACMD urges cooperation with the courts', January-February: 2.

Druglink (1996) 'The effects of E on harm reduction', January-February: 4.

Duke, K and MacGregor, S (1997) *Tackling Drug Locally*, London: Stationery Office.

Dunant, S and Porter, R (eds) (1996) *The Age of Anxiety*, London: Virago.

Duster, T (1970) *The Legislation of Morality*, New York: Free Press.

Eck, J (1989a) 'The future of drug control efforts', a paper prepared for Future Issues in Policing Symposium, Canadian Police College, Ottawa, Ontario.

Eck, J (1989b) *Taking a Problem-oriented Approach to Drug Enforcement*, Washington, D.C: Police Executive Research Forum.

Eco, U (1979) *The Role of the Reader*, London: Hutchinson.

Edmunds, M et al. (1998) *Arrest Referral: Emerging lessons from research*, London: Home Office CDPU.

Ekblom, P and Heal, K (1982) *The Police Response to Calls from the Public*, London: Home Office.

Erikson, K (1966) *Wayward Puritans*, New York: John Wiley.

Ferrell, J and Sanders, C (eds) (1995) *Cultural Criminology*, Boston: Northeastern University Press.

File on Four (1990) 'Crack on the front line', BBC Radio 4, 10 April.

Fraser, A and George, M (1996) 'Southern England, drugs and music: Policing the impossible?', in N. Dorn et al. (eds) *European Drug Policies and Enforcement*, Basingstoke: Macmillan.

Fraser, P (1996) 'Social and spatial relationships and the 'problem' inner city', *Critical Social Policy*, no. 49: 43-65.

Furedi, F (1997) *Culture of Fear*, London: Cassell.

Gallup (1989) *Political Index*, London: Gallup.

Garland, D (1990) *Punishment and Modern Society*, Oxford: Clarendon Press.

Gaus, G (1995) 'Taking drugs and rights seriously', *Criminal Justice Ethics*, Winter-Spring issue.

George, M and Fraser, A (1989) 'Changing trends in drug use: A second follow-up of a local heroin using community', *British Journal of Addiction*, 84: 1461-66.

Giddens, A (1987) *Sociology and Modern Social Theory*, Cambridge: Polity.

Gilman, M and Pearson, G (1991) 'Lifestyles and law enforcement', in D. Whynes and P. Bean (eds) *Policing and Prescribing*, Basingstoke: Macmillan.
Gilroy, P (1987a) *There Ain't No Black in the Union Jack*, London: Hutchinson.
Gilroy, P (1987b) 'The myth of black criminality', in P. Scraton (ed) *Law, Order and the Authoritarian State*, Milton Keynes: Open University Press.
Gilroy, P (1993) *Small Acts*, London: Serpents Tail.
Goldberg, D (1993) 'Polluting the body politic', in M. Cross and M. Keith (eds) *Racism, the City and the State*, London: Routledge.
Goode, E (1989) *Drugs in American Society*, third edition, New York: McGraw-Hill.
Goode, E and Ben-Yehuda, N (1994) *Moral Panics: The social construction of deviance*, Oxford: Blackwell.
Goodsir, J (1993) 'Civil rights and civil liberties surrounding the use of cocaine and crack', in P. Bean (ed) *Cocaine and Crack*, Basingstoke: Macmillan.
Gould, A (1994) 'Sweden's syringe exchange debate', *Journal of Social Policy*, 23: 195-217.
Green, P (1996) 'Drug couriers: The construction of a public enemy', in P. Green (ed) *Drug Couriers*, London: Quartet.
Griswold-Ezekoye, S (1986) 'The multicultural model in chemical abuse prevention and intervention', in S. Griswold-Ezekoye *et al.* (eds) *Childhood and Chemical Abuse*, New York: Haworth Press.
Gusfield, J (1963) *Symbolic Crusade*, Connecticut: Greenwood Press.
Hackney Community Defence Association (1992) *Fighting the Lawmen*, London: HCDA.
Hall, S, Critcher, C, Jefferson, T, Clarke, J and Roberts, B (1978) *Policing the Crisis: Mugging, the state and law and order*, London: Macmillan.
Hammersley, R *et al.* (1989) 'The relationship between crime and opiod use', *British Journal of Addiction*, 84: 1029-43.
Hargreaves, C (1992) *Snowfields*, London: Zed.
Hay, C (1995) 'Mobilization through interpellation', *Social and Legal Studies*, 4: 197-223.
Hayeslip, D (1989) 'Local-level drug enforcement: New strategies', *NIJ Reports*, no. 213: 2-6.
Headley, V (1992) *Yardie*, London: X Press.
Headley, V (1993) *Excess*, London: X Press.
Helmer, J (1975) *Drugs and Minority Oppression*, New York: Seabury Press.
Henderson, S (1997) *Ecstasy: Case unsolved*, London: Pandora.

Henham, R (1994) 'Criminal justice and sentencing policy for drug offenders', *International Journal of the Sociology of Law*, 22: 223-38.
HM Government (1995) *Tackling Drugs Together*, Cm 2846, London: HMSO.
HM Government (1998a) *Tackling Drugs to Build a Better Britain*, Cm 3945, London: Stationery Office.
HM Government (1998b) *Tackling Drugs to Build a Better Britain*, Guidance Notes, London: Stationery Office.
Home Affairs Committee (1985) *Misuse of Hard Drugs*, interim report, London: HMSO.
Home Affairs Committee (1989) *Crack: The threat of hard drugs in the next decade*, London: HMSO.
Home Office (1990) *UK Action on Drug Misuse: The government's strategy*, London: HMSO.
Home Office (1996) *Statistics of Drug Seizures and Offenders dealt with, United Kingdom 1995*, Statistical Bulletin 25/96, London: Home Office.
Home Office (1998) *Statistics of Drug Seizures and Offenders dealt with, United Kingdom 1996*, Statistical Bulletin 10/98, London: Home Office.
Hope, T and Shaw, M (eds) *Communities and Crime Reduction*, London: HMSO.
Hough, M (1996) *Drugs Misuse and the Criminal Justice System*, London: Home Office CDPU.
Howard, R et al. (1993) *Across the Divide*, London: Department of Health.
Hunt, A (1997) "Moral panic' and moral language in the media', *British Journal of Sociology*, 48: 629-48.
Husak, D (1992) *Drugs and Rights*, Cambridge: Cambridge University Press.
Inciardi, J (ed) (1991) *The Drug Legalization Debate*, Newbury Park: Sage.
Inciardi, J and McBride, D (1991) 'The case against legalization', in J. Inciardi (ed) *The Drug Legalization Debate*, Newbury Park: Sage.
Ives, R (1986) 'The rise and fall of the solvents panic', *Druglink*, July-August: 10-12.
Jefferson, T and Grimshaw, R (1987) *Interpreting Policework*, London: Allen & Unwin.
Jenkins, P (1992) *Intimate Enemies*, New York: Aldine de Gruyter.
Johnson, B (1989) 'Crime and compulsory treatment', *Druglink*, May-June: 12- 13.
Kaplan, J (1988) 'Taking drugs seriously', *The Public Interest*, 2 (92): 32-65.
Katz, J (1988) *Seductions of Crime*, New York: Basic Books.
Kay, J (not dated) 'Problem drug users in custody - information, advice and

treatment: lessons from a joint research project', Manchester: Lifeline Project.
Keith, M (1992) 'Angry writing', *Environment and Planning D: Society and Space*, 10: 551-568.
Keith, M (1993) *Race, Riots and Policing*, London: UCL Press.
Keith, M and Cross, M (1993) 'Racism and the postmodern city', in M. Cross and M. Keith (eds) *Racism, the City and the State*, London: Routledge.
Kendall, R E (1990) 'The international problem of criminal gangs', *International Criminal Police Review*, March-April.
Kinsey, R, Lea, J and Young, J (1986) *Losing the Fight against Crime*, Oxford: Blackwell.
Kleiman, M (1989) *Marijuana: Costs of abuse, costs of control*, New York: Greenwood Press.
Kleiman, M (1991) 'Modelling drug markets', paper presented at the American Society of Criminology, San Francisco.
Kleiman, M. and Smith, K (1990) 'State and local drug enforcement', in M. Tonry and J. Q. Wilson (eds) *Drugs and Crime*, Chicago: University of Chicago Press.
Kohn, M (1987) *Narcomania*, London: Faber.
Kohn, M (1992) *Dope Girls*, London: Lawrence & Wishart.
Kohn, M (1993) 'The Enemy Within', BBC Radio 4, 19 August.
Kraska, P (1990) 'The unmentionable alternative', in R. Weisheit (ed) *Drugs, Crime and the Criminal Justice System*, Ohio: Anderson Publishing.
Lash, S and Urry, J (1994) *Economies of Signs and Space*, London: Sage.
Lea, J and Young, J (1984) *What is to be done about law and order?*, Harmondsworth: Penguin.
Lee, M (1996) 'London: Community damage limitation?', in N. Dorn *et al.* (eds) *European Drug Policies and Enforcement*, Basingstoke: Macmillan.
Leishman, F and Savage, S (1993) 'The Police service', in D. Farnham and S. Horton (eds) *Managing the New Public Services*, Basingstoke: Macmillan.
Leitner, M, Shapland, J and Wiles, P (1993) *Drug Usage and Drugs Prevention*, London: HMSO.
McDermott, P (1992) 'Crack and the cropper', *The Guardian*, 17 June.
McLaughlin, E (1992) 'The Democratic Deficit', *British Journal of Criminology*, 32: 473-87.
McLaughlin, E and Murji, K (1995) 'The end of public policing?', in L. Noaks *et al.* (eds) *Contemporary Issues in Criminology*, Cardiff: University of Wales Press
McLaughlin, E and Murji, K (1996) 'Times change', in C. Critcher and D.

Waddington (eds) *Policing Public Order*, Aldershot: Avebury

McLaughlin, E and Murji, K (1997) 'The future lasts a long time', in P. Francis *et al.* (eds) *Policing Futures*, Basingstoke: Macmillan

McRobbie, A (1994) 'Folk devils fight back', *New Left Review*, 203: 107-16.

McRobbie, A and Thorton, S (1995) 'Rethinking 'moral panic' for multi-mediated social worlds', *British Journal of Sociology*, 46: 559-74.

Manderson, D (1997) 'Substances as symbols', *Social and Legal Studies*, 6: 383-400.

Manning, P (1980) *The Narcs' Game*, Cambridge, MA: MIT Press.

Media International Australia (1997) Issue on Panic: Media, morality, culture.

Meese, E and Carrico, B (1990) 'Taking back the streets', *Policy Review*, Fall, 22-30.

Metropolitan Police (1989) Memorandum of evidence, in Home Affairs Committee, *Drug Trafficking and Related Serious Crime*, vol. II, London: HMSO.

Miller, J (1996) *Search and Destroy*, Cambridge: Cambridge University Press.

Mirza, H, Pearson, G and Phillips, S (1991) *Drugs, People and Services*, London: Goldsmiths College.

Moore, M (1977) *Buy and Bust*, Lexington: DC Heath.

Moore, M (1979) 'Limiting supplies of drugs to illicit markets', *Journal of Drug Issues*, 9: 291-308.

Moore, M (1988) *Drug Trafficking*, NIJ Crime File Study Guide, Washington, D.C.: National Institute of Justice.

Moore, M (1990) 'Supply reduction and drug law enforcement', in M. Tonry and J. Q. Wilson (eds) *Drugs and Crime*, Chicago: University of Chicago Press.

Moore, M and Kleiman, M (1989) *The Police and Drugs*, Washington, D.C.: National Institute of Justice.

Morgan, R and Newburn, T (1997) *The Future of Policing*, Oxford: Oxford University Press.

Morley, D (1995) 'Theories of consumption in media studies', in D. Miller (ed) *Acknowledging Consumption*, London: Routledge.

Morris, N and Hawkins, G (1970) *The Honest Politician's Guide to Crime Control*, Chicago: Chicago University Press.

Murji, K (1998) 'White lines: Culture, 'race' and drugs', in N. South (ed) *Drugs: Controls, cultures and everyday life*, London: Sage.

Musto, D (1973) *The American Disease*, Oxford: Oxford University Press.

Nadelmann, E (1991) 'The case for legalization', in J. Inciardi (ed) *The Drug*

Legalization Debate, Newbury Park: Sage.
National Drugs Intelligence Unit (NDIU) (undated) 'Black Organised Crime - The Yardies', unpublished.
Neate, P (ed) (1995) *Scare in the Community: Britain in a moral panic*, London: Community Care/Reed Business Publishing.
Nee, C and Sibbitt, R (1993) *The Probation Response to Drug Misuse*, London: Home Office.
O'Connor, L et al. (eds) (1998) *Drugs: Partnerships for policy, prevention and education*, London: Cassell.
Open Eye (1990) 'In the Firing Line', Granada TV programme, 13 December.
Parker, H et al. (1988) *Living with Heroin*, Milton Keynes: Open University Press.
Parker, H et al. (1995) *Drug Futures*, London: ISDD.
Payton, C (1981) 'Substance abuse and mental health', *Public Health Reports*, 96: 20-25.
Pearson, G (1983) *Hooligan*, London: Macmillan.
Pearson, G (1987) *The New Heroin Users*, Oxford: Blackwell.
Pearson, G (1989) 'The street connection', *New Statesman and Society*, 15 September: 10-11.
Pearson, G (1990) 'Drugs, law enforcement and criminology', in V. Berridge (ed) *Drugs Research and Policy in Britain*, Aldershot: Avebury.
Pearson, G (1991) 'Drug-control policies in Britain', in M. Tonry and N. Morris (eds) *Crime and Justice*, Chicago: Chicago University Press.
Pearson, G (1992) 'Drugs and criminal justice: a harm reduction perspective', in P. O'Hare et al. (eds) *The Reduction of Drug-Related Harm*, London: Routledge.
Pearson, G (1995a) 'City of darkness, city of light', in S. MacGregor and A. Lipow (eds) *The Other City*, New Jersey: Humanities Press.
Pearson, G (1995b) 'Drugs, crime and aliens', paper presented at the American Society of Criminology, Boston.
Pearson, G, Gilman, M and McIver, S (1986) *Young People and Heroin*, London: Health Education Council.
Pearson, G et al. (1993) 'Cocaine in context', in P. Bean (ed) *Cocaine and Crack*, Basingstoke: Macmillan.
Pitts, J (1993) 'Thereotyping', in D. Cook and B. Hudson (eds) *Racism and Criminology*, London: Sage.
Platt, S (1988) 'The Yardies and the Yard', *New Society*, 22 April.
Platt, S (1995) 'Moral panic', *New Statesman and Society*, 24 November: 14-15.
Polich, J et al. (1984) *Strategies for Controlling Adolescent Drug Use*, Santa Monica: RAND.

Press, A (1987) *Piecing together New York's Criminal Justice System*, New York: NY Bar Association.
RCMP (Royal Canadian Mounted Police) (1988) *Monthly Digest of Drug Intelligence Trends*, October.
Ranger, C (1989) 'Race, culture and 'cannabis psychosis'', *New Community*, 15: 357-369.
Rattansi, A (1994) 'Western racisms, ethnicities and identities', in A. Rattansi and S. Westwood (eds) *Racism, Modernity and Identity*, Cambridge: Polity.
Read, M and Simpson, A (1991) *Against a Rising Tide*, Nottingham: Spokesman.
Reeves, J and Campbell, R (1994) *Cracked Coverage*, Durham, NC: Duke University Press.
Reinarman, C and Levine, H (1989) 'The crack attack', in J. Best (ed) *Images of Issues*, New York: Aldine de Gruyter.
Reiner, R (1988) 'British criminology and the state', in P. Rock (ed) *A History of British Criminology*, Oxford: Oxford University Press.
Reiner, R (1991) *Chief Constables*, Oxford: Oxford University Press.
Reiner, R (1992) *The Politics of the Police*, second edition, London: Harvester.
Rengert, G (1996) *The Geography of Illegal Drugs*, Boulder: Westview Press.
Reuter, P (1983) *Disorganized Crime*, Cambridge, MA: MIT Press.
Reuter, P (1992) 'The limits and consequences of US foreign drug control efforts', *The Annals of the American Academy*, 521: 151-62.
Reuter, P, Crawford, G and Cave, J (1988) *Sealing the Borders*, Santa Monica: RAND.
Reuter, P and Haaga, J (1989) *The Organization of High-Level Drug Markets: An exploratory study*, Santa Monica: RAND.
Reuter, P and Kleiman, M (1986) 'Risks and prices: An economic analysis of drug enforcement', in M. Tonry and N. Morris (eds) *Crime and Justice*, Chicago: University of Chicago Press.
Reuter, P and MacCoun, R (1995) 'Assessing the legalization debate', in G. Estievnart (ed) *Policies and Strategies to Control Drugs in Europe*, The Netherlands: Martinus Nijhoff.
Rouse, J and Johnson, B (1991) 'Hidden paradigms of morality in debates about drugs', in J. Inciardi (ed) *The Drug Legalization Debate*, Newbury Park: Sage.
Ruggiero, V (1995) 'Drug economics', *Capital & Class*, no. 55: 131-50.
Ruggiero, V and South, N (1995) *Eurodrugs*, London: UCL Press.
Ruggiero, V and South, N (1997) 'The late-modern city as a bazaar', *British*

Journal of Sociology, 48: 54-70.
Rumsey, S (1990) interview, reprinted in *HIV/AIDS and the Asian Communities*, report of a seminar at London Lighthouse, London: SHARE.
Sagarin, E and McNamara, D (1972) 'The problem of entrapment', in R. Dahl and G. Dix (eds) *Crime, Law and Justice Annual 1972*, Buffalo: W.S. Hein.
Sampson, A *et al.* (1988) 'Crime, localities and the multi-agency approach', *British Journal of Criminology*, 28: 478-93.
Saunders, N (1995) *Ecstasy and the Dance Culture*, London: N. Saunders.
Schlesinger, P and Tumber, H (1994) *Reporting Crime*, Oxford: Clarendon.
Schur, E (1965) *Crime without Victims*, Engelwood, NJ: Prentice-Hall.
Shapiro, H (1989) 'Crack: a briefing', *Druglink*, September-October.
Shapiro, H (1994) 'The crack report', *Druglink*, September-October.
Shapland, J and Vagg, J (1988) *Policing by the Public*, London: Routledge.
Sharkey, A (1996) 'Sorted or distorted?', *The Guardian*, 26 January: 2-3.
Sheptycki, J (1995) 'Transnational policing and the makings of a postmodern state', *British Journal of Criminology*, 35.
Sherman, L (1990) 'Police crackdowns', *NIJ Reports*, no. 219: 2-6.
Shiner, M and Newburn, T (1997) 'Definitely, maybe not?', *Sociology*, 31: 511-29.
Silverman, J (1993) 'Policing the media', in L. Gelsthorpe (ed) *Minority Ethnic Groups and Criminal Justice*, Cambridge: Institute of Criminology.
Silverman, J (1994) *Crack of Doom*, updated edition, London: Headline.
Skellington, R (1996) *'Race' in Britain today*, second edition, London: Sage.
Small, G (1995) *Ruthless: The global rise of the yardies*, London: Warner.
Solomos, J (1988) *Black youth, Racism and the State*, Cambridge: Cambridge University Press.
Southwark Arrest Referral Pilot Project [ARPP] Monitoring Group (1991) 'A report to the Home Office on the Southwark Arrest Referral Pilot Project', London: Southwark ARPP group.
Southwark Arrest Referral Pilot Project (1992) 'Preliminary report - Phase 2', London: Southwark Drugs Prevention Team.
Sparks, R (1992) *Television and the Drama of Crime*, Buckingham: Open University Press.
Stanley, C (1996) *Urban Excess and the Law*, London: Cavendish.
Stenson, K (1993) 'Community policing as a governmental technology', *Economy and Society*, 22: 373-89.
Stutman, R (1989) 'Crack stories from the States', *Druglink*, September-October, edited version of speech to ACPO conference, April 1989.

Sumner, C and Sandberg, S (1990) 'The press censure of 'dissident minorities'', in C. Sumner (ed) *Censure, Politics and Criminal Justice*, Buckingham: Open University Press.
Sweeney, J (1989) 'Heirs to the Krays', *The Observer*, magazine section, 25 June.
Szasz, T (1992) *Our Right to Drugs*, New York: Praeger.
Taylor, I, Evans, K and Fraser, P (1996) *A Tale of Two Cities*, London: Routledge.
Tester, K (1994) *Media, Culture and Morality*, London: Routledge.
Thompson, K (1998) *Moral Panics*, London: Routledge.
Thompson, T (1995a) *Gangland Britain*, London: Hodder & Stoughton.
Thompson, T (1995b) 'Yardies: myth and reality', *The Guardian*, 19 September.
Tilley, N (1993) 'Crime prevention and the Safer Cities story', *Howard Journal of Criminal Justice*, 32.
Tonry, M (1994) *Malign Neglect*, New York: Oxford University Press.
Turnbull, P et al. (1996) *Get It While You Can*, London: Home Office CDPU.
Turner, D (1991) 'Pragmatic incoherence', in M. Krauss and E. Lazear (eds) *Searching for Alternatives*, Stanford: Hoover Institute.
US General Accounting Office (1984) *Investigations of Major Drug Trafficking Organizations*, Washington, D.C.: US GAO.
Waddington, D (1992) *Contemporary Issues in Public Disorder*, London: Routledge.
Waddington, P A J (1986) 'Mugging as a moral panic', *British Journal of Sociology*, 37: 245-259.
Waddington, P A J (1993) *Calling the Police*, Aldershot: Avebury.
Waddington, P A J (1994) *Liberty and Order*, London: UCL Press.
Wagstaff, A and Maynard, A (1988) *Economic Aspects of the Illicit Drug Market and Drug Enforcement Policies in the United Kingdom*, Home Office Research Study 95, London: HMSO.
Walter, T et al. (1995) 'Death in the news', *Sociology*, 29: 579-596.
Watney, S (1987) *Policing Desire*, London: Methuen.
Webster, C (1997) 'The construction of British 'Asian' criminality', *International Journal of the Sociology of Law*, 25: 65-86.
Weisheit, R (ed) (1991) *Drugs, Crime and the Criminal Justice System*, Ohio: Anderson Publishing.
Wilson, J Q (1978) *The Investigators: Managing FBI and narcotics agents*, New York: Basic Books.
Wilson, J Q (1985) *Thinking about Crime*, revised edition, New York: Vintage.

Wilson, J Q and Kelling, G (1982) 'Broken windows', *Atlantic Monthly*, March.
Wisotsky, S (1986) *Breaking the Impasse in the War on Drugs*, New York: Greenwood Press.
Woodiwiss, M (1988) *Crime, Crusades and Corruption*, London: Pinter.
Young, J (1971) *The Drugtakers*, London: Paladin.
Zatz, M (1987) 'Chicano youth gangs and crime', *Contemporary Crises*, 11.
Zimmer, L (1987) *Operation Pressure Point: The disruption of street-level drug trade on New York's lower east side*, New York: NY University School of Law.
Zimring, F and Hawkins, G (1992) *The Search for Rational Drug Control*, Cambridge: Cambridge University Press.

Index

ACPO 12, 125, 139, 140, 143, 144, 147, 152, 153, 162, 175
ACMD 5, 20, 22, 24, 36, 37, 39, 62, 70, 71, 110, 113-115, 160
AIDS 6, 56, 62, 72, 98, 103, 116, 130, 141, 152
Asians 160, 168, 174
Audit Commission 31
Autonomy, principle of 55, 70

Bean, P 53, 122, 131, 140, 146, 152, 155
Beckett, I 30, 31, 33, 34, 37, 43
Bennett, W 13, 17, 25, 54, 56, 57, 59-61, 142
Berridge, V 53, 141, 152, 155
Betts, Leah 6, 122-126, 128, 130, 132-134, 153
Brennan, J 167, 169, 174
Brixton 150
Buy bust 36

Cannabis 3, 4, 42, 51-53, 60, 61, 63, 74, 84, 97-100, 106, 115, 25, 127, 135, 140, 150, 154-156, 162
Cautioning 39, 62, 63, 71, 73, 74, 82, 97, 98, 101, 113, 115
Chatterton *et al.* 3
Clutterbuck, R 126, 140, 147, 148, 153, 155, 163,
Cocaine 16, 14, 18, 31, 39, 53, 54, 59, 60, 74, 140, 142, 143, 145, 148, 149, 152-156, 162, 165, 166, 168, 172, 173
Cohen, S 126, 128, 129, 141
Collison, M 12, 22, 40, 43, 44
Controlling user crime 22, 68
Counter-reaction, in the media 6, 122, 124-128, 132-135
Crack 6, 7, 31, 33, 41, 42, 60, 112, 113, 121, 122, 125, 130, 131, 139-141, 143-154, 156, 162-166, 168, 170-72
Crackdowns 24, 36, 121, 150
Crop programmes 12
Culturalism 7, 160, 175
Custody officers 76, 99

Davis, M 24, 36, 150, 170
Davison, J 146, 147, 149, 153, 162, 164-166, 168, 169
DEA 139, 162
Decriminalisation 3, 4, 11, 40, 51, 52, 59-61, 63, 126, 154
Demand management 2, 29, 30, 34, 36, 38, 43-46
Demand reduction 2, 12, 13, 24, 25, 30, 36, 39, 79, 141, 143
Disruptive policing 18, 20, 21
Dorn, N 1, 2, 11-14, 17, 19, 20, 23, 24, 29, 31, 36, 37, 39-41, 43, 44, 122, 125, 126, 128, 131, 140-142, 145, 150, 152-154, 156,

159, 163, 168, 172, 173
Dorn, N and Murji, K 12, 13, 20, 24, 36, 39, 40, 58, 59, 70, 142
Dorn, N and South, N 11-14, 17, 24, 36, 44, 54
Drug enforcement 1, 11, 12, 16, 24, 29, 36, 43,139, 169
Drug markets 2, 11, 12, 14, 17, 18, 20, 23, 24, 36, 42, 44, 58, 126
Drugs and crime 22, 57, 58, 111

Eck, J 19, 36, 38
Ecstasy 4, 6, 13, 33, 51, 53, 97, 121-127, 129, 130, 132, 134, 139, 153, 162
Elasticity of demand 15, 16, 22

Family Referral 67-69, 115
Folk devils 7, 129
Fraser, A and George, M 2
Front lines 150

Generic referral 104, 107, 109
George, M and Fraser, A 16, 24, 58
Gilman, M and Pearson, G 16, 21, 39, 68
Gilroy, P 149, 161, 165, 168, 173
Goode, E and Ben-Yehuda, N 128, 132, 143, 154
Green, P 7, 56, 168
Guns 55, 146, 150, 162, 164, 165, 169, 170

Hall *et al.* 128, 130, 143, 149, 154, 160, 161
Harm reduction 20, 44, 62, 63, 71, 73, 74, 77, 79, 80, 130, 131

Harm principle 55
Heroin 15, 17, 18, 21-24, 53, 54, 60, 73, 74, 83, 100, 112, 121, 126, 129-131, 139, 140, 148, 149, 154-156, 162
High level enforcement 12
HIV 45, 62, 72, 79, 93, 98, 103, 116, 130, 141
HM Government 2, 3, 6
Home Affairs Committee 139, 140, 143, 145, 149, 164
Home Office 5, 29, 30, 39, 63, 69, 71, 80, 81, 97, 125, 162, 168, 169

Illegal immigration 155
Inciardi, J 12, 13, 45, 51, 59, 60, 62, 141
Inconvenience policing 22, 23, 39
Informants 4, 21, 33, 68, 111, 146, 168, 169
Interdiction 14

Keith, M 33, 133, 146, 149, 150, 161, 162, 171, 173
Kleiman, M 13-15, 17, 18, 22, 24, 25, 29, 41, 58, 68
Kleiman, M and Smith, K 13, 17, 18, 22, 24, 25, 68
Kohn, M 53,128, 140, 155, 161, 162, 165
Kraska, P 24, 51, 56, 59, 61

Legalisation 3, 4, 11, 24, 40, 51, 52, 54, 55, 57, 59-62, 126, 131, 135, 143, 144, 150, 154
Localisation 3, 29, 30
LSD 13

Mafia 17, 29, 56, 146, 147, 149, 151, 162, 163, 170-173, 175
Managerialism 3, 30, 31, 45
Manning, P 24, 35, 43
Merseyside 4, 40, 67, 69, 71, 73-77, 79, 80, 83, 91, 93, 108, 131
Money laundering 168
Moore, M 12-18, 20, 21, 23, 35-37, 39, 41, 44, 58
Moral panic 6, 7, 121, 122, 124, 128-132, 139-141, 151, 152, 156
Moral enterprise 143
Moss Side 151
Mugging 130, 143, 144, 149, 160, 161
Musto, D 52, 53, 155, 162

Nadelmann, E 19, 36, 56, 60
National Crime Squad 1, 11
NDIU 145, 163, 164, 167, 168, 173, 174
Norfolk 102, 104, 108, 110
Normalisation 4

Operation Dalehouse 146, 165
Operation Lucy 145, 146
Operation Pressure Point (OPP) 18-20, 36-38
Organised criminal networks 11, 56

Paternalism, principle of 55
Pearson, G 12, 16, 17, 20-24, 36, 39, 44, 62, 68, 73, 125, 128, 131, 139, 146, 150, 154, 155, 162
Platt, S 124, 128, 132, 145
Polich *et al.* 15
Prices 14-18, 20, 57, 59, 60, 152

Problematisation 7
Prohibitionists 52, 55-57, 59-63
Public relations 34, 35, 41, 42, 45, 97, 100, 101

Raids 31, 35, 36, 41, 144, 150
RCMP (Royal Canadian Mounted Police) 163, 164, 168, 169, 174
Reactive enforcement 37
Referral leaflet 76, 78, 100, 107, 109
Regional Crime Squads 1, 11, 12
Reid, V 149, 151, 171
Reinarman, C 58, 121, 122, 128, 131, 140, 155
Reuter, P 13-15, 17, 18, 20, 24, 44, 51, 52, 54, 57, 58, 62
Reuter, P and Kleiman, M 13-15, 17, 18, 24, 58
Ruggiero, V 160

Search time 15, 20, 23
Selective policing 21
Shapiro, H 57, 61, 140, 149, 151, 154
Sharkey, A 124, 125, 127, 128, 132, 134
Sherman, L 18, 19, 36
Silverman, J 36, 37, 41, 139, 140, 150, 164, 166, 168
Social censures 7
Social reaction 6, 7, 139, 141, 145, 147, 149, 151, 153
Social prevention 38-40, 69
Southwark 67
Stutman, R 139, 140, 143-145, 147-149, 151-154, 162, 163
Sumner, C 7, 130, 153
Supply reduction 12, 14-17, 20, 25
Sweeps 19, 36

Symbolic crusade 6, 141, 143, 151, 156

Threat 20, 29, 41, 60, 125, 126, 128-130, 139, 143, 145, 146, 149, 155, 156, 163,
Trafficking 1, 2, 11, 12, 16, 17, 53, 125, 141-143, 159-161, 164, 168, 170
Trafford 4, 67, 69, 71-73, 83, 91
Treatment 1, 2, 5, 6, 16, 21, 22, 24, 25, 29, 39, 45, 54, 56, 63, 67-72, 79, 83, 85, 93, 98, 101, 102, 108, 115
Triad 173

United Nations Special Session on the World Drug Problem 2
User accountability 12, 59, 141

Vigilantism 40
Violence 169, 170

Wagstaff, A and Maynard, A 14-16, 24, 58
War on drugs 1, 25, 41, 56, 58, 141, 147, 151
Weisheit, R 25, 56, 58
Wilson, J Q 16, 17, 20-23, 31, 35, 37, 38, 43, 68

Yardies 6, 7, 145-149, 151, 154, 156, 159-175

Zero tolerance 12, 59, 63, 142
Zimmer, L 18, 19, 36